CHANGING OUR OWN WORDS

Shahraz

Changing Our Own Words

ESSAYS ON CRITICISM, THEORY, AND WRITING BY BLACK WOMEN

Cheryl A. Wall, Editor

RUTGERS UNIVERSITY PRESS

New Brunswick and London

Second printing, 1991

Copyright © 1989 by Rutgers, The State University
All Rights Reserved
Manufactured in the United States of America

Library of Congress Cataloging-in-Publication Data
Changing our own words : essays on criticism, theory, and writing by
  Black women / Cheryl A. Wall, editor.
    p. cm.
    Proceedings of a conference held at Rutgers University in Oct.,
  1987.
    Includes bibliographies and index.
    Contents: Reading family matters / Deborah E. McDowell — The
  permanent obliquity of an in(pha)llibly straight / Hortense J.
  Spillers — Allegories of Black female desire / Claudia Tate — But
  what do we think we're doing anyway / Barbara Christian — What is
  your nation? / Abena P. A. Busia — Living on the line / Gloria T. Hull
  — I shop therefore I am / Susan Willis — Speaking in tongues / Mae Gwendolyn
  Henderson — Black feminist theory and the representation of the
  "other" / Valerie Smith.
    ISBN 0-8135-1462-2 (cloth)   ISBN 0-8135-1463-0 (pbk.)
    1. American literature—Afro-American authors—History and
  criticism—Theory, etc.—Congresses.   2. American literature—Women
  authors—History and criticism—Theory, etc.—Congresses.   3. Afro-
  American women—Intellectual life—Congresses.   4. Women and
  literature—United States—Congresses.   I. Wall, Cheryl A.
  PS153.N5C44   1989
  810'.9'9896073—dc20   89-6126
                                                             CIP
British Cataloging-in-Publication information available

To the community of black women writing
and to Barbara Smith for pointing
"toward a black feminist criticism"

C O N T E N T S

viii

CONTENTS

ACKNOWLEDGMENTS

I am grateful first to the critics whose essays make up this volume for so graciously accepting my invitation and acceding to the long list of requests that followed. They have taught me much about feminist critique and community. My thanks go as well to Houston Baker, Hazel Carby, and Mary Helen Washington for the scholarly example and their collegial support. I am especially indebted to Paule Marshall whose presence, like her fiction, is luminous.

Most of the essays collected here were originally presented at a symposium funded by the following programs and departments at Rutgers University whose contributions I gratefully acknowledge: the Institute for Research on Women, the Rutgers University Research Council, the Voorhees Assembly Board, the Paul Robeson Cultural Center, the Center for Critical Analysis of Contemporary Culture, and the Office of Assistant Vice President for Academic Affairs. For their generous support, intellectually and financially, I thank Mary Hartman, Dean of Douglass College, Catharine Stimpson, Dean of the Graduate School-New Brunswick, Tilden Edelstein, formerly Dean of the Faculty of Arts and Sciences, and Thomas Van Laan, former chair of the English department. The contribution of Carol Smith, director of the Institute for Research on Women, and her staff including Arlene Nora, Guida West, and especially Ferris Olin, was invaluable.

I thank as well the poet Cheryl Clarke and other colleagues at Rutgers including Abisola Gallagher and Renee Larrier who served on the planning committee. As always, I received encouragement and wise counsel from my past and present colleagues Adrianne Baytop, Wesley Brown, Donald Gibson, and Arnold Rampersad.

At Rutgers University Press, I thank Kathryn Gohl, Ann Sweeney, Tricia Zeller, and most of all, Leslie Mitchner, for her keen intelligence, boundless energy, and unwavering support.

Finally, I thank Camara Rose for being my sweet inspiration.

Cheryl A. Wall
New Brunswick, N.J.
June 1989

Introduction
Taking Positions and Changing Words

> We are the subjects of our own narrative, witnesses to and parti-
> cipants in our own experience, and, in no way coincidentally,
> in the experiences of those with whom we have come in
> contact. . . . And to read imaginative literature by and about
> us is to choose to examine centers of the self and to have the
> opportunity to compare these centers with the 'raceless' one
> with which we are, all of us, most familiar.
> —Toni Morrison

> Ah change jes ez many words ez Ah durn please!
> —Zora Neale Hurston

In the words of critic Hortense Spillers, "the community of black
women writing in the United States now can be regarded as a vivid
new fact of national life." [1] Certainly the impact of such writers as
Audre Lorde, Paule Marshall, Toni Morrison, Ntozake Shange, and
Alice Walker—to name only a few of the most visible members of
the community—cannot be gainsaid. Over the last two decades,
Afro-American women have written themselves into the national
consciousness. Their work is widely read, frequently taught, and increasingly the object of critical inquiry. Wherever it is met, black
women's writing elicits impassioned responses from readers across
boundaries of race and gender. Indeed, the readers now writing about
black women's writing are an extremely heterogenous group. Equally
diverse are the positions from which they approach it.

The contributors to this volume are academic critics who in the
main have a primary professional commitment to black women's
writing. The commitment is not merely professional; to borrow from
Cheryl Clarke, black women's writing has been for us "necessary
bread." As women, most of whom are black, we bring to our work
a critical self-consciousness about our positionality, defined as it is by
race, gender, class, and ideology. The position or place we are

assigned on the margins of the academy informs but does not determine the positions or stances we take. From the margins various strategies may be deployed, and varied, indeed contradictory, propositions set forth. Making our positionality explicit is not to claim a "privileged" status for our positions. Black and white male critics have written perceptively about black women's texts.[2] Making our positionality explicit is, rather, a response to the false universalism that long defined critical practice and rendered black women and their writing mute.

This gesture is, I think, congruent with the stance of those black women novelists and poets whose voices are at last being heard and whose words elicit and enable our own. What we offer here are propositions on reading and writing about their texts. Perhaps our words, like those texts, will have resonance beyond the community of black women writing.

In retrospect, events in 1970 signaled the emergence of that community. *The Black Woman,* an anthology edited by Toni Cade, presented itself as "a beginning—a collection of poems, stories, essays, formal, informal, reminiscent, that seem best to reflect the preoccupations of the contemporary Black woman in this country."[3] Rejecting the definitions imposed by experts ("all male") and resisting encouragement to locate themselves in the emergent definitions of women by white feminists, the anthology heralded an effort by black women to define themselves. In a memorable phrase, contributor Frances Beale entitled her essay "Double Jeopardy: To Be Black and Female." That phrase suggested one historical context for the reading of black women's fiction. Another was signaled by the reprinting that year of Zora Neale Hurston's classic volume of folklore, *Mules and Men.* Despite the republication of *Their Eyes Were Watching God* five years earlier, Hurston then remained, in biographer Robert Hemenway's words, "one of the most significant unread authors in America."[4] Hurston's writing would in time suggest another context for reading black women's fiction that would focus on shared narrative and rhetorical strategies as much as themes.

Of more immediately recognizable significance in 1970 was the publication of extraordinary first novels by Toni Morrison, *The Bluest Eye,* and Alice Walker, *The Third Life of Grange Copeland.* Powerfully written and deeply unsettling in their exploration of family violence, sexual oppression and abuse, and the corrosive effects of racism and poverty, these novels ran counter to the prevailing mood. Although *I Know Why the Caged Bird Sings,* the first volume of Maya Angelou's popular series of memoirs, partook more in that mood of righteous anger and triumphant struggle, its dramatic center, as in Morrison's novel, was the rape of a girl. In a society ordered by hierarchies of power based on race, class, and gender, no one is more powerless, hence more vulnerable, than a poor black girl. In these texts, such characters anchor the critique of social ideology. Necessarily, the fierce young female characters who are survivors rather than victims are trenchant social critics; Morrison's Claudia and Walker's Ruth define themselves and position themselves respectively as potential and active agents of social change.

To cite one last example from that watershed year, Audre Lorde's 1970 poem, "Who Said It Was Simple?" might be read as a gloss on the foregoing texts and a challenge to their critics.[5]

> There are so many roots to the tree of anger
> that sometimes the branches shatter
> before they bear.
>
> Sitting in Nedicks
> the women rally before they march
> discussing the problematic girls
> they hire to make them free
> An almost white counterman passes
> a waiting brother to serve them first
> and the ladies neither notice nor reject
> the slighter pleasures of their slavery.
> But I who am bound by my mirror
> as well as my bed
> see causes in Colour
> as well as sex
>
> and sit here wondering
> which me will survive
> all these liberations.[6]

What is now called black feminist criticism was one response to the richness and complexity of this writing. Without attempting to trace its history—and recognizing that bits of it are told in the essays that follow—I mark a few transformative moments.

Among the pioneering essays were Mary Helen Washington's articles "Zora Neale Hurston: The Black Woman's Search for Identity," "Black Women Image Makers," and the introduction to her first anthology, *Black-Eyed Susans.* In the last Washington asserted: "what is important about the black woman writer is her special and unique vision of the black woman."[7] Reductive though this statement now sounds, Washington's analysis conveyed her appreciation for the complex representation of black female character in the writing she surveyed. Writing in *Black World,* a journal that was generally devoted to the dissemination of positive images, Washington argued for the value of images so "powerful" and "realistic" that they could combat whatever stereotypes of black women still persisted.

Washington warned against giving too much scrutiny to such stereotypes, for to do so was to keep "looking backward." Looking ahead meant keeping one's critical attention fixed on the prose and poetry of such writers as Angelou, Toni Cade Bambara, Gwendolyn Brooks, Marshall, and Walker. If white feminists were apt to locate themselves on the margins of discourse, Washington and other black feminist critics in the 1970s and early 1980s tended to position themselves and the writing they addressed at the center. It proved to be an enabling perspective.

In her landmark 1977 essay, "Toward a Black Feminist Criticism," Barbara Smith gave the perspective a name and a firmer definition. Meeting the challenge laid down in Lorde's poem, Smith called "a black feminist approach to literature that embodies the realization that the politics of sex as well as the politics of race and class are crucially interlocking factors in the works of Black women writers . . . an absolute necessity."[8] She wrote angrily about the exclusion of black writers from the white feminist critique, the omission and condemnation of women writers in criticism authored by black men, and the absence of black lesbian writers everywhere. But she emphasized that the case she was making for a black feminist criticism was not merely reactive. Rather, the critic "should work from the assumption that Black women writers constitute an identifiable literary tradition" that could be abstracted from the study of their use of "black women's language and cultural experience."[9] Smith ended the essay with her controversial reading of *Sula* as a lesbian novel.

Despite the refinement of her terms by other critics, Smith's outline of the black feminist project has remained influential. Indeed, some critics refine the terms so they might join the project. Deborah McDowell, for example, points out the untenability of the concept of a monolithic black female language as well as Smith's imprecise definition of lesbian. In her "New Directions for Black Feminist Criticism," McDowell argues, naïvely, that Smith's approach runs the risk of yoking political ideology and aesthetic judgment. To the contrary, Smith's explicitly ideological stance was a response to the neglect of writing by black women on implicitly ideological grounds. More valid is McDowell's claim that a reading of *Sula* that "overlooks the novel's density and complexity, its skillful blend of folklore, omens, and dreams, its metaphorical and symbolic richness," is incomplete. She calls for a criticism that combines a consideration of context, both historical and political, with "rigorous textual analysis."[10] Like Smith, she would undertake the task of defining a black women's literary tradition, but recognizes the extreme difficulty of doing so.

To a degree, both Smith and McDowell here respond to Alice Walker's "In Search of Our Mothers' Gardens," perhaps the best-known critical essay by an Afro-American woman. Walker posits a theory of black female creativity and defines a tradition of black women's art in which she can locate her own. Opening with an analysis of Jean Toomer's *Cane* and drawing throughout on the model of Virginia Woolf's *A Room of One's Own*, Walker connects her work to existing Afro-American and female Anglo-American literary traditions. To construct her own "motherline" (to borrow Susan Willis's coinage), Walker recasts Woolf's famous query about the fate of Shakespeare's sister to ask: "What did it mean for a black woman to be an artist in our grandmother's time? In our great-grandmothers' day? It is a question with an answer cruel enough to stop the blood."[11] Even in the face of such cruel history, Walker imagines generations of black women artists—both those defeated and "driven to a numb and bleeding madness" by that creativity for which they could find no release and those who released their creativity in song and the crafts of quilt making, baking, and gardening which Walker reevaluates as art. Walker's portrait of her mother is surely the portrait of an artist: "Ordering the universe in the image of her personal conception of Beauty."[12]

By redefining art, Walker expands the universe of those entitled to be called artists; in the process she collapses the distance between her world and work and her mother's. Walker's gesture responds to the imperative that many of her sister writers heed, whether like Morrison they invoke the presence of the ancestors, or in Marshall's appellation, the "poets in the kitchen." To them, Marshall attributes the best of her work: "it stands as testimony to the rich legacy of language and culture they so freely passed on to me in the wordshop of the kitchen."[13]

Walker numbers only three literary foremothers in her essay: Phillis Wheatley, Nella Larsen, and Zora Neale Hurston. In the past decade, scholars have discovered that there have in fact been generations of black women writers. Reclamation projects have been carried out by Henry Louis Gates (Harriet Wilson), Gloria Hull (Alice Dunbar-Nelson), and Jean Fagan Yellin (Harriet Jacobs). McDowell's Black Women Writers series for Beacon Press has brought back into print such twentieth-century authors as Marita Bonner, Alice Childress, Ann Petry, and Carlene Hatcher Polite. By far the most extensive and potentially influential project is the Schomburg Library of Nineteenth-Century Black Women Writers, published under the general editorship of Henry Louis Gates in 1988. This series includes volumes by thirty authors, many of them unheard of and certainly unread until now. With the availability of all these texts, the task of identifying and analyzing what Smith termed the thematic, stylistic, and linguistic commonalities in black women's writing becomes possible, even as the dimensions of the task are made clear.

Surely, much has been accomplished. In relatively short order, black feminist critics and other critics of black women's writing have restored a lost tradition.[14] They have begun, in fact, to rethink the very concept of tradition. As Washington observes, tradition "is a word that nags the feminist critic. A word that has so often been used to exclude or misrepresent women." In the afterword to *Conjuring: Black Women, Fiction and Literary Tradition,* the anthology she co-edited, Spillers names many novels by black women that seem *not* to exist in intertextual relation. She draws a typically provocative conclusion: "I would want to say that 'tradition' for black women's writing community is a matrix of literary *discontinuities* that partially articulate various periods of consciousness in the history of an African-American people." In *Reconstructing Womanhood: The Emergence of the Afro-American Woman Novelist,* Hazel Carby eschews the term *tradition* altogether; she advocates instead that "black feminist criticism be regarded as a problem, not a solution, as a sign that should be interrogated, a locus of contradictions."[15]

Carby's position and the language in which she formulates it point to another transformation. Carby introduces her ground-breaking study by noting the emergence of two fields of academic inquiry during the period her book was conceived, researched, and written— black feminist literary criticism and black women's history. From the perspective of the pioneers of black feminist literary criticism at least, it might be more accurate to say that during the decade separating Smith's manifesto and Carby's study, the American academy entered the age of theory.

According to Elizabeth Bruss, some of the same sociopolitical forces that gave visibility to the community of black women writing impelled the move to theory; these included the challenge to academic authority and to traditional humanism, the advent of a more diverse student body and the attendant curricular changes, notably the teaching of nontraditional literatures.[16] Yet the intersection was delayed. In her essay "The Race for Theory," Barbara Christian explains that she first ignored what she terms the "takeover in the literary world by Western philosophers" because she felt she had "more pressing and interesting things to do, such as reading and studying the history of black women." Here Christian suggests one important reason the debate over the utility of poststructuralist theory has come rather late to the interpretive community most concerned with writing by black women.[17]

Leaving no doubt about where she stands, Christian proclaims:

The race for theory, with its linguistic jargon, its emphasis on quoting its prophets, its tendency towards 'Biblical' exegesis, its refusal even to mention specific works of creative writers, far less contemporary ones, its preoccupations with mechanical analyses of language, graphs, algebraic equations, its gross

CHERYL A. WALL

generalizations about culture, has silenced many of us to the extent that some of us feel we can no longer discuss our literature, while others have developed intense writing blocks and are puzzled by the incomprehensibility of the language set adrift in literary circles.[18]

Undoubtedly, these words touch a responsive chord in many of Christian's readers. She reminds us that in the "race for theory," black feminist critics should not forsake the work with which they have been concerned. Their enterprise has given us clarifying readings of key texts. And while the world may or may not need more readings of *King Lear* and *Light in August,* it certainly needs more readings of *Incidents in the Life of a Slave Girl* and *Iola Leroy.* These texts went uninterpreted for nearly a century. We need as well readings of the new novels and books of poetry that are appearing, readings of *Sarah Phillips* and *Mama Day, Ridin' the Moon to Texas* and *Under a Soprano Sky.*

Yet there is other work for critics to do. After or concurrent with these first readings should come more relational readings that put individual texts in dialogue. As Jonathan Culler observes in "Beyond Interpretation," since texts "participate in a variety of systems—the conventions of literary genres, the logic of story and the teleologies of emplotment, the condensations and displacements of desire, the various discourses of knowledge that are found in a culture—critics can move through texts towards an understanding of the systems and semiotic process which make them possible." [19]

Black women's writing may be read, then, alongside both those cultural artifacts like blues which are produced by Afro-American women and those artifacts of literary and popular culture which may or may not construct representations of black women but with whose production black women have nothing to do. It is not that we need literary theory to help us recognize that blues are, in Houston Baker's phrase, a "generative source" of black women's writing; but perspectives informed by literary theory may help us move beyond identifying blues metaphors and celebrating blues singers as artistic models to understanding how blues aesthetics and ethics are inscribed. Similarly, by reading black women's writing in the context of African and European philosophical and religious systems, we may mark when and how this writing privileges "other" ways of knowing. In a complementary move, we may begin to ask the same questions about race, gender, and class of "canonical" texts (and "noncanonical" texts by white men, black men, white women, men and women of color, everybody) that we ask of those by black women. We should continue to locate black women's writing in its multiple contexts.

Among its most intriguing possibilities, relational reading may allow us to reemphasize the connection between what Gayatri Spivak calls the verbal text and the social text. This connection is problematized in Afro-American literary study generally, because Afro-American literature has so often been misread as mimetic representation or sociology. In other words, the verbal text has been treated as if it merely mirrored the social text. To read that way is inanely reductive, but to read black writing as if it has no relation to political reality is to vitiate its power. Writing out of a complex of explicitly ideological and theoretical positions, Spivak suggests a tactical reversal when she argues that the strategies of literary criticism may be extremely useful in "interpreting and changing the social text." [20]

Spillers's "Interstices: A Small Drama of Words" enacts such a move, as it theorizes the construction of black women as sexual subjects. Spillers warns that "it is no use trying to decide whether or not discourse about discourse, or the impure good of theory is 'good' or 'bad,' [the] apparent reality is that it *is*." Black women's absence from the "privileged mode of feminist expression,' the nonfictional feminist text, allows white women who dominate the discussion to define issues such as sexuality, using their experience as normative. [21] Spillers's stance in the essay is not that she wishes to appropriate existing theories; she wants to create her own. Her theory will conflate critical discourse and the testimony of the women who live the experience she wishes to theorize. Consequently she draws on sources as diverse as Freud and Foucault, Kenneth Burke and Bessie Smith, and most notably the women whose testimonies John Gwaltney records in *Drylongso: A Self-Portrait of Black America*. Spillers's essay is stunning in its reach, as I hope my crude simplification conveys. What is striking to me as well is the continuity suggested by her "privileging" of the first-order naming of Gwaltney's informants.

In resisting the perspective of poststructuralism that would distrust any appeal to experience, Spillers sustains a view widely held in the community of black women writing. Appeals to experience need not be essentialist and ahistorical, because the experience of Afro-American women is unmistakably polyvalent. The simultaneity of oppressions in their lives resists essentialist conclusions. Black women are indeed "witnesses to and participants in [their] own experience, and, in no way coincidentally, in the experience of those with whom [they] have come in contact." The concept of a "multiple, shifting, and often self-contradictory identity, a subject that is not divided in, but rather at odds with language, an identity made up of heterogenous and heteronomous representations of gender, race, and class," which Teresa de Lauretis asserts is now emerging in feminist writings, sounds very much like that set forth almost twenty years ago by Audre Lorde. Who said it was simple, indeed?[22]

THIS VOLUME RECORDS ONE AND, I HOPE, CREATES another moment in an intense and extended conversation among black women writers and their readers. In October 1987, a group of critics and scholars participated in a conference at Rutgers University entitled "Changing Our Own Words: A Symposium on Criticism, Theory, and Literature by Black Women." [23] Speakers were asked to reflect on the following questions: What are the most fruitful contexts for the analysis of writing by black women? What can be learned from recent developments in literary theory? Can and should theories particular to black women's writing be developed? If so, what would the sources of such theories be? How might the literature under discussion alter traditional critical categories, categories of genre for example? The overarching question was how to bring the terms *criticism, theory,* and *writing by black women* into conjunction.

The title "Changing Our Own Words" is derived from a recurrent figure in the prose of Zora Neale Hurston. An idiom in the Afro-American vernacular—though not unique to it—"changing words" is an expression Hurston had either or perhaps both grown up hearing and transcribed in her field notes. A telling example of the use to which she put it in her fiction occurs in the opening scene of *Jonah's Gourd Vine.* Here a husband and wife argue over their children, their domestic arrangements, and the impact of slavery's legacy on their lives. When the argument grows ugly, the husband threatens violence if the wife does not keep silent: "Don't you change so many words

wid me, 'oman! Ah'll knock yuh dead ez Hector. Shet yo' Mouf!''
Amy Crittenden responds in typical Hurston style: "Ah change jez
ez many words ez Ah Durn please! Ahm three times seben and uh
button.'' [24]

Speech is an adult right that Amy, like so many other female characters in Hurston's and other black women's writing, must struggle
to assert. The risks of speaking are never small—not for Amy or Janie
Crawford, Pecola Breedlove or Nel Wright, Selina Boyce or Avey
Johnson, but claiming the right to speak is a requisite part of claiming
a self. As bell hooks asserts, "moving from silence into speech is for
the oppressed, the colonized, the exploited, and those who stand and
struggle side by side a gesture of defiance that heals, that makes new
life and growth possible. It is that act of speech of 'talking back,' that
is no mere gesture of empty words, that is the expression of our
movement from object to subject—the liberated voice." [25]

The doubled difficulty for black women to claim the right to speak
is represented clearly in *Jonah's Gourd Vine,* whose protagonist is a
male preacher. Implicitly a contrast is drawn between the relation to
language of characters like Amy and the major female character,
Lucy, and that of the protagonist, John. In contrast to John's vividly
metaphorical and public preaching, Lucy's talk, rich in wit and apho-
rism, is overheard in the home; only children respond to its imperatives. His words earn money, status, and respect. Hers evoke his
silence and enmity.

In recent writing, monologues become a favored device to represent the inability of women to "talk back" outside the home as well
as the refusal of men to engage in dialogue within it. This strategy is
employed by Marshall and Morrison and, in a more surreal aspect,
by playwright Adrienne Kennedy. For example, in *The Bluest Eye,*
Claudia describes her mother's monologues or "fussing soliloquies"
as "interminable, insulting, and although indirect (Mama never
named anybody—just talked about folks and *some* people), extremely
painful in their thrust.'' [26] Her daughters alone hear and respond to
this mother's pain. Only when Morrison puts this mother's voice in
dialogue with other voices in the novel can the objects of the mother's
anger be identified and her pain assuaged.

What bell hooks calls the "liberational voice" is not this mother's
voice (which is freed only in the daughter's representation) but the
voice, like Janie Crawford's specifying on Joe Starks, that is heard by

those it addresses. In the ideal case, this voice, like Celie's in *The Color Purple,* may liberate speaker and auditor alike.

The figure "changing words," derived, as it is from a form of the word *exchange* in which the weakly stressed syllable has been dropped, retains the idea of dialogue. What Hurston's Amy Crittenden seeks and her husband denies her is the reciprocal give and take of ideas. Happily, the spirit of exchange is at the heart of this volume's conversation. Its contributors exchange ideas with black women writers, with critics, with theorists (feminist theorists, theorists of Afro-American literature and culture, Marxist and Freudian theorists, poststructuralist theorists, et al.), and with each other. In the process they collapse more than a few of these categories.

THE CRITICAL PARADIGM THAT MAE HENDERSON DE-vises in "Speaking in Tongues: Dialogism, Dialectics, and the Black Woman Writer's Literary Tradition," answers the challenge Henry Louis Gates issues in *Figures in Black.* The critic of Afro-American literature should not, Gates says, "shy away from literary theory, but rather . . . translate it into the black idiom, renaming principles of criticism where appropriate, but especially naming indigenous black principles of criticism and applying these to explicate our own texts."[27] "Speaking in Tongues" does just that. Heteroglossia and glossalalia, Henderson's tropes for intertexuality and revision, are defined in terms of Bakhtin and Gadamer as well as in terms of the religious practices of the Afro-American Sanctified church. The perspectives she brings from literary theory help her produce the stunning readings of *Sula* and *Dessa Rose* that ground her argument. But Henderson builds as well on the work that has preceded hers in the black feminist project. When she suggests that black women's writing elicits the sustained responses it does because of the simultaneity of its discourse, she brings that idea full circle, picking it up where Barbara Smith and Audre Lorde began.

For Valerie Smith, black feminist literary theory "seeks to explore representations of black women's lives through techniques of analysis which suspend the variables of race, class, and gender in mutually interrogative relation." Such fluidity and questioning surely characterize her essay, "Black Feminist Theory and the Representation of the 'Other.'" In Smith's view, because black feminist criticism has grown ever more self-reflexive, a turn toward deconstruction is therefore inevitable. Some black feminist critics would question any such inevitability, but almost all share Smith's belief that it is crucial that their enterprise remain oppositional. Given the current popularity of black women's writing in the academic curriculum and the increasing institutionalization of its criticism, sustaining that opposition may be problematic. Smith suggests why it need not be impossible.

In "But What Do We Think We're Doing Anyway: The State of Black Feminist Criticism(s) or My Version of a Little Bit of History," Barbara Christian offers a view that is far less sanguine. Narrating her personal history, she emphasizes the hostility of the academy to black feminist criticism at its inception and warns against the academy becoming its exclusive site. An oppositional perspective, Christian argues, must be tied to a "literary activism." She makes the compelling point that far from a vogue—manufactured, sustained, and soon to be concluded by commercial publishers—as some of its opponents have been claiming it to be for almost twenty years, black women's writing is sustained within the Afro-American community. Indeed, novels by Morrison, Naylor, and Alice Walker seem to me to be the counterparts of the broadsides and chapbooks that were passed from hand to hand during the 1960s.

Deborah McDowell's "Reading Family Matters" unpacks the issues at the core of the contentious debate over the work of certain black women writers, notably Alice Walker. Reception theory is one tool McDowell draws on to analyze critical and fictional texts by the black feminist writer and the resisting black male reader. If the debate's issues turn on the shifting concepts of identity and narrative, the stakes are at once mundane—professional reputations and money—and profound—the right to write the family romance. In the latter instance, two deeply felt desires collide: the desire on the part of some for the family's recuperation and the restitution of the father's place in it, and the equally urgent desire on the part of others to imagine the family anew.

In "Allegories of Black Female Desire," Claudia Tate reads family matters through what she terms "nineteenth-century sentimental narratives of black female authority." Complementing one aspect of the preceding essay, Tate demonstrates how long-standing is the desire for the recuperation of the family. But the nineteenth-century woman writer and her female characters welcomed marriage and the family it promised with a level of equanimity that no twentieth-century black writer could muster. The critical problem Tate addresses is why traditional Afro-American scholarship has produced pejorative readings or none at all of novels by such writers as Frances Harper, Pauline Hopkins, Amelia Johnson, Emma Dunham Kelly, and Harriet Wilson. Tate contends that we have to read texts synchronically, with an awareness of historical shifts in values and meaning. Her essay facilitates our access to long lost narratives.

The depth of the desire for the family's recuperation and the inversions through which it is expressed are concerns Hortense Spillers addresses in "The Permanent Obliquity of an In(pha)llibly Straight." She interrogates the applicability of Freudian theory to the African-American situation, where, she argues historically, the African woman and man enslaved in the New World stood outside patriarchal law. When the African woman assumed the female roles sanctioned under patriarchy, she was not granted the protection of law. In a legal system where children of slaves, unlike all other children, followed the status of the mother, father was not a role the African man could assume. Spillers suggests that the recurrent representations of incest in modern black fiction are symbolic projections of this violent dispossession. Through detailed readings of two illustrative texts—one "canonical," *Invisible Man,* and one heretical, Alice Walker's "The Child Who Favored Daughter"—Spillers argues that incest here speaks for the black family's "losses, confusions, and its imposed abeyance of order and degree." Out of these losses, new configurations of the family might emerge.

The last three essays offer diverse examples of close and relational reading. "Living on the Line" is the supple and apt metaphor Gloria Hull develops to frame her study of Audre Lorde's poetry. In the view of her readers/admirers, Lorde, a black lesbian feminist who often assumes the persona of secular witness, places her life ever on the line. Pitching her oracular voice "at different frequencies," Lorde has challenged conventions of family, community, and nation. In its analysis of the recurrence of lines, edges, border, margins, and boundaries as figures in Lorde's work, Hull's essay exemplifies the ways close reading may be fruitfully combined with a consideration of historical and political context. Her discussion of Lorde's "ceaseless negotiations of a positionality from which she can speak" restates a key concern of this volume.

Susan Willis in "I Shop Therefore I Am" reads black women's fiction in relation to artifacts of mass culture, such as advertisements, toys, and popular music. Extending an element of the argument she developed in *Specifying: Black Women Writing the American Experience,* Willis asserts that black women's writing offers a forceful critique of the mass culture that dispenses commodities and values across gender, race, and class lines. It valorizes the *differences* mass culture denies. Of particular concern to her analysis is the way in which that culture merchandises Afro-Americans and co-opts the vernacular culture that is the wellspring of the utopian visions in contemporary black women's fiction.

Finally, in "What Is Your Nation?" Abena Busia presents another context in which to read writing by black American women, one that would include their sister writers in Africa and the Caribbean. Like Paule Marshall, Ama Ata Aidoo, Michelle Cliff, and Maryse Conde revalidate for their readers nonwritten cultural forms, particularly storytelling but also rituals of song, dance, and drama. To read their fictions well, Busia argues, we must develop a "diaspora literacy" of the kind manifested throughout her perceptive reading of Marshall's *Praisesong for the Widow.* To do so is not only to apprehend the theme of personal and cultural restoration in a single text, but to become aware of a larger project in which women writers across the African diaspora participate.

Rereading these essays conjures up another meaning intrinsic to our title. Changing words means transforming words. Not only has the criticism of black women's writing been transformed over the past two decades; this criticism has transformed other critical discourses as well. To paraphrase a title so resonant that it is quoted frequently below, all the blacks are (not) men, all the women are (not) white, but some critics are (still) brave. The extent to which feminist and Afro-Americanist writing and, yes, even the criticism that claims the center are more inclusive than they were twenty years ago owes much to black women's writing and its critics changing as many words as they pleased. The challenging essays collected here should produce more "(ex)changes."

Speaking in Tongues: Dialogics, Dialectics, and the Black Woman Writer's Literary Tradition

I am who I am, doing what I came to do, acting
upon you like a drug or a chisel *to remind you of your me-ness, as
I discover you in myself.*
                    —Audre Lorde, *Sister Outsider* (emphasis mine)

> There's a noisy feelin' near the cracks
> crowdin' me . . . slips into those long, loopin' "B's"
> There's a noisy feelin' near the cracks
> crowdin' me . . . slips into those long, loopin' "B's"
> of Miss Garrison's handwritin' class;
> they become the wire hoops I must jump through.
> It spooks my alley, it spooks my play,
> more nosey now than noisy,
>   lookin' for a tongue
>   lookin' for a tongue
>   to get holy in.
> Who can tell this feelin' where to set up church?
> Who can tell this noise where to go?
> A root woman workin' . . . a mo-jo,
> just to the left of my ear.
>   —Cherry Muhanji, *Tight Spaces*

Some years ago, three black feminist critics and scholars edited an anthology entitled *All the Women Are White, All the Blacks Are Men, But Some of Us Are Brave,*[1] suggesting in the title the unique and peculiar dilemma of black women. Since then it has perhaps become almost commonplace for literary critics, male and female, black and white, to note that black women have been discounted or unaccounted for in the "traditions" of black, women's, and American literature as well as in the contemporary literary-critical dialogue. More recently, black women writers have begun to receive token recognition as they are subsumed under the category of woman in the feminist critique and the category of black in the racial critique. Certainly these "gendered" and "racial" decodings of black women authors present strong and revisionary methods of reading, focusing as they do on literary discourses regarded as marginal to the dominant literary-critical tradition. Yet the "critical insights" of one reading might well become the "blind spots" of another reading. That is, by privileging one category of analysis at the expense of the other, each of these methods risks setting up what Fredric Jameson describes as "strategies of containment," which restrict or repress different or alternative readings.[2] More specifically, blindness to what Nancy Fraser describes as "the gender subtext" can be just as occluding as blindness to *the race subtext* in the works of black women writers.[3]

Such approaches can result in exclusion at worst and, at best, a reading of part of the text as the whole—a strategy that threatens to replicate (if not valorize) the reification against which black women struggle in life and literature. What I propose is a theory of interpretation based on what I refer to as the "simultaneity of discourse," a term inspired by Barbara Smith's seminal work on black feminist criticism.[4] This concept is meant to signify a mode of reading which examines the ways in which the perspectives of race and gender, and their interrelationships, structure the discourse of black women writers. Such an approach is intended to acknowledge and overcome the limitations imposed by assumptions of internal identity (homogeneity) and the repression of internal differences (heterogeneity) in racial and gendered readings of works by black women writers. In other words, I propose a model that seeks to account for racial difference within gender identity and gender difference within racial identity. This approach represents my effort to avoid what one critic describes as the presumed "absolute and self-sufficient" *otherness* of the critical stance in order to allow the complex representations of black women writers to steer us away from "a simple and reductive paradigm of 'otherness.'"[5]

Discursive Diversity: Speaking in Tongues

What is at once characteristic and suggestive about black women's writing is its interlocutory, or dialogic, character, reflecting not only

MAE GWENDOLYN HENDERSON

a relationship with the "other(s)," but an internal dialogue with the plural aspects of self that constitute the matrix of black female subjectivity. The interlocutory character of black women's writings is, thus, not only a consequence of a dialogic relationship with an imaginary or "generalized Other," but a dialogue with the aspects of "otherness" within the self. The complex situatedness of the black woman as not only the "Other" of the Same, but also as the "other" of the other(s) implies, as we shall see, a relationship of difference and identification with the "other(s)."

It is Mikhail Bakhtin's notion of dialogism and consciousness that provides the primary model for this approach. According to Bakhtin, each social group speaks in its own "social dialect"—possesses its own unique language—expressing shared values, perspectives, ideology, and norms. These social dialects become the "languages" of heteroglossia "intersect[ing] with each other in many different ways. . . . As such they all may be juxtaposed to one another, mutually supplement one another, contradict one another and be interrelated dialogically." [6] Yet if language, for Bakhtin, is an expression of social identity, then subjectivity (subjecthood) is constituted as a social entity through the "role of [the] word as medium of consciousness." Consciousness, then, like language, is shaped by the social environment. ("Consciousness becomes consciousness only . . . in the process of social interaction.") Moreover, "the semiotic material of the psyche is preeminently the word—*inner speech*." Bakhtin in fact defines the relationship between consciousness and inner speech even more precisely: "Analysis would show that the units of which inner speech is constituted are certain *whole entities . . . [resembling] the alternating lines of a dialogue*. There was good reason why thinkers in ancient times should have conceived of inner speech as *inner dialogue*." [7] Thus consciousness becomes a kind of "inner speech" reflecting "the outer word" in a process that links the psyche, language, and social interaction.

It is the process by which these heteroglossic voices of the other(s) "encounter one another and coexist in the consciousness of real people—first and foremost in the creative consciousness of people who write novels," [8] that speaks to the situation of black women writers in particular, "privileged" by a social positionality that enables them to speak in dialogically racial and gendered voices to the other(s) both within and without. If the psyche functions as an internalization of heterogeneous social voices, black women's speech/writing becomes at once a dialogue between self and society and between self and psyche. Writing as inner speech, then, becomes what Bakhtin would describe as "a unique form of collaboration with oneself" in the works of these writers.[9]

Revising and expanding Teresa de Lauretis's formulation of the "social subject and the relations of subjectivity to sociality," I propose a model that is intended not only to address "a subject en-gendered in the experiencing of race," but also what I submit is *a subject "racialized" in the experiencing of gender.*[10] Speaking both to and from the position of the other(s), black women writers must, in the words of Audre Lorde, deal not only with "the external manifestations of racism and sexism," but also "with the results of those distortions internalized within our consciousness of ourselves and one another."[11]

What distinguishes black women's writing, then, is the privileging (rather than repressing) of "the other in ourselves." Writing of Lorde's notion of self and otherness, black feminist critic Barbara Christian observes of Lorde what I argue is true to a greater or lesser degree in the discourse of black women writers: "As a black, lesbian, feminist, poet, mother, Lorde has, in her own life, had to search long and hard for *her* people. In responding to each of these audiences, in which a part of her identity lies, she refuses to give up her differences. In fact she uses them, as woman to man, black to white, lesbian to heterosexual, as a means of conducting creative dialogue."[12]

If black women speak from a multiple and complex social, historical, and cultural positionality which, in effect, constitutes black female subjectivity, then Christian's term "creative dialogue" refers to the expression of a multiple *dialogic of differences* based on this complex subjectivity. At the same time, however, black women enter into a *dialectic of identity* with those aspects of self shared with others. It is Hans-Georg Gadamer's "dialectical model of conversation," rather than Bakhtin's dialogics of discourse, that provides an appropriate model for articulating a relation of mutuality and reciprocity with the "Thou"—or intimate other(s). Whatever the critic thinks of Gadamer's views concerning history, tradition, and the like, one can still find Gadamer's emphases—especially as they complement Bakhtin's—to be useful and productive. If the Bakhtinian model is primarily adversarial, assuming that verbal communication (and social interaction) is characterized by contestation with the other(s), then the Gadamerian model presupposes as its goal a language of consensus, communality, and even identification, in which "one claims to express the other's claim and even to understand the other better than the other understands [him or herself]." In the "I-Thou" relationship proposed by Gadamer, "the important thing is . . . to experience the 'Thou' truly as a 'Thou,' that is, not to overlook [the other's] claim and to listen to what [s/he] has to say to us." Gadamer's dialectic, based on a typology of the "hermeneutical experience," privileges tradition as "a genuine partner in communication, with which we have fellowship as does the 'I' with a 'Thou.'" For black and women writers, such an avowal of tradition in the subdominant order, of course, constitutes an operative challenge to the dominant order. It is this rereading of the notion of tradition within a field of gender and ethnicity that supports and enables the notion of community among those who share a common history, language, and culture. If Bakhtin's dialogic engagement with the Other signifies conflict, Gadamer's monologic acknowledgment of the Thou signifies the potential of agreement. If the Bakhtinian dialogic model speaks to the other within, then Gadamer's speaks to *the same within.* Thus, "the [dialectic] understanding of the [Thou]" (like the dialogic understanding of the other[s]) becomes "a form of self-relatedness." [13]

It is this notion of discursive difference and identity underlying the simultaneity of discourse which typically characterizes black women's writing. Through the multiple voices that enunciate her complex subjectivity, the black woman writer not only speaks familiarly in the discourse of the other(s), but as Other she is in contestorial dialogue with the hegemonic dominant and subdominant or "ambiguously (non)hegemonic" discourses. [14] These writers enter simultaneously into familial, or *testimonial* and public, or *competitive* discourses—discourses that both affirm and challenge the values and expectations of the reader. As such, black women writers enter into testimonial discourse with black men as blacks, with white women as women, and with black women as black women. [15] At the same time, they enter into a competitive discourse with black men as women, with white women as blacks, and with white men as black women. If black women speak a discourse of racial and gendered difference in the dominant or hegemonic discursive order, they speak a discourse of racial and gender identity and difference in the subdominant discursive order. This dialogic of difference and dialectic of identity characterize both black women's subjectivity and black women's discourse. It is the complexity of these simultaneously homogeneous and heterogeneous social and discursive domains out of which black women write and construct themselves (as blacks and women and, often, as poor, black women) that enables these women writers authoritatively to speak to and engage both hegemonic and ambiguously (non)hegemonic discourse.

Janie, the protagonist in Zora Neale Hurston's *Their Eyes Were Watching God,* demonstrates how the dialectics/dialogics of black and female subjectivity structure black women's discourse.[16] Combining personal and public forms of discourse in the court scene where she is on trial and fighting not only for her life but against "lying thoughts" and "misunderstanding," Janie addresses the judge, a jury composed of "twelve more white men," and spectators ("eight or ten white women" and "all the Negroes [men] for miles around" [274]). The challenge of Hurston's character is that of the black woman writer—namely, to speak at once to a diverse audience about her experience in a racist and sexist society where to be black and female is to be, so to speak, "on trial." Janie not only speaks in a discourse of gender and racial difference to the white male judge and jurors, but also in a discourse of gender difference (and racial identity) to the black male spectators and a discourse of racial difference (and gender identity) to the white women spectators. Significantly, it is the white men who constitute both judge and jury, and, by virtue of their control of power and discourse, possess the authority of life and death over the black woman. In contrast, the black men (who are convinced that the "nigger [woman] kin kill . . . jus' as many niggers as she please") and white women (who "didn't seem too mad") read and witness/oppose a situation over which they exercise neither power nor discourse (225, 280).

Janie's courtroom discourse also emblematizes the way in which the categories of public and private break down in black women's discourse. In the context of Janie's courtroom scene, testimonial discourse takes on an expanded meaning, referring to both juridical, public, and dominant discourse as well as familial, private, and nondominant discourse. Testimonial, in this sense, derives its meaning from both "testimony" as an official discursive mode and "testifying," defined by Geneva Smitherman as "a ritualized form of . . . communication in which the speaker gives verbal witness to the efficacy, truth, and power of some experience in which [the group has] shared." The latter connotation suggests an additional meaning in the context of theological discourse where testifying refers to a "spontaneous expression to the church community [by whomever] feels the spirit." [17]

Like Janie, black women must speak in a plurality of voices as well as in a multiplicity of discourses. This discursive diversity, or simultaneity of discourse, I call "speaking in tongues." Significantly, glossolalia, or speaking in tongues, is a practice associated with black women in the Pentecostal Holiness church, the church of my childhood and the church of my mother. In the Holiness church (or as we called it, the Sanctified church), speaking unknown tongues (tongues known only to God) is in fact a sign of election, or holiness. As a trope it is also intended to remind us of Alice Walker's characterization of black women as artists, as "Creators," intensely rich in that spirituality which Walker sees as "the basis of Art." [18]

Glossolalia is perhaps the meaning most frequently associated with speaking in tongues. It is this connotation which emphasizes the particular, private, closed, and privileged communication between the congregant and the divinity. Inaccessible to the general congregation, this mode of communication is outside the realm of public discourse and foreign to the known tongues of humankind.

But there is a second connotation to the notion of speaking in tongues—one that suggests not glossolalia, but heteroglossia, the ability to speak in diverse known languages. While glossolalia refers to the ability to "utter the mysteries of the spirit," heteroglossia describes the ability to speak in the multiple languages of public discourse. If glossolalia suggests private, nonmediated, nondifferentiated univocality, heteroglossia connotes public, differentiated, social, mediated, dialogic discourse. Returning from the trope to the act of reading, perhaps we can say that speaking in tongues connotes both the semiotic, presymbolic babble (baby talk), as between mother and child—which Julia Kristeva postulates as the "mother tongue"—and the diversity of voices, discourses, and languages described by Mikhail Bakhtin.

Speaking in tongues, my trope for both glossolalia and heteroglossia, has a precise genealogical evolution in the Scriptures. In Genesis 11, God confounded the world's language when the city of Babel built a tower in an attempt to reach the heavens. Speaking in many and different tongues, the dwellers of Babel, unable to understand each other, fell into confusion, discord, and strife, and had to abandon the project. Etymologically, the name of the city Babel sounds much like the Hebrew word for "babble"—meaning confused, as in baby talk. Babel, then, suggests the two related, but distinctly different, meanings of speaking in tongues, meanings borne out in other parts of the Scriptures. The most common is that implied in 1 Corinthians 14—the ability to speak in unknown tongues. According to this interpretation, speaking in tongues suggests the ability to speak in and through the spirit. Associated with glossolalia—speech in unknown tongues—it is ecstatic, rapturous, inspired speech, based on a relation of intimacy and identification between the individual and God.

If Genesis tells of the disempowerment of a people by the introduction of different tongues, then Acts 2 suggests the empowerment of the disciples who, assembled on the day of Pentecost in the upper room of the temple in Jerusalem, "were filled with the Holy Spirit and began to speak in other tongues." Although the people thought the disciples had "imbibed a strange and unknown wine," it was the Holy Spirit which had driven them, filled with ecstasy, from the upper room to speak among the five thousand Jews surrounding the temple. The Scriptures tell us that the tribes of Israel all understood them, each in his own tongue. The Old Testament, then, suggests the dialogics of difference in its diversity of discourse, while the New Testament, in its unifying language of the spirit, suggests the dialectics of identity. If the Bakhtinian model suggests the multiplicity of speech as suggested in the dialogics of difference, then Gadamer's model moves toward a unity of understanding in its dialectics of identity.

It is the first as well as the second meaning which we privilege in speaking of black women writers: the first connoting polyphony, multivocality, and plurality of voices, and the second signifying intimate, private, inspired utterances. Through their intimacy with the discourse of the other(s), black women writers weave into their work competing and complementary discourses—discourses that seek both to adjudicate competing claims and witness common concerns.[19]

Also interesting is the link between the gift of tongues, the gift of prophecy, and the gift of interpretation. While distinguishing between these three gifts, the Scriptures frequently conflate or conjoin them. If to speak in tongues is to utter mysteries in and through the Spirit, to prophesy is to speak to others in a (diversity of) language(s) which the congregation can understand. The Scriptures would suggest that the disciples were able to perform both. I propose, at this juncture, an enabling critical fiction—that it is black women writers who are the modern day apostles, empowered by experience to speak as poets and prophets in many tongues. With this critical gesture, I also intend to signify a deliberate intervention by black women writers into the canonic tradition of sacred/literary texts.[20]

A Discursive Dilemma

In their works, black women writers have encoded oppression as a discursive dilemma, that is, their works have consistently raised the problem of the black woman's relationship to power and discourse. Silence is an important element of this code. The classic black woman's text *Their Eyes Were Watching God* charts the female protagonist's development from voicelessness to voice, from silence to tongues. Yet this movement does not exist without intervention by the other(s)—who speak for and about black women. In other words, it is not that black women, in the past, have had nothing to say, but rather that they have had no say. The absence of black female voices has allowed others to inscribe, or write, and ascribe to, or read, them. The notion of speaking in tongues, however, leads us away from an examination of how the Other has written/read black women and toward an examination of how black women have written the other(s)' writing/reading black women.

Using the notion of "speaking in tongues" as our model, let us offer a kind of paradigmatic reading of two works which encode and resist the material and discursive dilemma of the black woman writer. Sherley Anne Williams's *Dessa Rose* and Toni Morrison's *Sula* are novels that emphasize respectively the *inter*cultural/racial and *intra*cultural/racial sites from which black women speak, as well as the signs under which they speak in both these milieus.[21] Artificial though this separation may be—since, as we have seen, black women are located simultaneously within both these discursive domains—such a distinction makes possible an examination of black women's literary relations to both dominant and subdominant discourse. These works also allow us to compare the suppression of the black female voice in the dominant discourse with its repression in the subdominant discourse.[22] Finally, they provide models for the disruption of the dominant and subdominant discourse by black and female expression, as well as for the appropriation and transformation of these discourses.

The heroine of Sherley Anne Williams's first novel, *Dessa Rose,* is a fugitive slave woman introduced to the reader as "the Darky" by Adam Nehemiah, a white male writer interviewing her in preparation for a forthcoming book, *The Roots of Rebellion in the Slave Population and some Means of Eradicating Them* (or, more simply, *The Work*). The opening section of the novel is structured primarily by notations from Nehemiah's journal, based on his interactions with the slave woman during her confinement in a root cellar while awaiting her fate at the gallows. The latter section, describing her adventures as a fugitive involved in a scam against unsuspecting slaveholders and traders, is narrated primarily in the voice of Dessa (as the slave woman calls herself) after she has managed, with the assistance of fellow slaves, to escape the root cellar. At the end of the novel, the writer-interviewer, Adam Nehemiah, still carrying around his notes for *The Work,* espies the fugitive Dessa.

Brandishing a poster advertising a reward for her recapture, and a physical description of her identifying markings (an R branded on the thigh and whip-scarred hips), Adam Nehemiah coerces the local sheriff into detaining Dessa for identification. Significantly, Adam Nehemiah, named after his precursor—the archetypal white male namer, creator, and interpreter—attempts not only to remand Dessa into slavery but to inscribe her experiences as a slave woman through a discourse that suppresses her voice. Like the Adam of Genesis, Nehemiah asserts the right of ownership through the privilege of naming. Not only is his claim of discursive and material power held together symbolically in his name, but his acts and his words conflate: Nehemiah not only wishes to capture Odessa (as he calls her) in words that are instructive to the preservation of slavery, but he wishes to confine her in material slavery. Just as the biblical Nehemiah constructed the wall to protect the Israelites against attack by their enemies, so Williams's Nehemiah sets out to write a manual designed to protect the American South against insurrection by the slaves. Ironically, the character of Nehemiah, a patriot and leader of the Jews after the years of Babylonian captivity, is reread in the context of the Old South as a racist and expert on the "sound management" of the slaves.[23]

Dessa fears that exposure of her scars/branding will confirm her slave status. As she awaits the arrival of Ruth, the white woman who abets in the perpetration of the scam, Dessa thinks to herself, "I could feel everyone of them scars, the one roped partway to my navel that the waist of my draws itched, the corduroyed welts across my hips, and R on my thighs" (223). What interests me here is the literal inscription of Dessa's body, signified by the whip marks and, more specifically, the branded R, as well as the white male writer-cum-reader's attempt to exercise discursive domination over Dessa. Seeking to inscribe black female subjectivity, the white male, in effect, relegates the black woman to the status of discursive object, or spoken subject. The location of the inscriptions—in the area of the genitalia—moreover, signals an attempt to inscribe the sign *slave* in an area that marks her as *woman* ("Scar tissue plowed through her pubic hair region so no hair would ever grow there again" [154]). The effect is to attempt to deprive the slave woman of her femininity and render the surface of her skin a parchment upon which meaning is etched by the whip (pen) of white patriarchal authority and sealed by the firebrand. Together, these inscriptions produce the meaning of black female subjectivity in the discursive domain of slavery.[24] Importantly, the literal inscription of the flesh emphasizes what Monique Wittig, insisting on "the *material* oppression of individuals by discourses," describes as the "unrelenting tyranny that [male discourses] exert upon our *physical* and *mental* selves" (emphasis mine).[25] Dessa is ordered by the sheriff to lift her skirt so that these inscriptions can be "read" by her potential captors. (Perhaps we should read the R on Dessa's thigh as part of an acrostic for *Read.*) The signifying function of her scars is reinforced when Dessa recognizes that "[Nehemiah] wouldn't have to say nothing. Sheriff would see [i.e., read] that for himself" (223). Her remarks also suggest the mortal consequence of such a reading, or misreading:[26] "This [the scars] was what would betray me. . . . these white mens would kill me" (223).

If Williams's *Dessa Rose* contains a representation of the inscription of *black female* in the dominative white and male discourse, then Morrison's *Sula* contains a representation of *female* ascription in black subdominative discourse. If in the context of the white community's discourse Dessa is suppressed as woman *and* black, in the discourse of the black community she is repressed as woman.

Like Dessa, Sula is marked. Unlike Dessa, Sula is marked from birth. Hers is a mark of nativity—a biological rather than cultural inscription, appropriate in this instance because it functions to mark her as a "naturally" inferior female within the black community.[27] The birthmark, "spread[ing] from the middle of the lid toward the eyebrow" (45), is associated with a series of images. For her mother, Hannah, Sula's birthmark "looked more and more like a stem and a rose" (64). Although in European and Eurocentric culture the rose is the gift of love as well as the traditional romantic symbol of female beauty and innocence (lily-white skin and rose blush), it is a symbol that has been appropriated by black women writers from Frances Harper, who uses it as a symbol of romantic love, to Alice Walker, who associates it with sexual love.[28]

Jude, the husband of Nel, Sula's best friend, refers to the birthmark as a "copperhead" and, later, as "the rattlesnake over her eye." If the image of the rose suggests female romantic love and sexuality, then the snake evokes the archetypal Garden and the story of Eve's seduction by the serpent.[29] The association is significant in light of the subsequent seduction scene between Jude and Sula, for it is Jude's perception of the snake imagery which structures his relationship with Sula, suggesting not only that the meaning he ascribes to the birthmark reflects the potential of his relationship with her, but that, on a broader level, it is the "male gaze" which constitutes female subjectivity. At the same time, Morrison redeploys the role of Other in a way that suggests how the black woman as Other is used to constitute (black) male subjectivity.

The community, "clearing up," as it thought, "the meaning of the birthmark over her eye," tells the reader that "it was not a stemmed rose, or a snake, it was Hannah's ashes marking Sula from the very beginning" (99). (That Sula had watched her mother burn to death was her grandmother's contention and the community gossip.) If Jude represents the subject constituted in relation to the black woman as

Other, the community represents a culture constituted in relation to the black woman as Other:

> Their conviction of Sula's evil changed them in accountable yet mysterious ways. Once the source of their personal misfortune was identified, they had leave to protect and love one another. They began to cherish their husbands and wives, protect their children, repair their homes and in general band together against the devil in their midst. (102)

Sula signifies, for the community, the chaos and evil against which it must define and protect itself. Convinced that she bears the mark of the devil because of her association with Shadrack, the town reprobate, the community closes ranks against one who transgresses the boundaries prescribed for women.

For Shadrack, the shell-shocked World War I veteran who has become the community pariah, Sula's birthmark represents "the mark of the fish he loved"—the tadpole (134). A symbol of the primordial beginnings of life in the sea, the tadpole represents potential, transformation, and rebirth. Such an image contrasts with the apocalytic ending of life by fire suggested by the community's perception of Hannah's ashes.[30] As an amphibious creature, the tadpole has the capacity to live both terrestrially and aquatically. Etymologically, Sula's name is derived from the designation of a genus of seabird, again an image associated with a dual environment—aquatic and ariel. These contrasts suggestively position Sula at the crossroads or intersection of life and death, land and sea, earth and air. Thus both the mark and the designation are particularly appropriate for the black woman as one situated within two social domains (black and female) and, as such, implicated in both a racial and gendered discourse.

But it is the black community—the Bottom—which provides the setting for the action in Morrison's novel, and it is the men who have the final say in the community: "It was the men," observes the narrator, "who gave [Sula] the final label, who *fingerprinted* her for all time" (emphasis mine; 197). The men in the community speak a racial discourse that reduces Sula finally to her sexuality: "The word was passed around" that "Sula slept with *white* men" (emphasis mine; 97).

It is thus her sexuality, read through the race relation, which structures her subjectivity within the male-dominated discourse of the
black community.

The power of male discourse and naming is also suggested in the
epithet directed to the twelve-year-old Sula as she, along with her
friend Nel, saunters by Edna Finch's ice cream parlor one afternoon,
passing the old and young men of the Bottom:

> Pigmeat. The words were in all their minds. And one of them,
> one of the young ones, said it aloud. His name was Ajax, a
> twenty-one-year-old pool haunt of sinister beauty. Graceful and
> economical in every movement, he held a place of envy with
> men of all ages for his magnificently foul mouth. In fact he sel-
> dom cursed, and the epithets he chose were dull, even harmless.
> His reputation was derived from the way he handled words.
> When he said "hell" he hit the *h* with his lungs and the impact
> was greater than the achievement of the most imaginative foul
> mouth in town. He could say "shit" with a nastiness impossible
> to imitate. (43)

Not only does the language itself take on a special potency when exer-
cised by males, but the epithet "pigmeat" which Ajax confers on Sula
still has a powerful hold on her seventeen years later, when at twenty-
nine, having traveled across the country and returned to the Bottom,
she is greeted by the now thirty-eight-year-old Ajax at her screen
door: "Sula . . . was curious. She knew nothing about him except the
word he had called out to her years ago and the feeling he had excited
in her then" (110).

The images associated with Sula's birthmark connote, as we have
seen, a plurality of meanings. These images become not only symbols
of opposition and ambiguity associated with the stemmed rose, snake,
fire, and tadpole, but they evoke the qualities of permanence and mutability (nature and culture) inherent in the sign of the birthmark, the
meaning and valence of which changes with the reading and the
reader. At one point, Nel, Sula's complement in the novel, describes
her as one who "helped others define themselves," that is, one who
takes on the complementary aspect of the Other in the process of

constituting subjectivity. As if to underscore Sula's signifying function as absence or mutability, Sula is described as having "no center" and "no ego," "no speck around which to grow" (103). The plurality and flux of meaning ascribed to the birthmark share some of the characteristics of the Sign or, perhaps more precisely, the Signifier. Sula's association with the birthmark gradually evolves, through synecdoche, into an identification between the subject/object and the Sign. Thus her entry into the subdominative discursive order confers on her the status of "a free-floating signifier," open to diverse interpretations.

The inscription (writing) of Dessa and the ascription (reading) of Sula together encode the discursive dilemma of black women in hegemonic and ambiguously (non)hegemonic discursive contexts. However, these works also embody a code of resistance to the discursive and material dominance of black women. To different degrees and in different ways, Williams and Morrison fashion a counterdiscourse within their texts.

Disruption and Revision

In negotiating the discursive dilemma of their characters, these writers accomplish two objectives: the self-inscription of black womanhood, and the establishment of a dialogue of discourses with the other(s). The self-inscription of black women requires disruption, rereading and rewriting the conventional and canonical stories, as well as revising the conventional generic forms that convey these stories. Through this interventionist, intertextual, and revisionary activity, black women writers enter into dialogue with the discourses of the other(s). Disruption—the initial response to hegemonic and ambiguously (non)hegemonic discourse—and revision (rewriting or rereading) together suggest a model for reading black and female literary expression.

Dessa's continued rejection of Adam Nehemiah's inscription suggests that we must read with some measure of credence her claims of being mis-recognized. ("I don't know this master, Mistress," she says. "They mistook me for another Dessa, Mistress" [226–227].) Ultimately, Dessa's insistence on *meconnaissance* is vindicated in the failure of Nehemiah's attempts either to *con*fine her in the social system or *de*fine her in the dominant discourse.

Dessa not only succeeds in rupturing the narrator's discourse at the outset of the novel through a series of interventionist acts—singing, evasion, silence, nonacquiescence, and dissemblance—but she employs these strategies to effect her escape and seize discursive control of the story.[31] Moreover, Dessa's repeated use of the word *track* (a term connoting both pursuit and inscription) in reference to Nehemiah takes on added significance in the context of both her inscription and revision. Tracking becomes the object of her reflections: "Why this white man *track* me down like he owned me, like a bloodhound on my *trail*," and later, "crazy white man, *tracking* me all cross the country like he owned me" (emphasis mine; 225). In other words, Nehemiah *tracks* Dessa in an attempt to establish ownership—that is, the colonization—of her body. Yet tracking also suggests that Dessa's flight becomes a text that she writes and Nehemiah reads. His tracking (i.e., reading of Dessa's text) thus becomes the means by which he attempts to capture her (i.e., suppress her voice in the production of his own text).

If the pursuit/flight pattern emblematizes a strategic engagement for discursive control, Dessa's tracks also mark her emergence as narrator of her own story. It is her escape—loosely speaking, her "making tracks"—that precludes the closure/completion of Nehemiah's book. The story of Dessa's successful revolt and escape, in effect, prefigures the rewriting of *The Work*—Nehemiah's projected treatise on the control of slaves and the prevention of slave revolts. The latter part of the novel, recounted from Dessa's perspective and in her own voice, establishes her as the successful author of her own narrative. Tracking thus becomes a metaphor for writing/reading from the white male narrator's perspective, and a metaphor for revision (*re*writing/*re*reading) from Dessa's. Creating her own track therefore corresponds to Dessa's assumption of discursive control of the novel, that is, the telling of her own story. In flight, then, Dessa challenges the material and discursive elements of her oppression and, at the same time, provides a model for writing as struggle.

Nehemiah's inability to capture Dessa in print is paralleled, finally, in his failure to secure her recapture. As Dessa walks out of the sheriff's office, Nehemiah cries: "I know it's her . . . I got her down here in my book." Leaving, Dessa tells the reader, "And he reach and took out that little black-bound pad he wrote in the whole time I knowed him" (231). But the futility of his efforts is represented in the reactions of the onlookers to the unbound pages of Nehemiah's notebook as they tumble and scatter to the floor:

[Sheriff] Nemi, ain't nothing but some scribbling on here. . . . Can't no one read this.

[Ruth] And these [pages] is blank, sheriff. (232)

Finally, in two dramatic acts of self-entitlement, Dessa reaffirms her ability to name herself and her own experience. In the first instance, she challenges Nehemiah's efforts to capture her—in person and in print: "Why, he didn't even know how to call my name—talking about Odessa" (emphasis mine; 225). And in the second, after her release she informs Ruth, her white accomplice and alleged mistress, "My name Dessa, Dessa Rose. Ain't no O to it" (232). She is, of course, distinguishing between Odessa, an ascription by the white, male slave master and used by both Nehemiah and Ruth, and Dessa, her entitlement proper. Her rejection of the O signifies her rejection of the inscription of her body by the other(s). In other words, Dessa's repudiation of the O (Otherness?) signifies her always already presence—what Ralph Ellison describes as the unquestioned humanity of the slave. She deletes nothing—except the white, male other's inscription/ascription.[32]

At the conclusion of the novel, Dessa once again affirms the importance of writing oneself and one's own history. It is a responsibility that devolves upon the next generation, privileged with a literacy Dessa herself has been denied: "My mind wanders. This is why I have it down, why I has the child say it back. I never will forget Nemi trying to read [and write] me, knowing I had put myself in his hands. Well, *this* the childrens have heard from our own lips" (236). Yet, as Walker might say, the story bears the mother's signature.[33]

While Dessa, through interventions and rewriting, rejects white, male attempts to write and read black female subjectivity, Sula, through disruption and rereading, repudiates black male readings of black female subjectivity. (Significantly, black males, like white females, lack the power to *write,* but not the power to *read* black women.) If it is her sexuality which structures Sula within the confines of black (male) discourse, it is also her sexuality which creates a rupture in that discourse. It is through the act of sexual intercourse that Sula discovers "the center of . . . silence" and a "loneliness so profound *the word itself had no meaning*" (emphasis mine; (106). The "desperate terrain" which she reaches, the "high silence of orgasm" (112), is a nodal point that locates Sula in the interstices of the closed system of (black) male signification. She has, in effect, "[leapt] from the edge" of discourse "into soundlessness" and "[gone] down howling" (106). Howling, a unary movement of nondifferentiated sound, contrasts with the phonic differentiation on which the closed system of language is based. Like the birthmark, which is the symbolic sign of life, the howl is the first sound of life—not yet broken down and differentiated to emerge as intersubjective communication, or discourse. The howl, signifying a prediscursive mode, thus becomes an act of self-reconstitution as well as an act of subversion or resistance to the "network of signification" represented by the symbolic order. The "high silence of orgasm" and the howl allow temporary retreats from or breaks in the dominant discourse. Like Dessa's evasions and interventions, Sula's silences and howls serve to disrupt or subvert the "symbolic function of the language." It is precisely these violations or transgressions of the symbolic order that allow for the expression of the suppressed or repressed aspects of black female subjectivity. The reconstitutive function of Sula's sexuality is suggested in the image of the "post-coital privateness in which she met herself, welcomed herself, and joined herself in matchless harmony" (107). The image is that of symbiosis and fusion—a stage or condition represented in psychoanalysis as pre-Oedipal and anterior to the acquisition of language or entry into the symbolic order.[34]

It is through the howl of orgasm that Sula discovers a prediscursive center of experience that positions her at a vantage point outside of the dominant discursive order. The howl is a form of speaking in tongues and a linguistic disruption that serves as the precondition for Sula's entry into language. Unless she breaks the conventional structures and associations of the dominant discourse, Sula cannot enter through the interstices.[35] (This reading of *Sula,* in effect, reverses the bibical movement from contestorial, public discourse to intimate, familial discourse.)

In contrast to the howl, of course, is the stunning language of poetic metaphor with which Sula represents her lover and the act of love:

If I take a chamois and rub real hard on the bone, right on the ledge of your cheek bone, some of the black will disappear. It will flake away into the chamois and underneath there will be gold leaf. . . . And if I take a nail file or even Eva's old paring knife . . . and scrape away at the gold, it will fall away and there will be alabaster. . . . Then I can take a chisel and small tap hammer and tap away at the alabaster. It will crack then like ice under the pick, and through the breaks I will see the [fertile] loam. (112)

It is an eloquent passage—not of self-representation, however, but of representation of the male other. If Sula cannot find the language, the trope, the form, to embody her own "experimental" life, she "engage[s] her tremendous curiosity and her gift for metaphor" in the delineation of her lover. The poetic penetration of her lover through the layers of black, gold leaf, alabaster, and loam signals that her assumption of a "masculine" role parallels the appropriation of the male voice, prerequisite for her entry into the symbolic order. (Such an appropriation is, of course, earlier signaled by the association of the birthmark with the stemmed rose, the snake, the tadpole—a series of phallic images.)

I propose, however, in the spirit of the metaphor, to take it one step further and suggest that the imagery and mode of the prose poem form a kind of model for the deconstructive function of black feminist literary criticism—and to the extent that literature itself is always an act of interpretation, a model for the deconstructive function of black women's writing—that is, to interpret or interpenetrate the signifying structures of the dominant and subdominant discourse in order to formulate a critique and, ultimately, a transformation of the hegemonic white and male symbolic order.

If Williams's primary emphasis is on the act of rewriting, then Morrison's is on the act of rereading. Perhaps the best example of Sula's deconstructive rereading of the black male text is exemplified in her reformulation of Jude's "whiny tale" describing his victimization as a black man in a world that the "white man running":

I don't know what the fuss is about. I mean, everything in the world loves you. White men love you. They spend so much time worrying about your penis they forget their own. The only thing they want to do is cut off a nigger's privates. And if that ain't love and respect I don't know what is. And white women? They chase you all to every corner of the earth, feel for you under every bed. . . . Now ain't that love? They think rape soon's they see you, and if they don't get the rape they looking for, they scream it anyway just so the search won't be in vain. Colored women worry themselves into bad health just trying to hang on to your cuffs. Even little children—white and black, boys and girls—spend all their childhood eating their hearts out 'cause they think you don't love them. And if that ain't enough, you love yourselves. Nothing in this world loves a black man more that another black man. (89)

Adrienne Munich points out that "Jude's real difficulties allow him to maintain his male identity, to exploit women, and not to examine himself." Sula, she argues, turns "Jude's story of powerlessness into a tale of power." Through a deconstructive reading of his story, Sula's interpretation demonstrates how Jude uses "racial politics [to mask] sexual politics." [36]

If Sula's silences and howls represent breaks in the symbolic order, then her magnificent prose poem looks to the possibilities of appropriating the male voice as a prerequisite for entry into that order. Dessa similarly moves from intervention to appropriation and revision of the dominant discourse. As the author of her own story, Dessa writes herself into the dominant discourse and, in the process, transforms it. What these two works suggest in variable, but interchangeable, strategies is that, in both dominant and subdominant discourses, the initial expression of a marginal presence takes the form of disruption—a departure or a break with conventional semantics and/or phonetics. This rupture is followed by a rewriting or rereading of the dominant story, resulting in a "delegitimation" of the prior story or a "displacement" which shifts attention "to the other side of the story." [37] Disruption—the initial response to hegemonic and ambiguously (non)hegemonic discourse—and the subsequent response, revision (rewriting or rereading), together represent a progressive model for black and female utterance. I propose, in an appropriation of a current critical paradigm, that Sula's primal scream constitutes a "womblike matrix" in which soundlessness can be transformed into utterance, unity into diversity, formlessness into form, chaos into art, silence into tongues, and glossolalia into heteroglossia.

It is this quality of speaking in tongues, that is, multivocality, I further propose, that accounts in part for the current popularity and critical success of black women's writing. The engagement of multiple others broadens the audience for black women's writing, for like the disciples of Pentecost who spoke in diverse tongues, black women, speaking out of the specificity of their racial and gender experiences, are able to communicate in a diversity of discourses. If the ability to communicate accounts for the popularity of black women writers, it also explains much of the controversy surrounding some of this writing. Black women's writing speaks with what Mikhail Bakhtin would describe as heterological or "centrifugal force" but (in a sense somewhat different from that which Bakhtin intended) also unifying or "centripetal force." [38] This literature speaks as much to the notion of commonality and universalism as it does to the sense of difference and diversity.

Yet the objective of these writers is not, as some critics suggest, to move from margin to center, but to remain on the borders of discourse, speaking from the vantage point of the insider/outsider. As Bakhtin further suggests, fusion with the (dominant) Other can only duplicate the tragedy or misfortune of the Other's dilemma. On the other hand, as Gadamer makes clear, "there is a kind of experience of the 'Thou' that seeks to discover things that are typical in the behaviour of [the other] and is able to make predictions concerning another person on the basis of [a commonality] of experience." [39] To maintain this insider/outsider position, or perhaps what Myra Jehlen calls the "extra-terrestial fulcrum" that Archimedes never acquired, is to see the other, but also to see what the other cannot see, and to use this insight to enrich both our own and the other's understanding. [40]

As gendered and racial subjects, black women speak/write in multiple voices—not all simultaneously or with equal weight, but with various and changing degrees of intensity, privileging one *parole* and then another. One discovers in these writers a kind of internal dialogue reflecting an *intrasubjective* engagement with the *intersubjective* aspects of self, a dialectic neither repressing difference nor, for that matter, privileging identity, but rather expressing engagement with the social aspects of self ("the other[s] in ourselves"). It is this subjective plurality (rather than the notion of the cohesive or fractured subject) that, finally, allows the black woman to become an expressive site for a dialectics/dialogics of identity and difference.

Unlike Bloom's "anxiety of influence" model configuring a white male poetic tradition shaped by an adversarial dialogue between literary fathers and sons (as well as the appropriation of this model by Joseph Skerrett and others to discuss black male writers), and unlike Gilbert and Gubar's "anxiety of authorship" model informed by the white woman writer's sense of "dis-ease" within a white patriarchal tradition, the present model configures a tradition of black women writers generated less by neurotic anxiety or dis-ease than by an emancipatory impulse which freely engages both hegemonic and ambiguously (non)hegemonic discourse.[41] Summarizing Morrison's perspectives, Andrea Stuart perhaps best expresses this notion:

> I think you [Morrison] summed up the appeal of black women writers when you said that white men, quite naturally, wrote about themselves and their world; white women tended to write about white men because they were so close to them as husbands, lovers and sons; and black men wrote about white men as the oppressor or the yardstick against which they measured themselves. Only black women writers were not interested in writing about white men and therefore they freed literature to take on other concerns.[42]

In conclusion, I return to the gifts of the Holy Spirit: 1 Corinthians 12 tells us that "the [one] who speaks in tongues should pray that [s/he] may interpret what [s/he] says." Yet the Scriptures also speak to interpretation as a separate gift—the ninth and final gift of the spirit. Might I suggest that if black women writers speak in tongues, then it is we black feminist critics who are charged with the hermeneutical task of interpreting tongues?

Black Feminist Theory and the Representation of the "Other"

In her now classic review essay "Critical Cross-Dressing: Male Feminists and the Woman of the Year," Elaine Showalter considers the ways in which a number of prominent English and American male theorists—among them Wayne Booth, Robert Scholes, Jonathan Culler, and Terry Eagleton—have employed feminist criticism within their own critical positions. Although Showalter praises Culler's ability to read as a feminist and confront "what might be implied by reading as a man and questioning or [surrendering] paternal privileges," she suggests that often male theorists, specifically Eagleton, borrow the language of feminism to compete with women instead of examining "the masculinist bias of their own reading system." [1] This general direction by male theorists, she argues, resembles a parallel phenomenon in popular culture—the rise of the male heroine. Her discussion of *Tootsie* indicates that Dorothy Michaels, the woman character Dustin Hoffman impersonates in the movie, derives her power not in response to the oppression of women but from an instinctive male reaction to being treated like a woman. For a man to act/write like/as a woman is thus not necessarily a tribute to women, but more likely a suggestion that women must be taught by men how to assert themselves.

In her essay Showalter problematizes the function of feminist criticism in response to a growing tendency among Western white male theorists to incorporate feminism in their critical positions. Because the black feminist as writer of both critical and imaginative texts appears with increasing frequency in the work of male Afro-Americanists and Anglo-American feminists, I consider here the place of the black feminist in these apposite modes of inquiry. I begin by defining various stages of the black feminist enterprise within the context of changes in these other theoretical positions, and I suggest how the black feminist has been employed in relation to them. I then offer a reading of *Sarah Phillips* (1984) by Andrea Lee, a fictional text about an upper-middle-class young black woman that thematizes this issue of the status of the "other" in a text by and about someone simultaneously marginal and privileged.

It is not my intention to reclaim the black feminist project from those who are not black women; to do so would be to define the field too narrowly, emphasizing unduly the implications of a shared experience between "black women as critics and black women as writers who represent black women's reality."[2] Indeed, as the following remarks indicate, I understand the phrase *black feminist theory* to refer not only to theory written (or practiced) by black feminists, but also to a way of reading inscriptions of race (particularly but not exclusively blackness), gender (particularly but not exclusively womanhood), and class in modes of cultural expression. Rather, I examine black feminism in the context of these related theoretical positions in order to raise questions about the way the "other" is represented in oppositional discourse. This sort of question seems especially important now that modes of inquiry once considered radical are becoming increasingly institutionalized.

Feminist literary theory and Afro-Americanist literary theory have developed along parallel lines. Both arose out of reactive, polemical modes of criticism. Recognizing that the term *literature* as it was commonly understood in the academy referred to a body of texts written by and in the interest of a white male elite, feminist critics (mostly white) and Afro-Americanist critics (mostly male) undertook the archaeological work of locating and/or reinterpreting overlooked and misread women and black writers.

Black feminist criticism originated from a similar impulse. In reaction to critical acts of omission and condescension, the earliest practitioners identified ways in which white male, Anglo-American feminist, and male Afro-Americanist scholars and reviewers had ignored and condescended to the work of black women and undertook editorial projects to recover their writings. To mention but a few examples: Mary Helen Washington called attention to the ways in which the androcentric Afro-American literary tradition and establishment privileged the solitary, literate adventurers found in texts by male authors such as Frederick Douglass and Richard Wright and ignored the more muted achievements of the female protagonists featured in the work of women writers such as Harriet Jacobs, Zora Neale Hurston, and Gwendolyn Brooks.[3] Barbara Smith notes the ways in which not only Elaine Showalter, Ellen Moers, and Patricia Meyer Spacks, but also Robert Bone and Darwin Turner dismiss the writings of black women. And Deborah E. McDowell cites the omissions of Spacks, Bone, David Littlejohn, and Robert Stepto.[4] The legacy of oversights and condescension occasioned a number of editorial projects that recovered black women's writings; these much-needed projects continue to be undertaken.[5]

From the reactive impulse of these first-stage archaeological projects developed work of greater theoretical sophistication. More recent studies are less concerned with oversights in the work of others, involved instead with constructing alternative literary histories and traditions and exploring changes in assumptions about the nature of critical activity as assumptions about the nature of literature are transformed. As the kinds of questions Anglo-American feminists and male Afro-Americanists pose became increasingly self-referential—for instance, revealing the critics' own complicities and conceptualizing the links between various instances of practical criticism—they have each been drawn inevitably toward a third oppositional discourse: the discourse of deconstruction.

It should not surprise us that a number of Anglo-American feminists and Afro-Americanists have found contemporary theory compatible with the goals of their broader critical enterprise. The techniques and assumptions of deconstructive criticism destabilize the narrative relations that enshrine configurations according to genre, gender, culture, or models of behavior and personality. However, the alliances between contemporary theory on the one hand, and Anglo-American feminists or Afro-Americanists on the other, have raised inevitable questions about the institutionalization of each of these putatively marginal modes of inquiry. Anglo-American feminists as well as male Afro-Americanists are being asked to consider the extent to which their own adherence to a deconstructive practice, which by now has been adopted into the academy, undermines the fundamental assumptions of their broader, more profoundly oppositional enterprise.

The question of the place of feminist critical practice in the institution, for instance, prompted the 1982 dialogue in *Diacritics* between Peggy Kamuf and Nancy K. Miller. Kamuf argues that as long as mainstream feminists install writing by and about women at the center of their modes of inquiry and attempt to locate knowledge about women within an institutionalized humanistic discourse, they sustain the very ways of knowing that have historically excluded women's work:

> If feminist theory lets itself be guided by questions such as what is women's language, literature, style or experience, from where does it get its faith in the form of these questions to get at truth, if not from the central store that supplies humanism with its faith in the universal truth of man?[6]

In turn, Miller addresses what she perceives to be Kamuf's over-investment in deconstructive operations. Reasserting the significance of women as historical and material subjects, she suggests that the destabilization of all categories of identity, including the category "woman," may well serve the interests of a male hegemony whose own power is under siege. As she argues,

> What bothers me about the metalogically "correct" position is what I take to be its necessary implications for practice: that by glossing "woman" as an archaic signifier, it glosses over the *referential* suffering of women. . . . It may also be the case that having been killed off with "man," the author can now be re-thought beyond traditional notions of biography, now that through feminist rewritings of literary history the security of a masculine identity, the hegemony of homogeneity, has been radically problematized.[7]

Some of the most provocative and progressive work in Anglo-American feminist theory seeks to mediate these two positions. In *Crossing the Double-Cross: The Practice of Feminist Criticism,* Elizabeth A. Meese explores the possibilities of an interactive relation between feminist literary criticism and deconstruction. She argues for and illustrates a mode of feminist inquiry that employs the power of deconstruction's critique of difference even as it seeks to challenge and politicize the enterprise of critical theory.[8] Likewise, Teresa de Lauretis situates her collection of essays entitled *Feminist Studies/ Critical Studies* as a juncture in which "feminism is being both integrated and quietly suffocated within the institutions."[9] She urges a feminist model of identity that is "multiple, shifting, and often self-contradictory . . . an identity made up of heterogeneous and heteronomous representations of gender, race, and class, and often indeed across languages and cultures":[10]

> Here is where . . . feminism differs from other contemporary modes of radical, critical or creative thinking, such as postmodernism and philosophical antihumanism: feminism defines itself as a political instance, not merely a sexual politics but a politics of experience, of everyday life, which later then in turn enters the public sphere of expression and creative practice, displacing aesthetic hierarchies and generic categories, and which thus establishes the semiotic ground for a different production of reference and meaning.[11]

Recent work in Afro-American literary theory has occasioned a similar anxiety about institutionalization. Robert B. Stepto, Henry Louis Gates, and Houston A. Baker have been accused of dismantling the black subject when they bring contemporary theory to bear on their readings of black texts. In his 1984 study, *Blues, Ideology, and Afro-American Literature: A Vernacular Theory,* Baker himself argues that the presence of Afro-American critics in historically white academic institutions of higher learning has spawned a generation of scholars whose work is overly dependent on their white colleagues' assumptions and rhetoric.[12] To his mind, Stepto and Gates, two self-styled Reconstructionists, fall victim to this kind of co-optation in their early work. Both Stepto's "Teaching Afro-American Literature: Survey or Tradition: The Reconstruction of Instruction" and Gates's "Preface to Blackness: Text and Pretext" seek to explore the figurative power and complexity not only of Afro-American written art, but indeed of Afro-American cultural life more broadly defined.[13] Stepto's essay, like his book, *From Behind the Veil: A Study of Afro-American Narrative,* argues for the primacy of a pregeneric myth, the quest for freedom and literacy, in the Afro-American literary tradition.[14] But as Baker argues, Stepto's articulation of this myth underscores its apparent "agentlessness." According to Stepto, the pregeneric myth is simply "set in motion." Writes Baker, "the efficacy of motion suggested here seems to have no historically based community or agency or agencies for its origination or perpetuation."[15]

Gates's "Preface to Blackness" explores the extent to which social institutions and extraliterary considerations have intruded into the critical discourse about Afro-American literature. In order to reaffirm the textuality of instances of black written art, he argues for a semiotic understanding of literature as a system of signs that stand in an arbitrary relation to social reality. For Baker, such a theory of language, literature, and culture suggests that " 'literary' meanings are conceived in a nonsocial, noninstitutional manner by the 'point of consciousness' of a language and maintained and transmitted, without an agent, within a closed circle of 'intertextuality.' " [16] Baker's position indicates his concern that in their efforts to align the aims of Afro-American critical activity with the goals and assumptions of prevailing theoretical discourses, both Stepto and Gates extract black writers from their relationship to their audience and from the circumstances in which they wrote and were read.

Interestingly, Baker's critique of Stepto and Gates appears in revised form within the same work in which he develops his own considerations about ways in which contemporary theory may be used to explore the workings of the vernacular in black expressive culture. Whether he succeeds in his effort to adjust the terms of poststructuralist theory to accommodate the nuances of black vernacular culture remains debatable. For Joyce Ann Joyce, however, Gates, Stepto, and Baker have all adopted a critical "linguistic system" that reflects their connection to an elite academic community of theoreticians and denies the significance of race for critic and writer alike. The intensity of this debate among Afro-Americanists is underscored by the fact that Joyce's essay occasions strikingly acrimonious responses from both Gates and Baker.

At these analogous points of self-scrutiny, then, feminists and Afro-Americanists alike have considered the extent to which they may betray the origins of their respective modes of inquiry when they seek to employ the discourse of contemporary theory. When Anglo-American feminists have argued for the inclusion of Anne Bradstreet or Kate Chopin within the literary canon, and when male Afro-Americanists have insisted on the significance of Charles Chesnutt or Jean Toomer, what they have argued is a recognition of the literary activity of those who have written despite political, cultural, economic, and social marginalization and oppression. They argue, in other words, that to exclude the work of blacks and women is to deny the historical existence of these "others" as producers of literature. If feminists and Afro-Americanists now relinquish too easily the material conditions of the lives of blacks and women, they may well relinquish the very grounds on which their respective disciplines were established.

These debates from within feminist and Afro-Americanist discourse coincided with black feminist charges that the cultural productions of black women were excluded from both modes of inquiry. Audre Lorde, bell hooks (Gloria Watkins), Angela Davis, Barbara Smith, Mary Helen Washington, and Deborah McDowell, to name but a few, have all argued that the experiences of women of color needed to be represented if these oppositional discourses were to remain radical. The eruptions of these critical voices into feminist and Afro-Americanist literary theory, like their self-contained critical and theoretical utterances, question the totalizing tendencies of mainstream as well as reactive critical practice and caution that the hope of oppositional discourse rests on its awareness of its own complicities.

These twin challenges have resulted in an impulse among Anglo-American feminists and Afro-Americanists to rematerialize the subject of their theoretical positions. Meese, as I suggested earlier, examines the contributions deconstructive method can make to feminist critical practice, but only insofar as feminist assumptions repoliticize her use of theory. De Lauretis affirms the basis of feminism in "a politics of everyday life." And similarly, in his more recent work, for instance "The Blackness of Blackness: A Critique of the Sign of the Signifying Monkey," Gates argues for a material basis of his theoretical explorations by translating them into the black idiom, renaming principles of criticism where appropriate, and naming indigenous principles of criticism.

The black woman as critic, and more broadly as the locus where gender-, class-, and race-based oppression intersect, is often invoked when Anglo-American feminists and male Afro-Americanists begin to rematerialize their discourse. This may be the case because the move away from historical specificity associated with deconstruction resembles all too closely the totalizing tendency commonly associated with androcentric criticism. In other words, when historical specificity is denied or remains implicit, all the women are presumed white, all the blacks male. The move to include black women as historical presences and as speaking subjects in critical discourse may well then be used as a defense against charges of racial hegemony on the part of white women and sexist hegemony on the part of black males.

Meese ensures that the discourse of feminism grounds her explorations into deconstructive practice by unifying her chapters around the problems of race, class, and sexual preference. She thus offers readings not only of works by Mary Wilkins Freeman, Marilynne Robinson, Tillie Olsen and Virginia Woolf, but also of the fiction of Alice Walker and Zora Neale Hurston. The politics of de Lauretis's introduction are likewise undergirded in the material conditions of working women's lives. She buttresses, for instance, her observations about the conflicting claims of different feminisms with evidence drawn from a speech by the black feminist activist, writer, and attorney Flo Kennedy. And in her critique of the (white) feminist discourse in sexuality, she cites Hortense Spillers's work on the absence of feminist perspectives on black women's sexuality. Zora Neale Hurston, Phillis Wheatley, Alice Walker, and Rebecca Cox Jackson, the black Shaker visionary, ground Gates's essay "Writing 'Race' and the Difference It Makes," just as discussions of writings by Hurston and Linda Brent are central to Baker's consideration of the economics of a new American literary history.

That the black woman appears in all of these texts as a historicizing presence testifies to the power of the insistent voices of black feminist literary and cultural critics. Yet it is striking that at precisely the moment when Anglo-American feminists and male Afro-Americanists begin to reconsider the material ground of their enterprise, they demonstrate their return to earth, as it were, by invoking the specific experiences of black women and the writings of black women. This association of black women with reembodiment resembles rather closely the association, in classic Western philosophy and in nineteenth-century cultural constructions of womanhood, of women of color with the body and therefore with animal passions and slave labor. Although in these theoretical contexts the impulse to rehistoricize produces insightful readings and illuminating theories, and is politically progressive and long overdue, nevertheless the link between black women's experiences and "the material" seems conceptually problematic.

If *Tootsie* can help us understand the white male theorists' use of feminism, I suggest that Amy Jones's 1987 film *Maid to Order* might offer a perspective on the use of the black woman or the black feminist in Anglo-American feminist or Afro-Americanist discourse. *Maid to Order* is a comic fantasy about a spoiled, rich white young woman from Beverly Hills (played by Ally Sheedy) who is sent by her fairy godmother (played by Beverly D'Angelo) to work as a maid in the home of a ludicrously nouveau riche agent and his wife in Malibu. She shares responsibilities with two other maids—one black, played by Merry Clayton, and one Latina, played by Begona Plaza. From the experience of deprivation and from her friendship with the black maid, she learns the value of love and labor; she is transformed, in other words, into a better person.

With its subtle critique of the racist policies for hiring domestic help in Southern California, *Maid to Order* seems rather progressive for a popular fantasy film. Yet even within this context, the figure of the black woman is commodified in ways that are familiar from classic cinematic narratives. From movies such as John Stahl's 1934 version of *Imitation of Life* (or Douglas Sirk's 1959 remake) and Fred Zinnermann's 1952 *Member of the Wedding* to a contemporary film such as *Maid to Order,* black women are employed, if not sacrificed, to humanize their white superordinates, to teach them something about the content of their own subject positions. When black women operate in oppositional discourse as a sign for the author's awareness of materialist concerns, then they seem to be fetishized in much the same way as they are in mass culture.

If Anglo-American feminists and male Afro-Americanists are currently in the process of rematerializing their theoretical discourse, black feminists might be said to be emerging into a theoretical phase. The early, archaeological work gave way among black feminists as well to a period in which they offered textual analyses of individual works or clusters of works. Recent, third-stage black feminist work is concerned much less with the silences in other critical traditions; rather, the writings of Susan Willis, Hazel V. Carby, Mary Helen Washington, Dianne F. Sadoff, Deborah E. McDowell, Hortense Spillers, and others have become increasingly self-conscious and self-reflexive, examining ways in which literary study—the ways in which, for instance, we understand the meaning of influence, the meaning of a tradition, the meaning of literary periods, the meaning of literature itself—changes once questions of race, class, and gender become central to the process of literary analysis. In this third stage, then, black feminist theorists might be said to challenge the conceptualizations of literary study and to concern themselves increasingly with the effect of race, class, and gender on the practice of literary criticism.

Black feminist literary theory proceeds from the assumption that black women experience a unique form of oppression in discursive and nondiscursive practices alike because they are victims at once of sexism, racism, and by extension classism. However, as Elizabeth V. Spelman and Barbara Smith demonstrate separately, one oversimplifies by saying merely that black women experience sexism and racism. "For to say merely *that,* suggests that black women experience one form of oppression, as blacks—the same thing black men experience—and that they experience another form of oppression, as women—the same thing white women experience." [17] Such a formulation erases the specificity of the black woman's experience, constituting her as the point of intersection between black men's and white women's experience.

As an alternative to this position, what Smith calls the additive analysis, black feminist theorists argue that the meaning of blackness in this country shapes profoundly the experience of gender, just as the conditions of womanhood affect ineluctably the experience of race. Precisely because the conditions of the black woman's oppression are thus specific and complex, black feminist literary theorists seek particularized methodologies that might reveal the ways in which that oppression is represented in literary texts. These methods are necessarily flexible, holding in balance the three variables of race, gender, and class and destabilizing the centrality of any one. More generally, they call into question a variety of standards of valuation that mainstream feminist and androcentric Afro-Americanist theory might naturalize.

Proceeding from a point related to but different from the centers of these other modes of inquiry, black feminist critics demonstrate that the meaning of political action, work, family, and sexuality, indeed any feature of the experience of culture, varies depending on the material circumstances that surround and define one's point of reference. And as gender and race taken separately determine the conditions not only of oppression but also of liberation, so too does the interplay between these categories give rise to its own conception of liberation.

I want to resist the temptation to define or overspecify the particular questions that a black feminist theoretical approach might pose of a text. But I would characterize black feminist literary theory more broadly by arguing that it seeks to explore representations of black women's lives through techniques of analysis which suspend the variables of race, class, and gender in mutually interrogative relation.

The fiction of tradition represents one theoretical conception to which a number of black feminist theorists return. In a persuasively argued recent essay, Deborah McDowell examines the relationship between novels of racial uplift in the 1920s and recent black fiction.[18] Although Hazel V. Carby asserts in her book, *Reconstructing Womanhood,* that she is not engaged in the process of constructing the contours of a black female literary tradition, yet she establishes a lineage of black women intellectuals engaged in the ideological debates of their time. Mary Helen Washington and Dianne Sadoff likewise consider how race, class, and gender affect, respectively, the meaning of literary influence and the politics of literary reception. I focus here for a moment on the ways in which Washington's " 'Taming All That Anger Down': Rage and Silence in Gwendolyn Brooks's *Maud Martha* "[19] and Sadoff's "Black Matrilineage: The Case of Alice Walker and Zora Neale Hurston"[20] make use of these three variables in their reformulation of the fiction of literary tradition.

In this essay, as in much of her recent writing, Washington argues that the material circumstances of black women's lives require one to develop revisionist strategies for evaluating and reading their work. She demonstrates here that precisely because the early reviewers and critics failed to comprehend the significance of race and gender for both a black woman writer and a young black urban girl, they trivialized Brooks and her only novel, a text made up of vignettes which are themselves comprised of short, declarative sentences.

Contemporary reviewers likened Brooks's style "to the exquisite delicacy of a lyric poem," Washington writes. They gave it "the kind of ladylike treatment that assured its dismissal."[21] But by examining the subtext of color prejudice, racial self-hatred, sexual insecurity, and powerlessness that underlies virtually every chapter, Washington demonstrates that the structure and grammar of the novel enact not what one reviewer called the protagonist's "spunk," but rather her repressed anger. In her discussion of the historical conditions that circumscribe the lives of black women in the 1940s and 1950s, Washington suggests ways in which Maud's oppression recalls Brooks's own marginal position within the publishing industry. Brooks inscribes not only Maud Martha's frustration, then, but also her own.

Washington's discussion here considers as well Brooks's reluctance to represent black women as heroic figures as a further sign of her oppression by a racist and sexist literary establishment. She thus prompts not only new readings of the text, but also of the relation between author and character. Indeed, Washington's discussion, turning as it does on the representation of the circumstances of Maud's life, enables a redefinition of the way a range of texts in the Afro-American canon are read. In her words, "if Maud Martha is considered an integral part of the Afro-American canon, we will have to revise our conception of power and powerlessness, of heroism, of symbolic landscapes and ritual grounds." [22]

In her article, Dianne Sadoff argues that black women writers share neither the anxiety of influence Harold Bloom attributes to male writers nor the primary anxiety of authority Sandra Gilbert and Susan Gubar attribute to white women writers. Rather, she demonstrates that "race and class oppression intensify the black woman writer's need to discover an untroubled matrilineal heritage. In celebrating her literary foremothers, the contemporary black woman writer covers over more profoundly than does the white writer her ambivalence about matrilineage, her own misreading of precursors, and her link to an oral as well as a written tradition." [23]

Sadoff's examination of the relationship between Zora Neale Hurston and Alice Walker reveals a compelling tension between the explicit subjects of each author's work and the subversive material that underlies those surfaces. An ancestor claimed as significant by most recent black women writers, Zora Neale Hurston misrepresents herself within her fiction, Sadoff argues. *Their Eyes Were Watching God* may announce itself, for instance, as a celebration of heterosexual love, but Hurston manipulates narrative strategies to ensure that the male is eliminated and the female liberated. Sadoff goes on to show that Walker affirms her tie to Hurston by inscribing a similar double agenda throughout her work, problematizing the status of heterosexual love in similar ways. Moreover, while her essays document her enthusiastic pursuit of Hurston as a literary foremother, her novels display a profound anxiety about biological motherhood. Sadoff's readings demonstrate, then, that the peril of uniqueness compels an intense need on the part of black women writers to identify a literary matrilineage even as their historical circumstances occasion their ambivalence about the fact and process of mothering.

These two essays thus show that the black feminist enterprise, at this stage necessarily materialist, calls for a reconception of the politics of literary reception, the meaning of literary influence, and the content of literary tradition.

At this point in its evolution, black feminist literary theory does not yet appear to replicate the totalizing tendency I attributed to Anglo-American feminism and male Afro-Americanism earlier. No doubt because it has remained marginal, what has been primarily a heterosexual, Afro-American-centered feminist discourse has been concerned with refining its own mode of inquiry, perhaps at the expense of annexing to itself the experiences of "others" such as lesbians and other women of color.

Fiction by black women has, however, achieved significant visibility operating simultaneously as a body of texts both marginal and mainstream. Andrea Lee's *Sarah Phillips* thematizes this very issue and suggests that the very activity of conceptualizing the self as insider may occasion a fetishization of the "other."

The stories that make up Andrea Lee's *Sarah Phillips* appeared separately in *The New Yorker* magazine before they were collected and published together in 1984. This fact about the publishing history alone suggests that in at least one way this is a text of privilege; the content of the stories themselves also foregrounds the issue of class position. Each story is a vignette taken from the life of the title character, the daughter of a prosperous Baptist minister and his school-teacher wife. With the exception of the first, entitled "In France," the stories are arranged chronologically to sketch Sarah Phillips's girlhood and adolescence in private schools and progressive summer camps in and around Philadelphia, undergraduate years at Harvard, and obligatory expatriation to Europe after graduation.

In addition to their common subject, the majority of the stories share a common structure. Most of the stories establish a community of insiders, disparate voices brought into unison, poised in a continuous present. In each instance, the stasis achieved by the choice of verb tenses, imagery, and patterns of allusion is interrupted by the presence of an outsider, someone who is constituted as the "other" according to the characteristics and assumptions of the narrative community. In virtually every instance, the presence of this "other" serves to historicize a vignette that had existed for the narrator as a moment out of time. The stories thus enact a tension between the narrative of the community of privilege, posited as ahistorical, and a destabilizing eruption, posited as inescapably historical.

Contemporary reviews identified two problematic areas of the text—the significance of Sarah's class position and the ambiguous relation between narrator and protagonist. Mary Helen Washington places it in a tradition with William Wells Brown's *Clotel*, Frances E. W. Harper's *Iola Leroy*, and James Weldon Johnson's *Autobiography of an Ex-Colored Man*, all works about a privileged black narrator tenuously connected to his or her blackness who needs to escape the problematic meanings of that identity. Washington argues that in these other novels, in varying degrees the narrators recognize the complex interplay between issues of class and race. The narrator of *Sarah Phillips*, in contrast, participates in the character's capitulation to her own position. Washington writes: "By the fourth or fifth story, I felt that the privileged kid had become the privileged narrator, no longer willing to struggle over issues of race and class, unable to bear the 'alarming knowledge' that these issues must reveal." [24]

Sherley Anne Williams compares the text to Richard Wright's *Black Boy*, arguing that both works "literally and figuratively [renounce] oral culture and black traditions for personal autonomy." She remarks that *Sarah Phillips* holds up to mockery "not the pretensions of her upper middle class heroine, but the 'outworn rituals' of black community." [25]

Both reviews suggest a point of contrast between Lee on the one hand and other contemporary black women writers who construct fictional communities of privilege. Toni Morrison, like Paule Marshall, Gloria Naylor, and Ntozake Shange, to name but a few, occasionally centers her novels on middle-class black characters. But as Susan Willis has written, in Morrison's novels, black middle-class life is generally characterized by a measure of alienation from the cultural heritage of the black rural South. Her characters are saved from "the upper reaches of bourgeois reification" by "eruptions of 'funk' "—characters or experiences that invoke the characters' cultural past and repressed emotional lives.[26] The energy of the text is thus in every case with the characters who represent "funk": Sula, Pilate, Son, even Cholly Breedlove; Morrison consistently problematizes what it means to be black and privileged.

Lee's narrator, on the other hand, seems as alienated from outsiders as the protagonist does. The text is sufficiently invested in its own construction of what it means to be privileged that it marginalizes those different from the protagonist herself. Rather than disparage *Sarah Phillips* on the basis of its politics, however, I should like to consider ways in which the "other" is figured here. For it seems to me that like the examples drawn earlier from feminist and Afro-Americanist discourse, this text also equates that "other" with the historical or the material.

My argument focuses primarily on a story entitled "Gypsies," in which a family of itinerants disrupt the orderliness of Sarah's suburban girlhood and force at least a symbolic acknowledgment of her place in a broader historical reality. But I begin with a reading of "In France," the story with which the volume begins, for it establishes a perspective by means of which the other stories may be read.

"In France" violates the chronological arrangement of stories, since it recounts the most recent events in the protagonist's life. The story breaks the pattern of the other stories in the volume in yet another way, for it is the only one to situate Sarah as an alien in her environment. The reader learns at once that Sarah is an American in Paris, but her story is filtered through the account of another American living there, a girl named Kate who seems to be missing. Rumors circulate that Kate is being held hostage by her present lover and ex-boyfriend lover who were 'collecting her allowance and had bought a luxurious Fiat—the same model the Pope drove—with the profits." [27]

As it is recounted here, Kate's story invokes an absent double, underscoring Sarah's isolation. Moreover, the rumor of her mistreatment at the hands of her male friends presages the abuse Sarah's lover Henri and his friends inflict on her later in the story. We learn that after the death of her father and her graduation from Harvard, Sarah "cast off kin and convention in a foreign tongue" (4) and went to study French in Switzerland. Upon meeting Henri she leaves school and moves into the Paris apartment he shares with his friends Alain and Roger. Together they spend their time in cafés, museums, their apartment, and on occasional weekend expeditions into the country. The story turns on one such trip to the island of Jersey, when ostensibly harmless banter among the four of them suddenly turns nasty.

In this exchange Henri verbally assaults Sarah with racial insults, saying:

> Did you ever wonder . . . why our beautiful Sarah is such a mixture of races? . . . It's a very American tale. This *Irlandaise* was part redskin, and not only that but part Jew as well—some Americans are part Jew, aren't they? And one day this *Irlandaise* was walking through the jungle near New Orleans, when she was raped by a jazz musician as big and black as King Kong, with sexual equipment to match. And from this agreeable encounter was born our little Sarah, *notre Negresse pasteurisée.* (11)

Sarah responds in two ways. In the shock of the moment she recognizes that she cannot ignore this parody of miscegenation. Her class position notwithstanding, she plays some role in the drama of race relations from which such stereotypes derive. Several hours later, the meaning of the insult strikes her again, this time in a dream—one that impels her to return home: "I awoke with a start from a horrid dream in which I was conducting a monotonous struggle with an old woman with a dreadful spidery strength in her arms; her skin was dark and leathery, and she smelled like one of the old Philadelphia church-women who used to babysit with me" (14).

The dream prompts her to reflect more calmly on the fact that she will never be able to escape the call of her personal history. She remarks:

> I had hoped to join the ranks of dreaming expatriates for whom Paris can become a self-sufficient universe, but my life there had been no more than a slight hysteria, filled with the experimental naughtiness of children reacting against their training. It was clear, much as I did not want to know it, that my days in France had a number, that for me the bright, frank, endlessly beckoning horizon of the runaway had been, at some point, transformed into a complicated return. (15)

The story thus suggests that the past is inescapable. It anticipates Sarah's return home even though that return remains undramatized. I would argue that the subsequent stories, all of which center on events from Sarah's earlier life, function symbolically as that return home. The recurrent patterns that run through these other vignettes recapitulate the tension within the first story between escape and return. They indicate that the past may elude integration into the present, but it can also never be avoided.

In "Gypsies," the narrator attributes to Franklin Place, the street on which Sarah grows up, the ubiquity of a symbol. The opening description works against historical or geographical specificity, and instead represents the neighborhood in terms of the icons of upper-middle-class suburban culture. That is to say, in the opening paragraph the narrator locates the street in her dreams and nightmares, in her patterns of associations, before she locates it in a Philadelphia suburb. In this description, the suburb is represented as an abstraction, the fulfillment of a fantasy, distinct from the conditions of the world outside its boundaries:

> Franklin Place, the street that ran like a vein through most of my dreams and nightmares, the stretch of territory I automatically envisioned when someone said "neighborhood," lay in a Philadelphia suburb. The town was green and pretty, but had the constrained, slightly unreal atmosphere of a colony or a foreign enclave, that was because the people who owned the rambling houses behind the shrubbery were black. For them—doctors, ministers, teachers who had grown up in Philadelphia row houses—the lawns and tree-lined streets represented the fulfillment of a fantasy long deferred, and acted as a barrier against the predictable cruelty of the world. (39)

If this opening paragraph bestows a quality of unreality on the landscape against which this and several of the other stories take place, subsequent paragraphs render the world beyond the neighborhood even more ephemeral. From the narrator's perspective, historical events and political struggle represent levels of experience with which one may engage, but only imaginatively, the songs of cicadas providing a musical transition from Franklin Place to the world of those less privileged. As the narrator remarks:

For as long as I could remember, the civil rights movement had been unrolling like a dim frieze behind the small pleasures and defeats of my childhood; it seemed dull, a necessary burden on my conscience, like good grades or hungry people in India. My occasional hair-raising reveries of venturing into the netherworld of Mississippi or Alabama only added a voluptuous edge to the pleasure of eating an ice-cream cone while seated on a shady curb of Franklin Place. (39–40)

The image of the civil rights movement as a frieze fixes and aestheticizes the process of historical change, as if the inertia of Sarah's life had afflicted the world beyond the parameters of her neighborhood.

The illusion of timelessness and unassailability is sustained additionally by the narrator's tendency to cast the particular in terms of the habitual or familiar through her use of the second-person pronoun and the English equivalent of the French imperfect tense. For even as she narrows the focus of the story to the time of her encounter with the gypsies, the narrator describes that particular day in terms that homogenize or encompass, terms that, in other words, move away from particularity. Indeed, the impulse toward generalization and away from particularity is rendered nowhere more clearly than in the description of Sarah in which she is described as if she were a twin of her best friend Lyn Yancey.

On the day in question, a battered red pickup truck bearing its load of log furniture and a family of gypsies disturbs the peace of Franklin Place, a neighborhood of sedans, station wagons, and sports cars. Neither black nor white, the gypsies defy the categories available to Sarah and Lyn: the wife's breasts swaying back and forth in a way in which "the well-contained bosoms of [their] mothers never do" (43). Despite their marginal status, the gypsies articulate the assumptions about race and class shared by the majority culture. "It's a real crime for colored to live like this," says the wife. "You are very lucky little girls, very lucky, do you understand? When my son was your age he never got to play like you girls" (43).

At dinner that evening, Sarah repeats for her family her conversation with the gypsies. The exchange that ensues disrupts the veneer of family harmony, introducing social reality into the magic of the private sphere. Her father, ordinarily a man of great restraint, loses his sense of decorum. "Most of the world despises gypsies, but a gypsy can always look down on a Negro! Heck, that fellow was right to spit! You can dress it up with trees and big houses and people who don't stink too bad, but a nigger neighborhood is still a nigger neighborhood" (44).

Sarah and Lyn later meet at the swim club. The narrator's description of the pool at night betrays if not the young girls' yearnings, then her own nostalgia for the familiar tranquility. The language thus shifts dramatically from the father's clipped vernacular speech. Their rediscovered contentment lasts only until the return home, however, for on the street they confront the gypsies again, an insistent presence that cannot be ignored. The final paragraph of the story suggests that the protagonist's life has been altered profoundly. The narrator remarks, "nothing looked different, yet everything was, and for the first time Franklin Place seemed genuinely connected to a world that was neither insulated nor serene. Throughout the rest of the summer, on the rare occasions when a truck appeared in our neighborhood, Lyn and I would dash to see it, our hearts pounding with perverse excitement and a fresh desire for knowledge" (46). This final formulation resonates with a certain falseness; the narrator allows Sarah and Lyn the freedom to be entertained by historical events, as if the dim frieze of the civil rights movement might somehow amuse or stimulate them. Indeed, throughout the collection, stories conclude with similar ambivalence; Lee leaves unresolved the issue as to whether the insiders' acknowledgment of the other is symbolic or transformative.

The story thus constitutes a community of insiders rendered ahistorical and homogeneous by the allusions, descriptions, and grammar of the narrator. The presence of someone from outside of that community reminds the residents of Franklin Place of the contingencies on which their apparently stable lives are founded. Simultaneously, the outsider reminds the privileged community of the circumstances of their history. The exchange destabilizes the narrator's ability to totalize the experience the story describes.

Lee's persistent interest in eruptions into communities of privilege causes these stories to be useful texts within which to observe the relation between the presence of the "other" in theoretical discourse. The black woman protagonist in these stories locates herself within, rather than outside of, the normative community, be it an integrated camp for middle-class children, her neighborhood, or her family. Her very presence within these exclusionary communities suggests that the circumstances of race and gender alone protect no one from the seductions of reading her own experience as normative and fetishizing the experience of the other.

This essay offers three perspectives on the contemporary black feminist enterprise. It shows how black feminism is invoked in mainstream feminist and Afro-Americanist discourse, it presents in broad outlines the space black feminist theory occupies independently, and it suggests how one contemporary black woman novelist thematizes the relationship between those who occupy privileged discursive spaces and the "other."

I have approached the subject from three perspectives in part because of my own evident suspicion of totalizing formulations. But my approach reflects as well the black feminist skepticism about the reification of boundaries that historically have excluded the writing of black women from serious consideration within the academic and literary establishments. Since, to my mind, some of the most compelling and representative black feminist writing treads the boundary between anthology and criticism, or between cultural theory and literary theory, it seems appropriate that a consideration of this critical perspective would approach it from a variety of points of view.

But What Do We Think We're Doing Anyway: The State of Black Feminist Criticism(s) or My Version of a Little Bit of History

In August 1974, a rather unique event occurred. *Black World,* probably the most widely read publication of Afro-American literature, culture, and political thought at that time, used on its cover a picture of the then practically unknown writer Zora Neale Hurston.[1] Under Zora's then unfamiliar photograph was a caption in bold letters, "Black Women Image Makers," which was the title of the essay by Mary Helen Washington featured in the issue. Alongside the Washington essay were three other pieces: an essay now considered a classic, June Jordan's "On Richard Wright and Zora Neale Hurston: Notes Towards a Balancing of Love and Hate," an essay on major works of Zora Neale Hurston, "The Novelist/Anthropologist/Life Work," by poet Ellease Southerland, and a short piece criticizing the television version of Ernest Gaines's *The Autobiography of Miss Jane Pittman,* by black psychologist Alvin Ramsey. It was not particularly striking that the image of a black woman writer graced the cover of *Black World;* Gwendolyn Brooks's picture, for example, had appeared on a previous *Black World* cover. Nor was it especially noteworthy that literary analyses of an Afro-American woman writer appeared in that journal. That certainly had occurred before. What was so striking about this issue of *Black World* was the tone of the individual pieces and the effect of their juxtaposition.

Mary Helen Washington's essay sounded a strong chord—that there was indeed a growing number of contemporary Afro-American women writers whose perspective underlined the centrality of women's lives to their creative vision. June Jordan's essay placed Hurston, a relatively unknown Afro-American woman writer, alongside Richard Wright, who is probably the best known of Afro-American writers, and illuminated how their apparently antithetical worldviews were *both* necessary ways of viewing the complexity of Afro-American life, which Jordan made clear was not monolithic. Ellease Southerland reviewed many of Hurston's works, pointing out their significance to

Afro-American literature and therefore indicating the existence of major Afro-American women writers in the past. And in criticizing the television version of *The Autobiography of Miss Jane Pittman,* Ramsey objected that that commercial white medium had omitted the message of struggle in Ernest Gaines's novel and turned it into an individual woman's story—a foreshadowing of criticism that would be repeated when, periodically, images of black women from literature were translated into visual media.

What the configuration of the August 1974 *Black World* suggested to me, as I am sure it did to others, was the growing visibility of Afro-American women and the significant impact they were having on contemporary black culture. The articulation of that impact had been the basis for Toni Cade's edition of *The Black Woman* in 1970.[2] But that collection had not dealt specifically with literature/creativity. Coupled with the publication of Alice Walker's "In Search of Our Mothers' Gardens," only a few months before in the May issue of *Ms.,*[3] the August 1974 *Black World* signaled a shift in position among those interested in Afro-American literature about women's creativity. Perhaps because I had experienced a decade of the intense literary activity of the 1960s, but also much antifemale black cultural nationalist rhetoric, these two publications had a lightning effect on me. Afro-American women were making public, were able to make public, their search for themselves in literary culture.

I begin my reflections on the state (history) of black feminist criticism(s) with this memory because it seems to me we so quickly forget the recent past. Perhaps some of us have never know it. Like many of us who lived through the literary activism of the sixties, we of the eighties may forget that which just recently preceded us and may therefore misconstrue the period in which we are acting.

Less than twenty years ago, without using the self-consciously academic word *theory,* Mary Helen Washington articulated a concept that was original, startling even, to many of us immersed in the study of Afro-American literature, among whom were few academics, who knew little or cared less about this literature. In "Black Women Image Makers" Washington stated what for me is still a basic tenet of black feminist criticism: "We should be about the business of *reading, absorbing,* and giving *critical* attention to those writers whose understanding of the black woman can take us *further*" (emphasis mine).[4] The names of the writers Washington listed, with the exception of Gwendolyn Brooks, were then all virtually unknown; interestingly, after a period when poetry and drama were the preeminent genre of Afro-American literature, practically all of these writers—Maya Angelou, Toni Cade Bambara, Paule Marshall, Toni Morrison, Alice Walker—were practicing fiction writers. While all of the writers were contemporary, Washington implied through her analysis that their vision and craft suggested that previous Afro-American women writers existed. Hence Zora Neale Hurston's picture on the cover of this issue connoted a specific meaning—that of a literary foremother who had been neglected by Afro-Americanists of the past but who was finally being recognized by her daughters and reinstated as a major figure in the Afro-American literary tradition.

It is important for us to remember that in 1974, even before the publication of Robert Henenway's biography of Hurston in 1977 or the reissuing of *Their Eyes Were Watching God,* the articulation of the possibility of a tradition of Afro-American women writers occurred not in a fancy academic journal but in two magazines: *Ms.,* a new popular magazine that came out of the women's movement, and *Black World,* a long-standing black journal unknown to most academics and possibly scorned by some.

Walker's essay and *Black World's* August 1974 issue gave me a focus and are the recognizable points that I can recall as to when I consciously began to work on black women writers. I had, of course, unconsciously begun my own search before reading those pieces. I had spent some portion of the late sixties and early seventies asking my "elders" in the black arts movement whether there were black women who had written before Gwendolyn Brooks or Lorraine Hansberry. Younger poets such as Sonia Sanchez, Nikki Giovanni, Carolyn Rodgers, June Jordan, and Audre Lorde were, of course, quite visible by that time. And by 1974, Morrison and Walker had each published a novel. But only through accident or sheer stint of effort did I discover Paule Marshall's *Brown Girl, Brownstones* (1959) or Hurston's *Their Eyes Were Watching God* (1937)—an indication that the contemporary writers I was then reading might too fade into oblivion. Although in the sixties the works of neglected Afro-American male writers of the Harlem Renaissance were beginning to resurface, for example, Jean Toomer's *Cane,* I was told the women writers of that period were terrible—not worth my trouble. However, because of the conjuncture of the black arts movement and the women's movement, I asked questions I probably would not have otherwise thought of.

If movements have any effect, it is to give us a context within which to imagine questions we would not have imagined before, to ask questions we might not have asked before. The publication of the *Black World* August 1974 issue as well as Walker's essay was rooted in the conjuncture of those two movements, rather than in the theoretizing of any individual scholar, and most emphatically in the literature of contemporary Afro-American women who were able to be published as they had not been before, precisely because that conjuncture was occurring.

That the development of black feminist criticism(s) is firmly rooted in this conjuncture is crystal clear from a pivotal essay of the 1970s: Barbara Smith's "Toward a Black Feminist Criticism," which was originally published in *Conditions II* in 1977. By that time Smith was not only calling on critics to read, absorb, and pay attention to black women writers, as Washington had, but also to write about that body of literature from a feminist perspective. What *feminist* meant for Smith went beyond Washington's emphasis on image making. Critics, she believed, needed to demonstrate how the literature exposed "the brutally complex systems of oppression"[5]—that of sexism, racism, and economic exploitation which affected so gravely the experience and culture of black women. As important, Smith was among the first to point out that black lesbian literature was thoroughly ignored in critical journals, an indication of the homophobia existent in the literary world.

Because the U.S. women's movement had begun to extend itself into academic arenas and because women's voices had been so thoroughly suppressed, by the middle seventies there was a visible increase of interest among academics in women's literature. Yet despite the existence of powerful contemporary Afro-American women writers who continued to be major explorers of Afro-American women's lives—writers, such as Bambara, Jordan, Lorde, Morrison, Shange, Walker, Sherley Anne Williams (the list could be much longer)—little commentary on their works could be found in feminist journals. In many ways, they continued to be characterized by such journals as black, not women, writers. Nor, generally speaking, were critics who studied these writers considered either in the Afro-American or feminist literary worlds—far less the mainstream literary establishment—to be working on an important body of literature central to American letters. By 1977, Smith knew that the sexism of Afro-American literary/intellectual circles and the racism of white feminist literary journals resulted in a kind of homelessness for critical works on black women or other third world women writers. She underlined this fact in her landmark essay: "I think of the thousands and thousands of books which have been devoted by this time to the subject of Women's Writing and I am filled with rage at the fraction of these pages that mention black and other Third World women. I finally do not know how to begin, because in 1977 I want to be writing this for a black feminist publication." [6]

At that time, most feminist journals were practically all white publications; their content dealt almost exclusively with white women as if they were the only women in the United States. The extent to which the mid twentieth-century women's movement was becoming, like its nineteenth-century predecessor, infected by racism seemed all too clear, and the split between a black and a white women's movement that occurred in the nineteenth century seemed to be repeating itself.

Smith seemed to believe that the lack of inclusion of women-of-color writers and critics in the burgeoning literature on women's voices was due, in part, to "the fact that a parallel black feminist movement had been slower in evolving," and that that fact "could not help but have impact upon the situation of black women writers and artists and explains in part why during that very same period we have been so ignored." [7] My experience, however, suggests that other factors were more prominently at work, factors Smith also mentioned. In calling for a "body of black feminist political theory," she pointed out that such a theory was necessary since those who had access to critical publications—white male and, increasingly, black male and white female critics—apparently did not *know how* to respond to the works of black women. More accurately, I think these critics might have been resistant to this body of writing which unavoidably demonstrated the intersections of sexism and racism so central to Afro-American women's lives and therefore threatened not only white men's view of themselves, but black men and white women's view of themselves as well. Smith concludes that "undoubtedly there are other [black] women working and writing whom I do not know, simply because there is no place to read them."[8]

I can personally attest to that fact. By 1977 I was well into the writing of the book that would become *Black Women Novelists: The Development of a Tradition* (1980) and had independently stumbled on two pivotal concepts that Smith articulated in her essay: "the need to demonstrate that black women's writing constituted an identifiable literary tradition" and the importance of looking "for precedents and insights in interpretation within the works of other black women."[9] I found, however, that it was virtually impossible to locate either the works of many nineteenth-century writers or those of contemporary writers, whose books went in and out of print like ping-pong balls. For example, I xeroxed *Brown Girl, Brownstones* (please forgive me, Paule) any number of times because it simply was not available and I wanted to use it in the classes I had begun to teach on Afro-American women's literature. At times I felt more like a detective than a literary critic as I chased clues to find a book I knew existed but which I had begun to think I had hallucinated.

Particularly difficult, I felt, was the dearth of historical material on Afro-American women, that is, on the contexts within which the literature had evolved—contexts I increasingly saw as a necessary foundation for the development of a contemporary black feminist perspective. Other than Gerda Lerner's *Black Women in White America* (1973), I could not find a single full-length analysis of Afro-American women's history. And despite the proliferation of Afro-American and women's history books in the 1970s, I found in most of them only a few paragraphs devoted to black women, the favorites being Harriet Tubman in the black studies ones and Sojourner Truth in the women's studies ones. As a result, in preparation for my book, I, untrained in history, had created a patchwork quilt of historical facts gathered here and there. I remember being positively elated when Sharon Harley and Rosalyn Terborg Penn's collection of historical essays—*The Afro-American Woman* (1978)—was published. But by then, I had almost completed my manuscript. If Afro-American women critics were to turn to black women of the past for insights, their words and works needed to be accessible and had to be located in a cogent historical analysis.

As well, what was stunning to me as I worked on *Black Women Novelists* was the resistance I experienced among scholars to my subject matter. Colleagues of mine, some of whom had my best interest at heart, warned me that I was going to ruin my academic career by studying an insignificant, some said nonexistent, body of literature. Yet I knew it was fortunate for me that I was situated in an Afro-American studies rather than in an English department, where not even the intercession of the Virgin would have allowed me to do research on black women writers. I also found that lit crit journals were not interested in the essays I had begun to write on black women writers. The sustenance I received during those years of writing *Black Women Novelists* came not from the academic/literary world but from small groups of women in bookstores, Y's, in my classes and writers groups for whom this literature was not so much an object of study but was, as it is for me, life-saving.

Many contemporary Afro-American critics imply in their analyses that only those Afro-Americans in the academy—college faculty and students—read Afro-American literature. I have found quite the opposite to be true. For it was "ordinary" black women, women in the churches, private reading groups, women like my hairdresser and her clients, secondary school teachers, typists, my women friends, many of whom were single mothers, who discussed *The Bluest Eye* (1970) or *In Love and Trouble* (1973) with an intensity unheard of in the academic world. In fact most of my colleagues did not even know these books existed when women I knew were calling these writers by their first name—Alice, Paule, Toni, June—indicating their sense of an intimacy with them. They did not necessarily buy the books but often begged, "borrowed," or "liberated" them—so that book sales were not always indicative of their interest. I had had similar experiences during the 1960s. Postal clerks, winos, as well as the folk who hung out in Micheaux's, the black bookstore in Harlem, knew Baldwin's, Wright's, Ellison's works and talked vociferously about them when many of the folk at CCNY and Columbia had never read one of these writers. Ralph Ellison wrote an extremely provocative blurb for *Our Nig* when he pointed out that Harriet Wilson's novel demonstrated that there is more "free-floating" literacy among blacks than we acknowledge.

No doubt we are influenced by what publishers say people should read or do read. When I began sending out sections of *Black Women*

Novelists, practically all academic presses as well as trade presses commented that my subject was not important—that people were not interested in black women writers. Couldn't I write a book on the social problems of black women? Affected by the rhetoric à la Moynihan, most of these presses could hardly believe black women were artists—a point we might remember as some of us today minimize the craft and artistry of these writers in favor of intellectual or social analysis. In response to these comments I could not point to any precedents, for in 1978 there had not been published a full-length study of black women writers. I believe if it were not for the incredible publicity that Toni Morrison's *Song of Solomon* received in 1978, and the fact that one of my chapters was devoted to her work, I would not have been able to publish *Black Women Novelists* when I did. Smith was right on target when she suggested that there might be other black women critics writing and working about whom she did not know because there was no place to read them.

That situation began to change by 1980, however. And I think it is important for us to recall some of the major signs of that change. One such sign was the black sexism issue of the *Black Scholar* published in May/June of 1979 which grew out of black sociologist Robert Staples's extremely critical response to Ntozake Shange's play *for colored girls who have considered suicide when the rainbow is enuf* and Michele Wallace's critique of the sexism in the civil rights movement—*Black Macho and the Myth of the Superwoman* (1979).[10] In his critique of Shange and Wallace, Staples insinuated that black feminists were being promoted by the white media—a stance that would be reiterated years later by some critics in the *Color Purple* debate. Although the debate among the Afro-American women and men on the issue was not a specifically "literary" debate, its very existence indicated the effect Afro-American women's literature was having on Afro-American intellectual circles. What was also interesting about the debate was the intense involvement of Afro-American women writers themselves who unabashedly responded to Staples. Audre Lorde put it succinctly: "Black feminists speak as women and do not need others to speak for us."[11]

Such speaking had certainly ignited the literary world. In the 1970s black women published more novels than they had in any other decade. Some, like Morrison and Walker, were beginning to be acknowledged as great American novelists. Poets such as Lorde, Jordan, Sherley Williams, and Lucille Clifton, to mention a few, were clearly literary/political activists as well as writers in the Afro-American and women's communities. And many of these writers, most of whom were not academicians (e.g., Walker in "One Child of One's Own," Lorde in "The Uses of the Erotic"), were themselves doing black feminist criticism. Increasingly even academicians could not deny the effect this body of literature was having on various communities in American life. Simultaneously, critical essays and analysis began to appear in literary academic as well as in more generalized intellectual journals.

That a black feminist criticism was beginning to receive attention from the academic world was one basis for Deborah McDowell's essay "New Directions for Black Feminist Criticism," which originally appeared in an academic journal, *Black American Literature Forum,* in 1980.[12] In responding to Smith's call for a black feminist criticism, McDowell emphasized the need for clear definitions and methodologies, a sign as well of the increasing emphasis on theory surfacing in the academic world. She asked whether black feminist criticism was relegated only to black women who wrote about black women writers. Did they have to write from a feminist/political perspective to be black feminist critics? Could white women/black men/white men do black feminist criticism? a question which indicated that this literature was beginning to attract a wider group of critics.

McDowell's questions continue to have much relevance as more and more critics of different persuasions, genders, and races write critical essays on Afro-American women writers. Just recently, in April 1988, Michele Wallace published a piece in the *Village Voice* which seemed almost a parody of the August 1974 *Black World* issue.[13] The piece was advertised in the content listing with the titillating title "Who Owns Zora Neale Hurston: Critics Carve up the Legend," and featured on the first page of its text was a big photograph of Zora, who had become the darling of the literary world. Wallace counterpointed the perspectives of black women, black men, white women, even one prominent white male critic who had written about Hurston. Everyone apparently was getting into the act, though with clearly different purposes, as Wallace insinuated that Hurston had become a commodity. Wallace's own title for her piece, "Who Dat Say

Who Dat When I Say Who Dat?" spoken as if by Hurston herself, underlined the ironic implications of the proliferation of Hurston criticism, much of which, Wallace implied, was severed from Hurston's roots and most of which ignored Hurston's goddesslike mischievousness.

"Who Dat Say Who Dat When I Say Who Dat?" took me back to McDowell's essay and her suggestions of parameters for a black feminist criticism. In addition to the ones articulated by Washington in 1974 and Smith in 1977, McDowell emphasized the need for both contextual and textual analysis—contextual, in that the critic needed to have a knowledge of Afro-American history and culture, and women's situation within it, and textual, that is, paying careful attention to the individual text. If one were to combine Washington's, Smith's, and McDowell's suggestions, few of the critical works cited by Wallace would even come close to doing black feminist criticism. Wallace acceded that "Black literature needs a rainbow coalition," but she wondered if some critical approaches did not silence Hurston. While Hurston's and other Afro-American women's writing are deep enough, full enough to be approached from any number of perspectives, their work demands rigorous attention as does any other serious writing.

The question as to who the critic is and how that affects her/his interpretation was very much on my mind when I put together *Black Feminist Criticism* in 1983–1984.[14] In thinking about my own attempts to do such criticism, I increasingly felt that critics needed to let go of their distanced and false stance of objectivity and to expose their own point of view—the tangle of background, influences, political perspectives, training, situations that helped form and inform their interpretations. Inspired by feminist discussions about objectivity and subjectivity, I constructed an introduction to my volume that, rather than the usual formal introduction found in most lit crit books, was intended to introduce me in my specific context. It was a personalized way of indicating some of my biases, not the least of which was the fact that the literature I chose to study was central to an understanding of my own life, and not *only* an intellectual pursuit. Such exposure would, I thought, help the reader evaluate more effectively the choices I had made about the language I used, the specific issues I approached, the particular writers I emphasized. By then I realized I did not want

to write about every contemporary Afro-American woman writer—
some did not speak to me—and that the extent of my own personal
involvement with the writer's work was one aspect of my doing black
feminist criticism.

But even more to the point, I thought that black feminist criticism
needed to break some of the restricted forms, personalize the staid
language associated with the critic—forms that seemed opposed to the
works of the writers as well as the culture from which they came—
and forms that many readers found intimidating and boring. In the
introduction dialogue I used call and response, jazz riffs, techniques
found in writers like Hughes and Hurston, as well as the anecdote, a
device I had found so effective in the essays of Jordan and Walker, as
ways of reflecting on my own process.

In fact the form of the book was based on the idea of process as a
critical aspect of an evolving feminist approach—that is, a resistance
to art as artifact, to ideas as fixed, and a commitment to open-
endedness, possibility, fluidity—to change. These qualities were significant characteristics of the writers I studied. Inspired by Jordan's
adroit use of headnotes in *Civil Wars,* I compiled a collection not of
every essay I had written between 1975 and 1985 but examples of
writing events I considered necessary to doing black feminist criticism—most of which were not essays written originally for academic
outlets. For me, doing black feminist criticism involved a literary activism that went beyond the halls of academe, not because I had so
legislated but because in practice that is what it often, happily, had to
be.

I also intended the book to be a tracing of that journey some of us
had been making since 1974, a journey guided by what I considered
to be another important element of doing this type of criticism, that
is, on being a participant in an ongoing dialogue between the writer
and those who were reading the writer, most of whom were not academics and for whom that writing was life-sustaining, life-saving. As
the race for theory began to accelerate in 1984, I became concerned
that that dialogue was drying up as critics rushed to construct theories
in languages that many writers abhorred and which few readers understood or enjoyed or could use. In particular I was struck by a talk
I had had with one major writer who told me she had gone to a lit crit
panel on her work but could not comprehend one word, nor could she

recognize her work in anything that was said. To whom, she asked, were we critics speaking?

Finally, I used the phrase *Black Feminist Criticism* as the title of my book because it seemed to me, in 1984, as it still does that few black women critics were willing to claim the term *feminist* in their titles. *Women* was an acceptable term, but the political implications of the term *feminist* meant that it was fast giving way to the more neutral term *gender*. I believed it was important to place the term on the black literary map, so to speak, even if it were only a reminder of an orientation no longer in vogue.

My introduction was an appeal to practice as one decisive factor in defining a black feminist criticism. In 1985 Hortense Spillers contributed another point of view. Along with Marjorie Pryse, she edited a volume entitled *Conjuring: Black Women, Fiction and Literary Tradition*,[15] which included essays by black and white women as well as black men. The subtitle was particularly striking to me since the volume privileged fiction, as had the majority of such collections, including my own. And I began to wonder why, in this rich period of Afro-American women's poetry, that genre was being so summarily ignored.

Spillers's afterword, entitled "Cross-Currents, Discontinuities: Black Women's Fiction," made it clear that "the community of black women writing in the U.S. can be regarded as a vivid new fact of national life." She defines this community as "those composed of fiction writers, as well as writers of criticism who are also teachers of literature." [16] In emphasizing the overlapping of these categories, she saw that the academy was fast becoming the site of this community and pointed to one reason why perhaps criticism had taken the direction it had. She might have added as well that new development might be one reason criticism had become so focused on fiction. Perhaps intellectual analysis is more suited to fiction and the essay than it is to poetry and drama—genres that insist on the emotions, the passions, the senses as well as the intellect as equally effective ways of knowing.

In characterizing Afro-American women's fiction as a series of discontinuities and relating these discontinuities to other American writing—to Faulkner, Dreiser, Wright—Spillers constructed a picture of American literature unthinkable in the academic world of 1974. And by using language associated with "new" critical approaches, she demonstrated how an overview of Afro-American women's fiction converged with the more conventional American literary tradition. Her essay extended the perimeters of black feminist criticism(s) in that they could now be situated in the study of American letters as an entirety. Spillers was clearly responding to the impetus for revised canons by showing how Afro-American women's fiction intersected with the currents of other literatures in the United States.

Canon formation has become one of the thorny dilemmas for the black feminist critic. Even as white women, blacks, people of color attempt to reconstruct that body of American literature considered to the *the* literature, we find ourselves confronted with the realization that we may be imitating the very structure that shut our literatures out in the first place. And that judgments we make about, for example, the BBBs (Big Black Books) are determined not only by "quality," that elusive term, but by what we academicians value, what points of view, what genre and forms we privilege.

We finally must wonder about whether this activity, which cannot be value free, will stifle the literatures we have been promoting. For while few white male American critics feel compelled to insinuate "white" literary works into *our* characterizations of American history and culture, we are almost always in a position of having to insinuate our works into their schema.[17] Spillers concludes her afterword with a provocative statement: "The day will come, I would dare to predict, when the black American women's writing community will reflect the currents of both the New new critical procedures and the various literatures concurrent with them."[18] One might also turn that statement around. We might wonder, given that Afro-American women's writing is so clearly at the vortex of sex, race, and class factors that mitigate the notion of democracy at the core of "traditional" American literatures, whether one might want to predict the day when other literatures will reflect the currents of the black American women's writing community.

While Spillers was still concerned with Afro-American women's literature as a recognizable literary tradition, Hazel Carby, in the introduction to her *Reconstructing Womanhood* (1987), was positively negative about the use of the term *tradition*. In "Rethinking Black Feminist Theory," Carby insisted that black feminist criticism has "too frequently been reduced to an experiential relationship that is assumed to exist between black women as readers and black women as writers who represent black women's reality" and that "this reliance on a common or shared experience is essentialist and ahistorical." Her book, she stated, "does not assume the existence of a tradition or traditions of Afro-American intellectual thought that have been constructed as paradigmatic of Afro-American history."[19]

In what frame is her book situated? Carby tells us that her inquiry "works within the theoretical premises of societies—'structured in dominance' by class, by race, and by gender and is a materialist account of the cultural production of black women intellectuals within the social relations that inscribed them."[20] As Valerie Smith pointed out in her review of Carby's book in *Women's Review of Books, Reconstructing Womanhood* signals a new direction in black feminist criticism in that Carby is not as much interested in Afro-American women writers as she is in constructing a black female intellectual history.[21]

Ironically, in reconstructing that history, Carby turns to creative writers/novelists. Perhaps that is because Afro-American writers, female and male, are central, pivotal, predominant figures in Afro-American intellectual history. Why that is so would take volumes to investigate, but one explanation might be that the usual modes of European/American intellectual production were not accessible to or particularly effective for Afro-Americans. That is, the thoroughly rationalist approach of European intellectual discourse might have seemed to them to be too one-dimensional, too narrow, more easily co-opted than narratives, poetry, nonlinear forms where the ambiguities and contradictions of their reality could be more freely expressed and that in these forms they could address themselves to various audiences—their own folk as well as those readers of the dominant culture. In any case, a large number if not the majority of those considered intellectuals in the Afro-American world, female or male, were or attempted to be creative writers—which might account for some of the focus Afro-American intellectual critics have had on creative literature.

No doubt Carby's emphasis on the reconstruction of a black female intellectual history is needed. And that history can now be imagined and speculated about by her and others, as it could not have been even a decade ago, because the words and works of Afro-American women of the past are more accessible. Yet Carby's approach, as she articulates it, does not seem to allow for other emphases within the arena of black feminist criticism, and the work she can now do is possible because others pursued different orientations from her own. Twenty years ago, scholars who used the language and approach she uses (and it is indeed a primarily academic language) were completely opposed to the inclusion of gender as central to their analyses and in fact called that term "essentialist." Nor could Carby be doing the work she is doing unless a space for it was created by a powerful contemporary Afro-American women's literature which in part comes out of the very paradigm she denies. What, I wonder, would Frances Harper or Pauline Hopkins think of her denial of the possibility of Afro-American literary history?

In addition, as my and other overviews of the development of Afro-American literature suggest, there is more of an inclination in the academic and publishing worlds (and we might ask why) to accept sociological/political analyses of black writers—female, male—whether they be from a materialist or bourgeois point of view, than to conceive of them as artists with their own ideas, imagination, forms. This seems to be a privilege reserved for only a few selected white men. Finally one must ask whether the study of an intellectual tradition necessitates the denial of an imaginative, creative one? Who is to say that the European emphasis on rational intellectual discourse as the measure of a people's history is superior to those traditions that value creativity, expression, paradox in the constructing of their historical process?

Carby's introduction brings the debate as to what black feminist criticism is full circle, back to Mary Helen Washington's essay in the August 1974 *Black World* in that Washington's assumptions about the relationship between black women's writings and the reality of a shared experience among black women are held suspect—a question worth pursuing. What is so riveting to me is that the term *black feminist criticism* continues to be undefineable—not fixed. For many that might seem catastrophic; for me it is an indication that so much still needs to be done—for example, reading the works of the writers, in order to understand their ramifications. Even as I cannot believe all that has been accomplished in the last fifteen years—a complete revision of, conceptualization of nineteenth-century Afro-American literature, and a redirecting of definitions in contemporary life about women's sexuality, motherhood, relationships, history, race/class, gender intersections, political structures, spirituality as perceived through the lens of contemporary Afro-American women—there is so much yet to do.

So—what do we think we're doing anyway? More precisely, what might we have to do at this juncture, in 1990?

For one—we might have to confront the positives and negatives of what it means to become institutionalized in universities.

Does this mean we will no longer respond to the communal/erotic art that poetry and drama can be because it is so difficult to reduce these forms to ideological wrangling? As Audre Lorde has so profoundly expressed, it is often in poetry that we imagine that which we have been afraid to imagine—that poetry is an important source of imagining new ideas for change.

Does our emphasis on definitions and theories mean that we will close ourselves to those, the many, who know or care little about the intense debates that take so much of our time in universities? Can we conceive of our literary critical activities as related to the activism necessary to substantively change black women's lives?

Does our scholarly advancement mean that more and more of us will turn to the study of past writers as a safer pursuit in the university which apparently has difficulty engaging in the study of present-day literatures? As necessary as the study of the past is, it is just as important to be engaged in the history that we are now making—one that has been so powerfully ignited by the contemporary writers.

In spite of the critical clamor, how many of us have actually produced sustained readings, critiques?

Can we ignore the fact that fewer and fewer blacks are receiving Ph.D.s? In fact, only 820 in 1986. Although black women are not the only ones who can do feminist criticism, it would be a significant loss if they were absent from this enterprise.

BARBARA CHRISTIAN

Do we assume that this orientation will be here even at the turn of the century?

To whom are *we* accountable? And what social relations are in/scribing us?

Does history teach us anything about the relationship between ideas, language, and practice? By 2000 will our voices sound like women's voices, black women's voices to anyone?

What do we want to do anyway and for whom do we think we're doing it?

Reading Family Matters

> Possibly the real determinants of interpretation are the literary
> and cultural assumptions of particular communities in history.
> —Wallace Martin,
> *Recent Theories of Narrative*

> They were a family somehow and he was not the head of it.
> —Toni Morrison,
> *Beloved*

It is not late-breaking news that literary criticism is another form of
storytelling, of mythmaking. Nor is it news that literary texts take
shape in the minds of readers and critics who form disparate interpretive communities.[1] These communities are held together by shared
assumptions, values, and desires that influence if not determine *what*
they see when they read and *how* they receive and represent what they
read. Or, to borrow from Mary Louise Pratt, reading and reception
are "socially and ideologically-determined process[es]."[2] I use these
commonplace insights as departure points in a brief meditation on one
interpretive community—primarily male—and its reading and reception of a group of contemporary black female writers—those published since the 1970s. More specifically, I focus on the controversial
and adhesive charge surrounding their work—that it portrays black
males in an "unflinchingly candid and often negative manner" as
"thieves, sadists, rapists, and ne'er-do-wells."[3]
    Let me start with some preliminary observations. First, this debate
has been waged primarily in the popular, white, East Coast literary
media—the *New York Times Book Review, New York Review of Books,
New York Times Magazine*—though it has also spread to academic
journals and scholarly collections. Second, for all its intensity, the debate has centered primarily on a very small sample of writers: Toni
Morrison, Gayl Jones, Ntozake Shange, and, most frequently, Alice
Walker. Finally, but perhaps most importantly, it has tended to polar-
ize (though not neatly) along gender lines. With few exceptions,

female readers see an implicit affirmation of *black women,* while males see a programmatic assault on black men, though I grant that these two responses are not mutually exclusive.[4] This tendency has been reflected especially in responses to and reviews of Alice Walker's *The Color Purple,* though most have centered disproportionately and inappropriately on Steven Spielberg's film adaptation of the novel.[5]

Why focus on a debate that seems to have outlived its interest and usefulness? Why focus, especially, since the controversy has in no way affected the reputations of the writers in question? Why spend time picking apart straw men whose arguments are so easily discredited? Why? Because for all their questionable arguments, from the perspective of readers more informed, these are men whose judgments help to influence the masses of readers largely untutored in Afro-American literature, who take their cues of what and how to read from the *New York Times Book Review, New York Review of Books,* and other organs of the literary establishment. As Richard Ohmann notes, the *New York Times Book Review* has "several times the audience of any other literary periodical" in the United States, a circulation that grants it a powerful and prestigious role in mediating the terms by which the writers and writings it selects will be received and understood. Further, such periodicals as *NYTBR* work with their counterparts—the college classroom and academic journal—and together they become, Ohmann adds, "the final arbiters of literary merit and even of survival."[6] The route Ohmann traces from prestigious literary journal to academic journal to college classroom to literary survival is surely not so direct, but useful nonetheless for mapping some of the salient points and problems of this debate. Finally, to borrow from Cathy Davidson, there is an "unequal distribution of story time" in this debate[7] Mainly we see men telling *their* stories about the writings of black women, but seldom a counterresponse from a woman. While I do not presume to resolve the tensions on either side, I think that the debate over contemporary writings by black women might profit from my attempt to uncover and suggest something of what is fundamentally at issue and at stake here.

Lest what follows be read as the critical companion of the alleged fictional attack on black men, let me rush to point out that here follows no composite portrait of "*the* black male reader." Because all readers experience and express complex and often contradictory positions, it is näive to suggest that any readership, male or female, can be so simply abstracted. It is possible and necessary, however, even despite dangers and limitations of a different order, to historicize readers, to refer, after Paul Smith, "to specific modes of production, to definite societies at historically specific moments and conjunctures." [8] That is my modest attempt here.

I leave aside for the moment speculations about why the most influential literary publications tend mainly to employ black men to review and comment on the literature of black women, and speculations about whose interests are really served in this debate. While I am interested in these critical questions, I am equally interested in what this debate illuminates about the inflections of gendered ideologies in the reading process. [9] As Maureen Quilligan rightly argues, "To pose questions about the gender of the reader is to pose questions that open the texts' relations to the political arrangements of their audiences." [10] The relation between this specific group of readers and the texts they review might be seen as the product of certain political arrangements. One could argue, for example, that the shifting power relations between black men and women in the literary sphere informs and partly explains the terms of this controversy, terms defined mainly by black men.

IF THIS DEBATE IS BUT PART OF THE DESIGN OF A larger pattern, it is useful to trace it, if only telescopically. Actually, this is the second round of a debate sparked in 1976 by the blockbuster success of Ntozake Shange's choreopoem *for colored girls who have considered suicide when the rainbow is enuf*. It spread with the publication of Michele Wallace's *Black Macho and the Myth of the Superwoman* (1980). [11] These two works were the subject of widespread and acrimonious debate from many sectors of the black community. Vernon Jarret of the *Chicago Defender* likened *for colored girls* to the pro–Ku Klux Klan film *Birth of a Nation,* and dismissed it as "a degrading treatment of the black male" and "a mockery of the black family." [12] Perhaps the most controversial statement about Shange and Wallace, however, was an article by Robert Staples, "The Myth of Black Macho: A Response to Angry Black Feminists," published in *The Black Scholar* in March/April 1979. Identified significantly as "the noted *sociologist* on black sex roles," Staples reflects in his essay a tendency in the current debate (as in most discussions of Afro-American literature) to read literature in terms that are overwhelmingly sociological.[13]

Staples argues that Shange and Wallace were rewarded for their "diatribes against black men," charging *for colored girls* with whetting black women's "collective appetite for black male blood." He attributes their rage, which "happily married women" lack, to "pent up frustrations which need release." And he sympathizes with the black male need for power in the only two institutions left to black control: the church and the family. During the 1960s, Staples continues, "there was a general consensus—among men and women—that black men would hold the leadership positions in the movement." Because "black women had held up their men far too long, it was time for the men to take charge." But as those like Shange and Wallace came under the powerful sway of the white feminist movement, he continues, they unleashed the anger black women had always borne silently. For witnessing this anger, he concludes, they were promoted and rewarded by the white media.[14]

A la Freud, I categorize this story that Staples tells as a family romance, defined by Janet Beizer as the "attempt to rewrite origins, to replace the unsatisfactory fragments of a . . . past by a totalizing fiction" that recuperates loss and fulfills desire.[15] This family romance is de-romanticized in writings by the greater majority of black women. Text meets countertext, and the "confrontation" might be described, to borrow from Christine Froula, as between the "daughter's story and the father's law." Froula argues compellingly that "the relations of literary daughters and fathers resemble . . . the model . . . describ[ing] the family situation of incest victims: a dominating, authoritarian father; an absent, ill, or complicitous mother; and a daughter who [is] prohibited by her father from speaking about abuse."[16] Not surprisingly, it is for narrating, for representing male abuses within "the family," that contemporary black women are most roundly criticized in the family plots that follow. Though this narrative of the family romance inserted itself most aggressively in the discourse of the 1960s, this story of the Black Family cum Black Community headed by the Black Male who does battle with an oppressive White world, continues to be told, though in ever more subtle variations. In Staples's version, as in the other essays discussed here, the rupture in the unified community, the haven against white racism, is the white woman offering the fruit of feminist knowledge. [17]

While his story has a subtlety that Staples's lacks, David Bradley's enlists the same rhetoric of family to argue that "Alice Walker has a high level of enmity toward black men." In "Telling the Black Woman's Story," published in the *New York Times Magazine*, January 1984, Bradley sets out to explain this enmity through pop psychobiography, tracing Walker's antagonism toward black men to a childhood accident when her brother shot her with a BB gun. "After that accident," Bradley explains, "she felt her family had failed her," specifically her father. [18]

Philip Royster goes Bradley one better to argue, in an obvious riff on her famous essay, that Walker "may be in search of not so much our mother's gardens as our fathers' protecting arms." Royster reads all of her fiction as an example of Walker's desire "to be the darling of older men and her bitterness toward younger ones." He compares her work to Morrison's in which "if a woman learns to be a daughter, then she will be able to be a wife to a black man and a mother to black children and a nurturer and preserver of black people." [19] Just what work by Morrison he has in mind here I am not sure, since so much of Morrison's work features what Susan Willis calls "three women households" that do not permit "male domination to be the determining principle for living and working relationships of the group." [20] The epigraph from *Beloved* alludes to another of these three-women households: "They were a family somehow and he was not the head of it."

Apart from their attempt to psychoanalyze Walker, using the language of family, the essays by Bradley and Royster reach a common conclusion and judgment: Walker's involvement with feminism has placed her outside the family of the larger black "community." In Bradley's essay there are repeated references to Gloria Steinem, feminism, and *Ms.* magazine, a world he describes as a "steam-driven meat grinder, and [Walker] the tenderest of meat." [21] Royster would like to see her escape the meat grinder, would like to welcome Walker back to what he calls "the extended family, the unity of the tribe," but on one condition: she, along with other black women, "may have to feel a greater loyalty towards black men . . . than towards women throughout the world." [22]

DEBORAH E. McDOWELL

Mel Watkins offers another variety of a domestic story transplanted in critical soil. His much-discussed "Sexism, Racism, and Black Women Writers" appeared in the June 15, 1986, issue of the *New York Times Book Review.* He continues the charge that black women writers "have chosen black men as a target" of attack. In so doing, they "have set themselves outside a tradition that is nearly as old as black American literature itself." They have broken an "unspoken but almost universally accepted covenant among black writers" "to present positive images of blacks." [23]

In Watkins's version of the family romance, Afro-American literary history is written in a way that emphasizes family unity. Here we have a family of *writers* who were unified until contemporary black women decided, in Watkins's words, that "sexism is more oppressive than racism." In his abridged new literary history the ancestral keepers of the tradition are William Wells Brown, W.E.B. DuBois, James Weldon Johnson, and Richard Wright, all of whom shared a commitment to "establishing humane, positive images of blacks." Though a negative character, according to Watkins, even Bigger Thomas "is presented within a context," absent in black women's writings, that "elucidated the social or psychological circumstances that motivate[]" Bigger. [24] Partially agreed. How else could the reader of any gender absorb Bigger's enjoyment of the "agony" he inflicts on his girlfriend Bessie? He enjoys "seeing and feeling the worth of himself in her bewildered desperation." And after he bludgeons her to death with a brick and throws her body down the airshaft, it occurs to him that he has done a "dumb thing"—"throwing her away with all that money in her pocket." [25]

I cite this passage not to take the cheap route of tit for tat, but to suggest something about the critical double standard that glosses over the representation of violence, rape, and battering in Richard Wright's work and installs him in a "family portrait" of black writers, but highlights that representation in *The Bluest Eye, The Third Life of Grange Copeland,* and *The Color Purple,* to justify "disinheritance." Watkins's literary history conforms strikingly to what Marilyn Butler describes in her essay "Against Tradition: The Case for a Particularized Literary Method." Butler argues forcefully that

traditions are features of all regularized practices in all societies, for they are a basic tool of selecting and ordering the past in order to validate activities and people in the present. The literary critic calls on tradition when he draws up a genealogy or family tree of writers. . . . Transmission down the line is usually described as easy and harmonious, though there is often a gap, which tends to occur near to the present day.[26]

The gap in Watkins's family tree of writers is created by the contemporary black *feminist* writers who are the subject of his essay.

Watkins's rhetoric of boundaries, parameters, of public speech about private matters figure as well in Darryl Pinckney's essay "Black Victims, Black Villains" which appeared in the January 29, 1987, issue of the *New York Review of Books*. Following its appearance, I concluded that Pinckney's essay was the winter season's family narrative and Watkins's the summer season's, in this open season on contemporary black women writers in the establishment literary media.

Pinckney attempts a joint review of Walker's *The Color Purple*, Spielberg's film adaptation, and Ishmael Reed's novel *Reckless Eyeballing*. Why it was published in the first place is unclear, since *The Color Purple* had already been reviewed in *NYRB* along with Ishmael Reed's novel *The Terrible Twos*.[27] Pinckney repeats this media match featuring Reed and Walker, but with a new twist on the family plot. This time it is the black male locked outside the family fold, and, borrowing from Morrison's *The Bluest Eye*, "his own kin had done it."

The first part of the three-part essay reads *The Color Purple*, book and film, as stories of excessive violence that present black women as the helpless victims of brutal black men. Part two briefly reviews *Reckless Eyeballing*, after a disproportionately long preface anatomizing the deterioration of the civil rights movement and the simultaneous rise of U.S. feminism. This shift "had a strong effect on Afro-American literature," Pinckney argues. "Black women writers seemed to find their voices and audiences," while "black men seemed to lose theirs." One such loser is Ishmael Reed, a thinly disguised Ian Ball in *Reckless Eyeballing*. Ball, a black playwright, has been "sexlisted" for not writing according to the feminist line and may well be the Flower Phantom who shaves the heads of black women whom he believes to be "collaborating with the enemies of black men."[28] Pinckney calls this subplot "a little nasty" and rushes to quote a long passage from the novel describing such a collaboration.

DEBORAH E. McDOWELL

In part three Pinckney returns to *The Color Purple* and the Walker/ Spielberg connection and links the work with other "highly insular stories" told by Hurston, Morrison, and Gayl Jones in which the white world has disappeared and with it the reason for the "struggling black families" whose stories these novels tell. This structuration should not go unnoticed, for it cleverly and subtly replicates Pinckney's argument. His review of Reed has been compressed and eclipsed, veritably sandwiched between Walker and Spielberg. The victims and villains of part one trade places in part two, as black males become the victims of a partnership between Alice Walker and Steven Spielberg, a black woman and a white man. Their power to eliminate the publishing options of the black male is made pointedly and metaphorically clear by part three, in which Reed has been erased altogether. An old folk expression reasserts itself here—"the freest people on earth are a black woman and a white man"—to explain the vagaries of the literary marketplace.[29]

Haki Madhubuti's reading of the U.S. publishing industry centers not on how and why it has excluded black men, but rather on how it has neglected some black women. In two essays on Sonia Sanchez and Lucille Clifton, Madhubuti explains their critical neglect in terms of "the exchange nature of the game played daily in the publishing world; the only business more ruthless and corrupted is Congress." Clifton is neglected because she "does not live in New York, may not have 'connections' with reviewers nor possess Madison Avenue visibility."[30] Likewise, Sanchez "does not have the national celebrity that her work and seriousness demand" because "she does not compromise her values, her art, or her people for fame or gold."[31] In these two essays Madhubuti relies on archetypal distinctions between "good" and "bad" women, accordingly reserving condemnations for some (Alice Walker, Toni Morrison, and Ntozake Shange) and commendations for others (Lucille Clifton, Sonia Sanchez, Mari Evans, and Gwendolyn Brooks). And one does not have to search for the real basis for the distinctions: attitudes about family. He praises Sonia Sanchez and Lucille Clifton for being "cultural workers" who refuse to "become literary and physical prostitutes" in order to "make it." He takes care to note that for Sanchez, writing poetry is combined with "raising . . . her children, maintaining a home, [and] working fourteen-hour days." Her poetry, he continues, "highlights Black women as mothers, sisters, lovers, wives, workers, and warriors" committed to the "Black family and the Black woman's role in building a better world." "In a real fight," he concludes, Sanchez is "the type of black woman you would want at your side." [32]

In his essay on Clifton, the references to family proliferate. Madhubuti begins by describing Clifton as a "full-time wife, overtime mother, part-time street activist and writer of small treasures" whose focus is "the children, the family." He even speculates that she suffers neglect because "the major body of her work is directed toward children." He commends Clifton for her "unusually significant and sensitive" treatment of black male characters, ascribing it to "her relationship with her father, brothers, husband, and sons. Generally, positive relationships produce positive results." In his closing passages, Madhubuti tellingly quotes Clifton's poem "to a dark moses," demonstrating unambiguously the ideological basis of his critique: "you are the one I am lit for/come with your rod that twists and is a serpent/I am the bush/I am burning/I am not consumed." Not surprisingly, Madhubuti concludes, "I am excited about [Clifton's] work because she reflects me; she tells my story." [33]

WHAT IS THE LEGIBLE SUBTEXT OF THESE MALE READings of black women writers? Let me make a direct and certainly predictable claim: this debate over black women writers' portrayal of black males is not principally about *this* issue (if it is at all). Rather, what lies behind this smoke screen is an unacknowledged jostling for space in the literary marketplace (certainly apparent in the essays by Haki Madhubuti mentioned above) which brings to mind Hawthorne's famous complaint about the "damn'd mob of scribbling women" of the 1850s. Furthermore, to enlist Judith Fetterley's remarks from a different context, this debate is a lament for "the sense of power derived from the experience of perceiving one's self as central, as subject, as literally because literarily the point of view from which the world is seen." This community of male readers brings to the reading of black women's texts a complex of powerful assumptions, not the least of which is "the equation of textuality with masculine subjectivity and masculine point of view." [34] This equation has operated historically in discourses about blackness. Calvin Hernton does well to note that

DEBORAH E. McDOWELL

historically, the battle line of racial struggle in the U.S. has been drawn exclusively as a struggle between the men of the races. Everything having to do with race has been defined and counter-defined by the men as a question of whether black people were or were not a race of Men. The central concept and the universal metaphor around which all aspects of the racial situation revolve is "Manhood." [35]

It should not go unnoticed that critics leading the debate have lumped all black women writers together and have focused on one tiny aspect of their immensely complex and diverse project—the image of black men—despite the fact that, if we can claim a center for these texts, it is located in the complexities of black female subjectivity and experience. In other words, though black women writers have made black women the subjects of their own family stories, these male readers/critics are attempting to usurp that place for themselves and place it at the center of critical inquiry.

The desire of these black male readers to see themselves reflected favorably back to themselves is aggressively unfulfilled in the work of contemporary black women's literature. And the ideas and ideals of masculinity and femininity upheld by the nuclear family deeply entangled in this desire are actively opposed in black women's literature. This emphatic desire for the family's recuperation and the father's restitution to his "rightful" place within it surges ironically at the very moment that this vision and version of family seem forever out of reach. In other words, as the fabric of the nuclear family progressively frays, the desire to be enfolded in it gathers force. Of course this ancient, urgent longing for the family's healing hold is not intrinsically masculine, nor does it always mask a naked will to power.

While this "regressive longing for the stem family of their nostalgic imagination" [36] must be seen as part of a much wider cultural trend, the frequency with which it has appeared in a variety of recent work by black men is suggestive. To choose a few random examples: In his moving autobiography *Brothers and Keepers,* John Wideman implies that the power of the family as a social unit could secure foundations badly shaken by the criminal activities of a brother. On the front jacket of the first edition is a jailed man in shadow, but on the back is a portrait of Wideman's family harmoniously gathered in front of the house: mother *and* father, children and grandchildren lined up in neat and orderly rows, faces smiling at each other, their bodies erect and composed. The family becomes the framing rhetoric and logic of Houston Baker's suggestive monograph *Modernism and the Harlem Renaissance*. Baker writes below a block of family photographs beginning with a picture of his wife's father, "the family signature is always a renewing renaissancism that ensures generation, generations."[37]

Finally, in *The Truly Disadvantaged: The Inner City, the Underclass, and Public Policy*, Wilson Julius Wilson, a black sociologist, lays the problem of an ineradicable underclass to intergenerational female-headed households. His solution, as Adolph Reed astutely notes, is not to appeal for "pay equity, universal day care and other initiatives to buttress women's capacities for living independently in the world," but rather to increase the pool of black "marriageable" men.[38]

Wilson too narrates a family romance with a sociological twist. He recalls nostalgically the time when "lower class, working-class, and middle-class black families all lived more or less in the same communities . . . sent their children to the same schools, availed themselves of the same recreational facilities, and shopped at the same stores."[39] So powerful is the desire to recuperate the family and a safe and uncomplicated black community that Wilson ignores, according to Reed, that the "glue" holding these earlier communities together "was not so much nuclear, 'intact' families as the imperatives of racial segregation." Reed continues pointedly that "the new concern with the black family—like the old concern with the black family . . . is . . . a moralistic ideology that . . . enforce[s] patriarchal institutions by appealing to a past that may have been largely mythical . . . and one that was certainly predicated on the subordination of women."[40]

This narrative of a fantasy family is unfulfilled in the majority of writings by contemporary black women. Much of their work exposes black women's subordination within the nuclear family, rethinks and configures its structures, and places utterance outside the father's preserve and control. But while this work refuses to offer comforting and idealized fantasies of family life, it understands their origins and the needs they fill. To cite just one example, in her first novel, *The Third Life of Grange Copeland*, Alice Walker captures poignantly the origins of Brownfield's daydream family in his childhood observations of his father's numbing life as a sharecropper. As Brownfield waits with his father for the truck to come, he sees "his father's face [freeze] into an unnaturally bland mask. . . . It was as if his father became a stone or robot . . . an object, a cipher." And when the white Mr. Shipley appears, Brownfield is "filled with terror of this man who could, by his presence alone, turn his father into something that might as well have been a pebble or a post or a piece of dirt, except for the sharp bitter odor of something whose source was forcibly contained in flesh." Brownfield's only way to cope with this dehumanization is to retreat to the comfort of a daydream that comforts him throughout his childhood:

> He saw himself grown-up, twenty-one or so, arriving home at sunset in the snow. . . . He pulled up to his house, a stately mansion with cherry-red brick chimneys . . . in a chauffeur-driven car . . . Brownfield's wife and children . . . a girl and a boy—waited anxiously for him just inside the door. . . . They jumped all over him, showering him with kisses. While he told his wife of the big deals he'd pushed through that day, she fixed him a mint julep.[41]

The text understands, then, this desire for the father's presence in the sanctity of the home, but it frustrates that desire and exposes this domestic space as the privileged site of women's exploitation.[42] It is telling, for example, that in Brownfield's idyllic fantasy, his wife and the cook are "constantly interchanged so that his wife was first black and glistening from cooking and then white and powdery to his touch."[43]

In the view of these reviews and essays, the possibilities for "wholeness" within the black family have been fractured by black women's consumption of the fruit of feminist knowledge, but more, by their affiliations with white women. Even signs of embattled reconciliation between them after long estrangement and distrust have made the black male a stranger in his own home, an outcast in his own family.

The scene in *Reckless Eyeballing* in which Becky French, a white woman, and Treemonisha Smarts, a black woman, decide the fate of Ball's play, *No Good Man,* captures the cross-racial reconciliation that demands the black male's sacrifice. As the two women exchange stares, Ball thinks

> of them in the same households all over the Americas while the men were away on long trips to the international centers of the cotton or sugar markets. The secrets they exchanged in the night when there were no men around, during the Civil War in America when the men were in the battlefield and the women were in the house. Black and white, sisters and half-sisters. Mistresses and wives. There was something going on here that made him, a man, an outsider, a spectator, like someone who'd stumbled into a country where people talked in sign language and he didn't know the signs.[44]

Quoting this passage in his review, Pinckney describes it as "a paranoid update" on a conspiratorial theme, and with that I can agree, but the passage suggests much more that bears directly on issues of gender and reading.

The male readers of this debate, whose gazes are fixed on themselves, seem to have entered a fictional territory marked by unreadable signs. Pinckney refers to this territory as the kitchen. He remembers when "Black women's concerns had belonged to what was considered the *private*, rather than the public, as if the kitchen range could not adequately represent the struggle. But it turned out that the concerns of the kitchen were big enough to encompass the lore of struggle and survival." [45]

Pinckney's distinction between public and private space is a distinction repeatedly deconstructed in the writings of the black women under review, for they understand the operations of power within intimate domains, operations captured in that now familiar axiom, "the personal is political." But more to the point, Pinckney's metaphor of the kitchen calls to mind Susan Glaspell's short story "A Jury of Her Peers." Feminist critics have read this story of a different form of family violence as a model of the workings of gender in the reading process. As the men of the story search for clues that will suggest a motive for Minnie's murder of her husband, they bypass the inside of the house and search its surroundings. They dismiss what one of them

DEBORAH E. McDOWELL

terms "the insignificance of kitchen things," and are consequently unable to "interpret this farm wife's world." [46]

While the story does not "exclude the male as reader," it attempts to educate him "to become a better reader." [47] In terms of our debate, that process of re-education begins with questioning and adjusting the categories and constructs, the values and assumptions that we bring to bear *when* reading that have almost always been formed *before* reading. Put another way, that process begins with questioning what Fredric Jameson calls "the always-already-read," the "sedimented layers of previous *interpretations*." [48]

Alice Walker's story "Source," from her collection *You Can't Keep a Good Woman Down,* offers a different model of reading. [49] Choosing "Source" as a model seems especially appropriate because, of all the black women writers under critique in this debate, Walker has been the object of the most savage, sustained, and partisan attack (primarily for *The Color Purple*) and the lightning rod for these reviewers' hostility to feminism. It is notably ironic, then, that well before that controversial novel was published, Walker, had, perhaps in an uncanny moment of prescience, staged in "Source" many general concerns and assumptions—both literary and cultural—at work in this debate.

The title announces the story's concern with origins, beginnings, with questions of male subjectivity and its relation to language and representation. Repeated references to Mt. McKinley function as figures of masculine potency and transcendence. In its parallel plot lines—one involving reading matters, the other family matters—the story stages competing words and conflicting discourses framed as a secular myth of origins. Further, it engages and complicates the salient and interlocking assumptions inherent in this controversy. For example, the story confronts head-on the twin beliefs inherent in these reviews: the belief in the text as *reflection* rather than *production* of self and world; the belief in a pre-given positive masculine identity. In the process, it poses questions about the nature of identification and recognition in the reading process.

source: from Latin *surgere*—to raise, rise; the point of origin; a generative force or stimulus; genealogical lineage.

A veritable reference work, "Source" alludes to a number of books, song titles, films, and historical figures, including "Eleanor Rigby," *Steppenwolf, Imitation of Life, Autobiography of an Ex-Colored Man, Confessions of Nat Turner, Birth of a Nation,* and *Louisa Picquet, the Octoroon: A Tale of Southern Slave Life.* These titles are suggestive and instructive, for they cast into bold relief the status of the story as *story,* as text. But more importantly, most of these titles comment on the constructed (not found) and contingent nature of identity and subjectivity. These allusions establish and announce the narrative's self-conscious insistence on its own *fictionality,* its own textuality, in a way that compares to Shari Benstock's reading of footnotes in the literary text. I agree with her that footnotes (and here I would substitute Alice Walker's various allusions to artistic works) "belong to a fictional universe, stem from a creative act . . . and direct themselves toward the fiction and never toward an external construct, even when they cite 'real' works in the world outside the particular fiction." [50]

The "real" works of Walker's story, the sources behind her "Source," instruct the reader about the disguises of identity, about identity as disguise. From the opening allusion to "Eleanor Rigby" (who keeps her face in a jar by the door) to *The Autobiography of an Ex-Colored Man* to *Steppenwolf* to *Louisa Picquet, the Octoroon,* the underlying issue is the same: identity is textually constructed, not pre-given or found. The "real" persons function similarly: "once 'inside' the fiction, both fictional characters and real personages exist at the same fictive level." [51]

While Walker liberally incorporates references to historical personages throughout her fiction, she seems fully aware of both their fictive status in her work *and* their "fictive" status in the world. She compounds the story's many ironies and self-complications by suggesting that such *actual* historical figures may even have *made* up their identities. The reference to Kathleen Cleaver is a case in point. Although readers familiar with the Black Panther party recognize her as one of its leaders, the narrative stresses that that identity is assumed, is made, is produced by the contingencies of time and place.

Anastasia's memory of her first meeting with Kathleen Cleaver "before *she* was Kathleen Cleaver" is suggestive. Male-identified, like Anastasia, Cleaver "sat in a corner all evening without saying a word. . . . Men did all the talking" (153). However, after the men are dead or jailed, Cleaver is forced to change; that change figures in her dress: in "boots and sunglasses and black clothes" she "poses for photographers [while] holding a gun" (153).

This dynamic, ever-changing historically and spatially situated nature of identity is counterposed to the static conception of identity embodied in Source, the title character, the only stationary figure in the text. While all move around him, Source sits on a bed and receives those who come to hear his static message: "the universe is unchangeable" (153). His name evokes the "original," "pre-given," positive racial self, historically and paradigmatically male. It is this conception of self that is demanded by these reviewers. Although the story's title leads the reader to expect a story *about* this guru/teacher/father figure, Source is not the work's center of reference. Rather, the nominal "center" is relocated to the margins of the text. His presence is deferred until the narrative action is well under way. And even at that, his appearance is brief and clearly subordinated to the narrative's dramatization of the reunion between Irene and Anastasia.

The narrative of this reunion brings to a head conflicting discourses about family and identity, discourses which the story figures through its controlling metaphor of teaching. It juxtaposes Source's method—requiring passive and unquestioning acceptance and transcription of his authority—to Irene's, requiring that her students "take an active part in their own instruction" (142).

These conflicting methodologies come to rest in Anastasia, who must negotiate between them and, in effect, between Irene and Source. As flower child and sometime mistress of Source, Anastasia finds unacceptable Irene's critique and rejection of Source's authority. In a section that dramatizes the family's site as production and construction of identity, especially the daughter's identity, Anastasia defends Source to a suspicious and judgmental Irene. Always painfully confused about her racial identity (she looks white but is considered black), Anastasia has spent much of her life drifting, changing identities as she changes "personal fashion" (143). After several such changes—"Southern Innocent," "New York Super Vamp," "Kathleen Cleaver type"—she meets Source who hastens her along to her next change to flower child. Significantly, Source describes their first meeting by remembering that Anastasia looked like Kathleen Cleaver, her "hair like an angry, wild animal bush." He tames her, substituting her "militancy" for calm, and renames her Tranquility.

Further, he helps her accept that "[she] is nothing," that "nobody's anything." More importantly, Source arranges the reunion between Anastasia and her family—arranges, more precisely, her reunion with her father who "now wrote of God's love, God's grace, God's assured forgiveness, and of his own happiness that his daughter, always at heart 'a good girl,' had at last embarked on the path of obedience . . . [which] alone led to peace everlasting in the new and coming system of the world" (148). It is this "new and coming system" that Irene's questioning presence threatens. She sits with "a clenched fist resting on the letters from Anastasia's father (148) and poses a challenge to the universal negatives of Source's teaching: "Nobody's anything." "You can't change anything." Ensuring the continued circulation of his words, Source has his daughter write them down.

Reading this new and coming system accurately as an age-old sanction for the daughter's seduction and submission, Irene is invited to leave. Irene's life work is teaching students to respect and inscribe "their own personal histories and their own experience" (142), not to reinscribe themselves in another's "universal truths." Structured into Irene's method of teaching "Advanced Reading and Writing" is a provision for students to write their own books, which effectively contravenes the assumption that "bearing a father's word," as Source's daughter does, is "women's only acceptable role with respect to language."[52] Source's daughter is literally and literarily bearing his word, as she is pregnant with his child. Here Margaret Homans's observations about women who "act as amanuenses . . . usually for men" are pertinent. "Like the mother of the Word, the woman who carries language from one place or state of being to another does not herself originate or even touch it, and she gets nothing for her labor, which she performs for others."[53] In addition, Irene's students are required to shift any identity constructs that lock them into a single reading persona or type.

"SOURCE" INCORPORATES VARIOUS CATEGORIES OF readers and scenes of instruction. And while each characterizes a woman reader, the implications are more broadly applicable. Fania represents one category. Like many of the men sustaining this debate, Fania is a "resisting reader," to borrow from Judith Fetterley, refusing to learn to read anything that hurt (145) or in which she failed to recognize herself. While the narrative clearly sympathizes with Fania's reading strategies, it challenges her to move beyond her resistance to explore her "undeveloped comprehension of [self and] world" (153). For Fania, that expansion begins with the slave narratives of black women. Significantly, Fania, "a stout, walnut-colored woman," identifies with the narrative of *Louisa Picquet, the Octoroon,* though she does not *recognize* Picquet as identical with herself.

While Irene succeeds in teaching Fania a way to read that effectively displaces the recognizable and the familiar as privileged conventions of reading, she is in like need of instruction. And in an interesting narrative twist, as readers witness her instruction, they are taught themselves. The narrative sets the reader up for the familiar and "recognizable" story of a deprived but socially committed black woman and an indulged, confused, and irresponsible mulatto with a "lack of commitment to anything . . . useful" (166); but happily the story swerves from such banalities, for while Irene casts herself in the role of Anastasia's teacher, their roles reverse in the course of the narrative and teacher becomes learner and learner teacher. This reversal captures the very issues of constructed identities and idealized self-definition with which the story wrestles and which are most pertinent to the controversy about black women writers.

Though Irene is partly represented as an idealist with a knowledge of self that qualifies her to represent the race, she falls far short of that carefully constructed and controlled ideal. (Walker clearly intends a parallel with Nella Larsen's similarly deluded narrator Irene in *Passing,* the seeming foil to Clare). Correlatively, Anastasia, who changes identities as she "changed fashion," helps Irene to "unmask her own confusion" about self and race.

The productive tension between Irene and Anastasia and the symbolic role reversals they undergo can only occur away from Source's watchful gaze and the influence of his teachings. Anastasia has bought these teachings uncritically, crediting them with reuniting her with her family. (Interestingly, while Anastasia accepts Source's teachings, which coincide with her father's words, she "never read the newsletter that Irene and her [students] published" [142]). But Anastasia pays for the family reunion, arranged on Sources's terms and turf, with her own psychic and physical health. Her recovery requires that she review Source's teachings and unmask their repressive aims.

While Source would teach that "the good of life is indifference" (suggesting undifferentiation, nondifference) and that "nobody's anything," Anastasia progressively distances herself from his rhetoric and his universalization of stasis. Arguing that "only a fascist would say nobody's anything," Anastasia changes Source's words and substitutes her own, emphatically: "Everybody's *some*thing. Some*body*." In rejecting Source's positivization of the negative, Anastasia begins the process of unnaming and the recognition of the arbitrary relation between the name and the thing that necessarily calls into question any confident claims about a positive black male identity. With "a permanent tremor under [her] eye," "constant colds, diarrhea, loose teeth and skin eruptions," Anastasia asks pointedly, "If I was so tranquil, why was this happening?" Implicitly renouncing the name that Source has given her—Tranquility—she has learned, to paraphrase a passage from *Invisible Man,* that "to call a thing by name is [not] to make it so." Similarly, Source, despite his name, is not the absolute source, the self-present origin, the namer, the author whose authority is unchallengeable.

Much the same might be said about Alice Walker as the source, the author, the originator of "Source"—suggestions not lost on Walker. The multiple listing of textual sources in the story might be read as Walker's commentary on the process of authorship, which implies a distance from received notions of a single author and the concept of single, self-identity it implies. Although, with that said, one cannot then take Walker's own words as Truth. It is nonetheless pertinent and useful to note that Walker's response to her critics takes the form of a discussion of self-identity. In "In the Closet of the Soul" she writes:

> crucial to our development . . . is an acceptance of our actual as opposed to our mythical selves. We are the mestizos of North America. We are black, yes, but we are "white," tan, and we are red. To attempt to function as only one, when you are really two or three, leads, I believe, to psychic illness. Regardless of who will or will not accept us, including perhaps, our "established" self, we must be completely (to the extent it is possible) who we are.[54]

It is precisely this question about self-identity that is thematized in "Source." Like *Sula,* the narrative exploits, complicates, and affirms a dynamic conception of identity that resists any notion of a single identity to be "positively" represented in fiction. More, both through its figuration of Anastasia's "identity changes" and through its unmasking of Irene's "self-saving vanity" (141), the text reveals the workings of desire in the construction of identity. In this richly textured story, then, Shoshana Felman's words come directly to mind: "Indeed it is not so much the critic [reader/reviewer] who comprehends the text, as the text that comprehends the critic." [55] The narrative understands the critics who would charge Walker and her black female contemporaries with shattering the "established" image, the positive identity. More to the point, the text understands what their rhetoric of family reveals and conceals.

Whether or not one agrees that the text comprehends the critics of Afro-American women novelists, it is certain that these reviewers have had a constraining influence on the writers they attack. Since this controversy began, certain black women writers have expressed their fear and concern about how their depictions of black men would be received, and, more sobering, others might even be said to have adjusted their aesthetic vision because of the pressures of negative publicity. To take just one example, Gloria Naylor admits to being "self-conscious" about her first novel. "I bent over backwards," she says, "not to have a negative message come through about the men. . . . I worried about whether or not the problems that were being caused by the men in the women's lives would be interpreted as some bitter statement I had to make about black men" [56]

Similarly, in a 1987 interview Ntozake Shange agreed with Brenda Lyons's perception that between the controversial *for colored girls* and her most recent novel *Betsey Brown* (1985), there was "a movement away from radical feminist politics . . . toward what seems a return to family-centered values." [57] There is of course no necessary causal connection between the controversy and Shange's aesthetic shift, but it should not go unnoticed that Shange moves aesthetically toward representing the very value system espoused in these reviews. And while family- and female-centered writing need not be seen as incompatible, it is significant that Shange dedicates *Betsey Brown* to her family. And the back flap of the first edition features a photograph of her beaming down admiringly at her daughter. Completing the portrait is Ishmael Reed's lone blurb, which praises Shange for her "uncanny gift for immersing herself within the situations and points of view of so many different types of women." By delimiting her audience to women, he continues, "she has achieved an almost oracular status among her female readers." Although a "writer of many masks," he concludes, "the masks come off" with *Betsey Brown*.

I leave it to the reader to speculate about what Reed might mean by Shange's masks, but what his description of her as a writer for *female* readers suggests is unambiguous. His comments that give, then take away, represent a shift, however feeble, to a more sanguine response to a black woman writer. But it is only a momentary shift, for he resurrects his venom in his roman à clef, *Reckless Eyeballing*. Ian Ball is a clear self-portrait whose story allegorizes Reed's now well-known and predictable perception that the work of talented black men is being eclipsed by the power bloc of black women writers midwifed and promoted by white feminists.

"Sex-listed" in a feminist publication suggestively titled *Lilith's Gang,* Ball goes on to experience a positive reversal of literary fortune. But the more interesting development is a parallel "reversal" for Treemonisha Smarts, a thinly disguised Ntozake Shange. At novel's end, drunk with what the narrative describes as the "skull and cross-bones" of literary success, Treemonisha has abandoned her successful career, moved to Yuba City, California, with a recovering drug addict and failed musician, renounced her involvement with voyeuristic white feminists, and resolved to "get fat, have babies, and write, write write." [58] Reed's fantasy, no doubt. In this scenario, writing for a woman is preceded by getting fat and having babies and is best not followed by the "skull and cross-bones" of literary success, although achieving that same success has been Ian Ball's driving ambition. With *Reckless Eyeballing,* we might say, Reed's "masks come off," revealing plainly to this reader that reading family matters.

But this controversy is clearly not reducible simply to conflictual interaction between the texts of contemporary black women and a group of resisting male readers. Thus, its resolution is no simple matter of "adjusting" identity constructs and altering reading strategies at the finite level of the text, for, in the language of "Souce," always "up there" is the Higher Power, the meta-structure, which has not only already textualized "identity," but has also already determined whether there will be "reading" at all.

The story is sharply alert to the political economy of reading and writing, and it understands the inextricable relation between the source of funding and the source of words. In talking to Anastasia about how federal cuts ended the Advanced Reading and Writing course she was teaching to poor women in the rural South, Irene explains, "In the beginning there was no funding" and "the two women could not help grinning in recognition of the somehow *familiar* sound of this" (143–44, emphasis in text). But Irene, like Walker, defamiliarizes the familiar (familial) and secularizes the sacred origins of the myth of creation. She understands the twin relation of church to state and underscores the vulnerability of women's reading and writing to the power of their entwined control.

Walker uses references to Mt. McKinley to allegorize white male dominance over language and representation and to illustrate how, through the erasure of difference, that power is institutionalized. The highest peak in North America, Mt. McKinley, was renamed for President William McKinley in 1896, replacing the Indian name Denali (The Highest One). And while it is clear that Walker associates the "great elusive" Mt. McKinley with a power wielded mainly by white men, she knows that black men are also inescapably the agents of that hegemony in many respects. The narrative establishes an equivalent relation between Source's "bare feet," which he "cover[s] and uncover[s]" with a "white robe" (150), and another mountain in Seattle mentioned, but unnamed, at story's end. Tourists pointing in the distance "thought they were finally seeing the great elusive [Mt. McKinley], a hundred miles away. They were not. It was yet another, nearer, mountain's very large feet, its massive ankles wreathed in clouds" (167).

While these male gazes are fixed on the texts of black women in which they seek to find idealized reflections of themselves, they fail to see the highest mountain, the meta-structure who has the naming power and in whose name and interests that power is secured. It is this looming, distant structure that orchestrates and dominates this literary battle royal, this already fixed match between black men and black women.[59] And one could argue that this fixed match reproduces an older meta-narrative written in the history of the slave master's hand. In that narrative, as in this, the bodies/texts of black women have become the "battlefield on and over which men, black and white, [fight] to establish actual and symbolic political dominance and to demonstrate masculine" control.[60] This attempt to control both black women's written *bodies* and their *written* bodies[61] must be read and its service to the family plot interpreted, for that plot makes women permanent daughters content merely to transcribe their father's words.

Allegories of Black Female Desire; or, Rereading Nineteenth-Century Sentimental Narratives of Black Female Authority

Key incidents in two prominent twentieth-century Afro-American novels are especially paradigmatic for representing (post)modernist attitudes about marriage because they measure that institution against individual wish fulfillment and reveal a growing apprehension, on the part of their respective central characters, that marriage does not enhance personal gratification. Each incident evolves from what Fredric Jameson calls "allegories of desire"[1] that are, in these instances, gender specific as well as generationally and racially specific. Thus, if we see these incidents referencing marriage as representations of individual and collective, male and female desire that are also historically conditioned, this understanding can instruct our strategies for (re)reading nineteenth-century sentimental texts of black female authority that categorically valorize the institution of marriage.

The first incident occurs in Richard Wright's *Black Boy* and involves Richard's stay at the Moss household in Memphis, where he encounters Bess Moss and her mother, Mrs. Moss, both of whom are very eager to have him marry Bess and settle down. Soon after meeting Richard, Mrs. Moss tells him that "[she'd] be happy when [she] died if [she] thought Bess had a husband like [him]."[2] A day or so later Mrs. Moss renews her offer: "You and Bess could have this house for your home. . . . You-all could bring up your children here" (197). Richard explains his desire to relocate in the North, an ambition that no doubt will be difficult to realize without the added burden of a wife and a new family. Understandably, he declines Mrs. Moss's offer as gracefully as he can. However, she becomes angry at his categorical rejection of what she considers to be an exceptionally generous offer and orders him to move out of her house. Although she later withdraws her demand, Richard sees that his freedom is in jeopardy and resolves to preserve his autonomy by escaping domestic entrapment.[3] In this incident, black women become emblematic of the loss of freedom; they represent compromised masculine desire and the dissolution of male autonomy. The measure of a black man's autonomy is, then, his steadfast desire for freedom, which is here portrayed as Richard's undaunted flight from female entanglement, the most definitive of which is marriage.

The second incident is in Zora Neale Hurston's *Their Eyes Were Watching God* and occurs immediately after Nanny sees Johnny Taylor kissing her sixteen-year-old granddaughter, Janie. Janie believes that the desire for romantic fulfillment culminates in marriage: "Ah wants things sweet wid mah marriage lak when you sit under a pear tree and think. Ah. . . ."[4] Nanny, however, does not entertain such notions. "Lawd have mussy!" she says, "Dat's de very prong all us black women gits hung on. Dis Love" (41)! Inasmuch as black female desire for freedom is doubly prohibited in a white patriarchal society, Nanny substitutes social (e.g., financial) security for that prohibition. In her estimation, marriage to a well-to-do black man is protection for a black woman. With this goal in mind, she arranges Janie's marriage to Logan Killicks. Nanny's experiential wisdom compels this match because she fully understands that biological vulnerability threatens her granddaughter's life. Life has taught Nanny the necessity of postponing her "dreams of whut a woman oughta be and to do" (31) in order to survive. For this reason, she encourages Janie to hold on to her dream, depicted here as female sexual desire, while simultaneously postponing its realization with the demand that she marry Killicks. After the ceremony, Janie sees marriage with growing apprehension; it is, first, a form of socially sanctioned brokerage in which women serve as currency in the circuit of patriarchal exchange; second, the culmination of socially regulated female sexual desire; and, third, a deterrent to achieving female subjectivity. From Nanny's perspective, though, marriage means keeping this dreamer "safe in life" (30).

To Vote and to Marry

The two modernist allegories of desire, one black male-centered and the other black female-centered, characterize marriage and freedom as antithetical. Marriage, in these two texts, mediates desire with promises of matrimonial bliss and respectability, as well as disavows individual subjectivity and, indeed, compromises individual freedom. These are the beliefs that we largely share and are likely to bring to Afro-American texts that depict marriage because, given our postmodernist conditioning, the subject of marriage signals its opposite—(unmarried) freedom—and because the genesis and general preoccupation for black literature places those texts automatically in a discourse on freedom. Thus, when we read texts that not only focus on marriage but privilege that institution as well, as in the case of nineteenth-century black women's sentimental fiction, we are likely to find ourselves conforming to patterns of value formation dictated by our historical moment rather than historicizing the texts and couching our readings in the black cultural ethos for the nineteenth century. We tend to applaud the discourse on freedom unconditionally, while the discourse on marriage is, for us, at best problematic.

As Robert B. Stepto had notably argued, to write and to be free were dual historical imperatives for black Americans in bondage.[5] Continuing to inscribe these imperatives in black literature has remained a central objective, with the subject of civil liberty assuming racially sanctioned discursive dominance. With this imperative in mind, the two twentieth-century incidents depicted above assist me in configurating a problematic for hypothesizing why traditional Afro-American scholarship has produced either particularly pejorative readings or none at all for nineteenth-century sentimental texts of black female authority.[6] That is, those texts written by black American women in which the narrative and central character evolve specifically from a black woman's perspective, values, and her material history, thus forming a black female subjectivity. In addition, that authority evolves from appropriating Victorian prescriptives about female decorum and social expectations, paramount among them marriage, and from adapting many formal conventions of sentimental fiction. My problematic arises from yoking together the discourses on matrimony and liberation from twentieth-century texts like the two cited and witnessing the resulting antagonism on the part of the principal characters who find that their notions about marriage and freedom do not peaceably coexist. Traditional scholarship also reflects this characteristically (post)modernist antagonism. These texts center marriage, whereas the scholarship has valorized freedom. In other words, the texts and the criticism have been mutually hostile. This antagonism, I suggest, largely accounts for the dearth of scholarly attention routinely accorded to black women's sentimental texts, and it further accounts for the history of their misreadings. The issue of history itself prompts other questions. What are the temporal limitations of this antagonistic union of marriage and freedom? Might there have been a time when a readership would have been conditioned to read marriage as liberational?

I am arguing, then, that modernist views on marriage, a metonym for female desire, and critical evaluations that privilege realistic depictions of the so-called race problem have been largely responsible for the low esteem that traditional Afro-American scholarship has routinely accorded nineteenth-century black women's sentimental narratives. However, we must be mindful that all critical practice arises from specific sets of historical circumstances. Historical time, then, is a central factor in formulating interpretations and making value judgments. Thus, a crucial enterprise, in a discussion about this writing, is, first, reconstructing how nineteenth-century black people may have regarded the institution of marriage and, second, specifically hypothesizing how black women may have translated their domestic ideals into literary representation. In other words, coming to the question hermeneutically prompts me further to ask whether nineteenth-century black people were apt to regard marriage like their twentieth-century counterparts, that is, as a negation of personal autonomy. Might a representative nineteenth-century black man have referred to his wife, even in jest, as "the ball and chain"? As an initial answer to these questions, I direct my attention to reconstructing nineteenth-century black people's attitudes about marriage and freedom before proceeding to reread selected antebellum and postbellum black women's sentimental narratives as political, indeed liberational, texts.

John Bouvier's *A Law Dictionary Adapted to the Constitution and Laws of the U.S.A.* and *Judicial and Statutory Definitions of Words and Phases,* collected, edited and compiled by members of the editorial staff of the National Reporter Association, provide the following composite of judicial and statutory definitions for marriage that are instructive for understanding the nineteenth-century ethos for marriage and especially for hypothesizing how the newly liberated black population regarded this institution. Marriage is defined as civil status, condition and relation, created by a contract, which is regulated by law, that involves the mutual agreement of a man and a woman, competent to contract, to live together as husband and wife for the purpose of civilized society.[7] "Unlike other contracts," [marriage] is the one instituted by God himself, and has its foundation in the law of nature" (*Judicial* 4390). Thus, marriage is the foundation of the family and indeed the very foundation of society, without which there would be neither civilization nor progress. Civilized society, then, is that management of human relationships and resources, serving to multiply, preserve, and improve the species through the procreation and education of children (*Judicial* 4390–93).

During the antebellum era, slaves could not enter into legal marriage because they had no civil status (Bouvier 1848:116). Although slaves might participate in slave marriages by "jump[ing] the broom" or "marry[ing] in blankets," a ceremony easily imagined, these extralegal marriages were not sanctioned by law, but were regulated by the caprice of slave owners.[8] The history of slavery as well as its literary representations record slaves marrying and practicing monogamy to the best of their ability. However, such marriages were routinely dissolved at the auction block where families were torn apart with bills of sale. In addition, because slave marriages existed outside of civil law, they also existed outside of Western concepts of morality, civilization, and human progress.

President Lincoln's Emancipation Proclamation of 1863 freed Negro slaves in the Confederate states still in rebellion. The Thirteenth Amendment to the Constitution completed the abolition of slavery throughout the United States in 1865. But it was the Fourteenth Amendment that granted all black people who were born or naturalized in the United States citizenship. Thus, with the ratification of this amendment in 1866, black people secured political status as civil entities. As citizens, black people became competent to enter into civil contractual obligations, of which marriage was clearly the most popular.

Herbert Gutman, in *The Black Family in Slavery and Freedom*, provides statistical evidence for the rates by which newly freed black people registered their slave marriages and, I suggest, affirmed their new civil status. He compares 1860 population figures for adult slaves throughout several southern states, county by county, to the actual number of ex-slave marriages in the same regions in 1866. He finds that astounding numbers of ex-slaves legally reaffirmed their "common law" marriages by purchasing "Negro Cohabitation Certificates" or securing marriage certificates by repeating their marriage vows, despite the fact that most former slave states had passed legislation automatically legalizing existing slave marriages.[9]

Nineteenth-century people, white and black, were well aware of the social ethos for their period. They staunchly sanctioned civil marriage as the vehicle for promoting family stability, social progress, and respectability; indeed, marriage was the sign of civilization. Black people, in particular, regarded marriage as an important index of their propensity for civilization and as uncontestable evidence for their moral commitment to social progress. In fact, many advocates for racial justice referred to the high marriage statistics for ex-slaves to counter popular arguments about the decline in morality among the newly freed blacks.[10] In this context, then, marriage has tremendous social value and utility. Exercising the civil right to marry, I argue, was as important to the newly freed black population as exercising another civil right, which was inscribed into the Constitution as the Fifteenth Amendment in 1870—Negro suffrage. For black people, the importance of marrying in the private sphere of domestic activity may have indeed paralleled that of voting in the public. Put another way, for black people, voting and marrying were the signs of the race's ascent to manhood and womanhood. To vote and to marry, then, were two civil responsibilities that nineteenth-century black people elected to perform; they were twin indexes for measuring how black people collectively valued their civil liberties.

If we look at black women's postbellum sentimental fiction written by such writers as Frances Harper, Pauline Hopkins, Victoria Earle, Emma Kelly, Amelia Johnson, and Katherine Tillman, for example, in this light, we are in need of reinterpreting this large body of writing and reevaluating its social and aesthetic value.[11] By historicizing this writing, the label "sentimental" becomes not merely a code word for describing domestic narratives that moralize about proper male and female spiritual, familial, and social conduct in the conventions of hyperbolic emotionality, but a term that is somewhat misleading for women's texts because they generally appropriate the conventions of sentimentality to mask the heroine's growing self-consciousness, rationality, and ultimately her desire to redefine feminine propriety.[12] However, before I show how we might reread selected antebellum and postbellum black women's texts, I examine briefly how the racial arguments differ in nineteenth-century narratives of both black male and female authority.

Current scholarship documents the tremendous popularity of white women's sentimental fiction during the nineteenth century, while also documenting how twentieth-century scholarship has marginalized this writing. That discussion is also pertinent to black women's writing; it suggests that gender shapes very different racial arguments in nineteenth-century black male and female narratives and that the manner of their presentation is likewise categorically distinct.[13] Both male and female texts inscribe racial oppression and black peoples' desire to participate in what was then an emergent bourgeois-capitalistic society; however, those inscriptions generally assume the form of racial protestation in male texts, such as Charles Chesnutt's *The House behind the Cedars* (1900) and Sutton Griggs's *Imperium in Imperio* (1899), and ideal familial formation in female texts such as Harper's *Iola Leroy* (1892), Amelia Johnson's *Clarence and Corinne* (1890), and Katherine Tillman's novella "Beryl Weston's Ambition" (1893). In similar antebellum narratives racial oppression appears in male and female texts alike as moral indignation at slavery; male authors such as Frederick Douglass, Henry Bibb, and Solomon Northrup make passionate petitions for civil liberty, while female authors such as Harriet Jacobs and Nancy Prince make that same petition, but as their outrage at the sexual oppression and abused maternal rights associated with slavery.[14]

One way of explaining the disproportionate amounts of attention that scholars have given to black male antebellum and postbellum texts as compared to female counterparts (aside from the fact that the scholars have been almost exclusively men) is to refer to the social value and power typically invested in what Jameson calls allegorical master narratives. Such allegories are, as he explains, "a persistent dimension of literary and cultural texts precisely because they reflect a fundamental dimension about our collective thinking and our collective fantasies about history and reality."[15] These master allegories are not simply gender specific, but in the case of black literature they are racially predetermined as well. By referring to this interpretative strategy, we can detect two master allegories in Frederick Douglass's *The Narrative of the Life* of 1845: the black liberational discourse and another about male struggle for patriarchal power, known in the modern Eurocentric context as the Oedipal complex. The forcefulness of two master allegories combined into one text, I suggest, transforms *The Narrative* into *the* prototypical black master text whose clear gender specificity characterizes the act of black heroic self-definition, or what Stepto calls "heroic self-transformation," as a masculine discursive event.[16] What is also important to see here is that this narrative inscribes violent and aggressive confrontation as the means for making one's psychological independence into a physical fact. In other words, asserting one's independence alone is insufficient for shaping a collective heroic fantasy. For example, two antebellum black women's texts—Harriet E. Wilson's *Our Nig* (1859) and Harriet Jacobs's *Incidents in the Life of a Slave Girl* (1861)—dramatize the act of self-affirmation; however, passive aggression is substituted for violent confrontation. In *Our Nig* Frado's psychic liberation occurs when she refuses to accept passively Mrs. Bellmont's repeated abuse. After Mrs. Bellmont knocks her to the ground, Frado announces that she will withhold her labor should Mrs. Bellmont ever strike her again. And in *Incidents* Linda liberates herself from her master's sexual harassment by giving herself willingly to another white man. Because both acts of self-affirmation are fundamentally compromised in that neither reflects women's, let alone men's, idealized "collective fantasies about their history and reality,"[17] their full claim to heroic stature is likewise compromised. Under these circumstances, the master text subsumes the entire category of black heroic liberational discourse and makes interracial violence the dominant medium for achieving heroic self-affirmation.

The allegorical master narrative is also present in black male, postbellum sentimental texts, like Chesnutt's *The Morrow of Tradition* (1901). A typical plotline for such novels would proceed as follows: in attempting to enact his prescribed role as the family patriarch and participate in a bourgeois-capitalistic economy, the black male-hero confronts civil injustice because he is black. The marriage story, then, provides the general social context for the hero to affirm his personal integrity. However, the story usually closes with racial bigotry defeating him, and the role of black patriarch assumes greater magnitude as a position to be desired. The marriage story not only supports the dominant racial discourse of protesting social injustice; it also sets the stage for the interracial contest. Black, bourgeois, male-heroic subjec-

CLAUDIA TATE

tivity does not achieve discursive dominance because that role is reserved for the racial discourse in postbellum male texts. The celebration of civil liberty as desire, consequently, is the male text's primary discursive enterprise, and it is dramatized as masculine ambition in the world of public affairs and measured against systems of value formation qualified by male voice, experience, and prerogative. Moreover, the lofty language of sentimentality, the ideology of romantic love and idealized character portrayals all serve to sanction the hero's frustrated claim to patriarchal dominion over the public and private spheres of black society. Thus, his defeat is not simply tragic; it is also instructive for readers because it fortifies their resolve to fight racism with greater vigilance. Black male sentimental narratives serve as sounding boards for emphatically explicit petitions for social justice; for this reason traditional Afro-American scholarship has inscribed them in literary history.

In sharp contrast the black, bourgeois female-heroic subjectivity is not only realized in corresponding female postbellum novels, such as Frances Harper's *Iola Leroy* (1892), Pauline Hopkins's *Contending Forces* (1900), Amelia Johnson's *Clarence and Corinne* (1890), and Emma Dunham Kelley's *Megda* (1891), which I discuss below; this subjectivity is decidedly emphasized, albeit within a closely circumscribed, idealized, intraracial social context. That is, black women's personal experiences, material history, and especially their desires constitute the text's controlling vision that forms a very different dominant story, which seems more a product of gender constructs than racial ones. These narratives not only culminate in marriage; they also idealize the formation of the family unit. Moreover, the marriage story and resulting domestic ideality assume discursive dominance in female narratives (whereas in male texts that position is reserved for the socially sanctioned racial story). This shift in narrative hegemony may be the source of ambivalent, indeed negative, readings from traditional scholars who have been schooled on masculine discourses of racial protest that privilege male desire. To compound the problem, black female texts seem overly preoccupied with middle-class propriety, civility, domesticity, and commodity consumption, all of which undercuts the sanctioned preeminence of the discourse on interracial hostility. But this focus on bourgeois propriety and material consumption may have indeed been a device to disrupt the popular conflation of race with class rather than a conspicuous display of wealth. Put another way, these texts call deliberate attention to the fact that black people were not categorically poor. For nineteenth-century society, material comfort was a sign of a virtuous life. In this context, then, what seems to be black women writers' general preoccupation with fine clothing and expensive household articles becomes the semiotics of an emergent bourgeois-capitalism in which black people are full participants. When read as mimetic representation, though, this preoccupation seems grossly out of touch with the actual material conditions of the majority of black people, thus traditional scholarship's contention that this writing is unrealistic, pretentious, and nonpolitical.[18] Rather than question its own reading strategies, this scholarship has expected black women's texts to sanction black male desire. Instead, black women writers have persistently privileged the objects of their own desire and written allegorical narratives in which black female subjectivity is the sole proprietary authority.

What is important to see here is that the representational modes for depicting the racial discourses in black female narratives are fundamentally different from those in their male counterparts; they privilege other signs in the discursive equation for social justice. The antebellum texts, both fictional and nonfictional, inscribe black women's moral indignation at the sexual and maternal abuses associated with slavery as the discursive equivalent to black men's moral outrage at the nation's refusal to respect their inalienable moral and civil rights as men. In similar postbellum texts, the racial discourse affirms a domestic ideality that centers a more equitable reconstruction of women's positions in their families and intraracial society. Black women's postbellum sentimental narratives, then, construct, deconstruct, and reconstruct Victorian gender conventions in order to designate black female subjectivity as a most potent force in the advancement of the race. In order to interpret selected antebellum and postbellum narratives as allegories of black female desire, I seek to reclaim a hermeneutical understanding of these texts as feminized mediations of what is conventionally understood as male power. In other words, by providing readings that are experiential encounters with black women's novelistic tradition and that speak through the work,[19] I propose to read black women's nineteenth-century sentimental narratives as discourses of liberation.

Mothering the Black Child/the Black Text

It hardly bears stating that slavery demanded slave women to be bearers of human chattel. Although slave women might appropriate the term *mother* for themselves, they were regarded as "mammies"; motherhood was an institution to which they had only biological claim. And matrimony was entirely out of the question inasmuch as all slaves were categorically excluded from the institution of civil marriage. Somewhat less polemical as a social institution, motherhood was also problematic for free black women, especially for those who were single parents. They faced extreme hardship trying to support themselves let alone their children. Possessing no political status then, black women, slave and free, largely appealed to moral law to justify their rights as mothers and to solicit public sympathy for their plight. Going public, however, demanded a vehicle. Some like Sojourner Truth lectured at public gatherings; others appropriated the written word as the means for transforming their private struggles into public testimony, and their books crossed the social boundaries between white and black, male and female, free and slave, public and private. By making their personal lives publicly visible for moral scrutiny, they dared to appropriate political power to change not only their own psychological and material conditions but those for all black people. Especially important for viewing nineteenth-century literary representations of black motherhood are Jacobs's *Incidents in the Life of a Slave Girl* and Wilson's *Our Nig*. Although *Incidents* undoubtedly contributed to the abolitionist cause, this book ironically fell into disrepute for more than one hundred years.[20] *Our Nig* was even less fortunate. The book's appeal for patronage failed, and immediately after publication it fell into obscurity for more than a century.

Referring to the discursive equations of protestion above, *Incidents* writes a female version of the racial discourse by aligning black women's moral outrage at the sexual abuses of slavery with black men's petition for liberty. One particular instance of Jacobs's affirming the sexual autonomy of her fictive self—Linda Brent—becomes especially instructive in this context. In recalling her interlude with Mr. Sands, she explains reflectively that "I will not try to screen myself behind the plea of compulsion from a master, for it was not so. . . . Neither can I plead ignorance or thoughtlessness. . . . I knew what I did, and I did it with deliberate calculation." Jacobs claims that she became a strategist in her sexual battle with Mr. Flint, but she effaces her assumption of an offensive role with her decision to "give [her]self, [rather] than to submit to compulsion" because she insists that this course of action is less degrading.[21] On one level we know what the act of giving herself was, but on another the text obscures the actual agent of this act. By reading what is implied but not explicitly stated, we see that Jacobs either initiated or, at the very least, encouraged the attention of Mr. Sands, who until the moment of utility in Jacobs's design had not appeared in the narrative. At this moment the text switches conventions from those for sentimental fiction to those for the novel of seduction in order to requalify the prescribed sexual character for the heroine from innocence to experience. The text also switches the gender network in the seduction story so that Jacobs can momentarily become the free agent. In other words, by reading the effaced seduction story, we can see Jacob playing the role of the seductress instead of the seduced victim. This is indeed radical, revolutionary autonomy for a woman to record in a public document, irrespective of her social status.

The most emphatic expression of protest in *Incidents*, however, involves Jacobs's incessant evocations of natural and divine law to affirm black women's rights to be respected as mothers, rather than being treated as "brood-sow[s]" to use Nanny's term in Hurston's *Their Eyes Were Watching God* (31). Jacobs insists that slave mothers "may be ignorant creature[s], degraded by the system that has brutalized [them] from childhood; but [they] have a mother's instincts, and [are] capable of feeling a mother's agonies" (16). Although Jacobs is ultimately successful in claiming her own children, many other slave women are not, and their stories form the tragic countertext to Jacobs's own story of personal triumph.

One story runs throughout the text and synthesizes black female oppression as that particularly experienced by black mothers. This is the story of Jacobs's grandmother's refusal to allow slavery to destroy her hope, integrity, and human compassion. Throughout the text, Jacobs especially underscores her grandmother's compassion with repeated references to the fact that she had to wean her own three-month-old daughter, Jacobs's mother, in order to breast-feed the sister of Jacobs's eventual mistress (who is Mrs. Flint in the narrative). From that point onward, her grandmother could never hold any malice toward either white woman because she had fed at least one of them at her breast. In this very material way the text juxtaposes this ideal mother with an ungrateful Mrs. Flint, who returns maternal nurturance with cold-heartedness and cruelty. Thus, by relying on nineteenth-century ethos, Jacobs demonstrates that Mrs. Flint is not only an unnatural (surrogate) daughter and therefore an unnatural woman, incapable of reproducing the compassionate generosity routinely ascribed to women; she also represents the cruelty generally ascribed to slave owners. Jacobs further characterizes her grandmother's ideal constancy and maternal love by recalling her unending struggle to buy some of her children out of slavery. Chapter 27, entitled "Aunt Nancy," serves as the epilogue to her grandmother's story. Aunt Nancy is her dead mother's twin; thus, she is Jacobs's ideal surrogate mother. Indeed, this is the only way Aunt Nancy can experience motherhood because although she gave birth to eight children, all of them died shortly after birth due to the incessant toil that "completely broke down her constitution" (143). Not only does Aunt Nancy attempt to nuture her motherless niece in the Flint household, but she also counters with steadfast encouragement her own mother's (and Jacobs's grandmother's) repeated expressions about the futility of trying to run away from slavery. Aunt Nancy holds on to one conviction in her repeated efforts to strengthen Jacobs's resolve to risk escape for her children's sake. Aunt Nancy tells her "[she] shan't mind being a slave all [her] life, if [she] can only see [her niece] and the children free" (129).

At the end of *Incidents* Jacobs secures freedom for herself and her children. Freedom here is both the dramatic conclusion to her story and its rhetorical strategy for closure. She writes, "Reader, my story ends with freedom; not in the usual way, with marriage" (210). This apostrophe acknowledges Jacobs's awareness that the appropriate conclusion for a sentimental narrative is marriage. However, she abandoned this expectation early in the text by publicizing sexual content that was conventionally concealed. Moreover, she inflects the act of heroic self-transformation with gender, and privatizes social justice for black people by redefining that ambition as a black woman's desire to obtain a home of her own for herself and her children, a home in which slavery has no domain. The text asserts political autonomy for maternity with its break from the conventional closure of marriage in sentimental fiction. In Jacobs's historical moment and from her perspective as a female slave, matrimony and slavery could find no compatible place in her text. Marriage and bondage, then, are not merely antithetical in *Incidents;* they are mutually exclusive. Thus, matrimony serves as the ideal sign of liberation.

Turning to Wilson's *Our Nig* (1859), we find a complex antebellum, autobiographical novel that utilizes conventions of nineteenth-century white women's sentimental fiction in order to protest racial oppression by focusing on the moral sanctity of maternity through its denial and subsequent affirmation.[22] The novel's social criticism, audience appeal, authorial posture, and discursive strategies evolve from problematizing the relationship between Frado, a black child, and her absent white mother. The story begins not with Frado, the central character and alias "our nig," but with the circumstances surrounding her abandonment at six. Although the dominant narrative subjectivity of *Our Nig* is that of the motherless child Frado, the last chapter—chapter 12, "Winding up the Matter"—and the extranarrative text located in both the preface and appendix underscore the presence of a complementary maternal discourse, that about the mature Frado as mother, struggling to fulfill her own maternal obligations.

Social conventions have historically designated mothers as the parent responsible for initially engendering the child's personal esteem. The mother's presence marks its likely formation, while her absence usually condemns the child to an acute sense of personal worthlessness, as Frado repeatedly demonstrates in her remarks about her condition:

I've got to stay here and die. I ha'n't got no mother, no home. I wish I was dead. (47)

Oh I wish I had my mother back; then I should not be kicked and whipped so. (51)

As the title of the familiar spiritual "Sometimes I Feel Like a Motherless Child" suggests, Frado aligns her motherlessness with her oppression. Thus, she accepts racial abuse as a consequence of the fact that she has no mother. Only when she becomes a young woman does she learn to relate her condition to racism. Blackness, then, becomes the revised justification for her oppression, from which death appears as the only means of escape: "Work as long as I can stand, and then fall down and lay there till I can get up. No mother, father, brother or sister to care for me, and then it is, You lazy nigger, lazy nigger— all because I am black! Oh, if I could die!" (75).

The maternal discourse here does not simply address the abused, motherless child who becomes the exploited mother; rather, it revises the condition of black people in general—free and enslaved, northern as well as southern—all of whom have been similarly oppressed by replacing the alienation inherent to that oppression with symbolic mother-love. Wilson's prefatory remarks—"Deserted by kindred, disabled by failing health, I am forced to some experiment which shall aid me in maintaining myself and child. . . . I sincerely appeal to my colored brethren universally for patronage"—modify the condition of black motherlessness not by altering the similarity between her own and her mother's materiality, but by altering Frado's response to her material circumstances. In this way the text gives expression to Frado's resolve to preserve the bond between herself and her child, and transforms that resolve into affirming her own autonomy as a black person who was a motherless child who became a woman who became a mother who was compelled to be a writer. Indeed, the very text *Our Nig* comes from the compatible resolution of what had to have been a difficult conflict arising from the coexistence of these multiple identities. These prefatory remarks also evoke the act of "heroic self-transformation" [23] in that Wilson resolved to break the cycle of psychological oppression by transforming herself into a heroic mother with material independence, albeit symbolic rather than economic. Significantly, she gave this transformation literary representation; she wrote a novel, a venture in which she vested her hope to provide a home for her child. However, *Our Nig* does not merely inscribe maternal responsibility; the novel is more importantly Wilson's vehicle for reproducing black self-esteem by displacing racial inferiority with maternal materiality. Black maternity here is the symbolic erasure of cyclic generational hopelessness with motherly love and determination.

Wilson cleverly inscribed the refusal to be bound to racist ideology by inscribing her psychological independence in irony on the title page: *Our Nig; or, Sketches from the Life of a Free Black, in a Two-Story White House, North. Showing that Slavery's Shadows Fall Even There. By "Our Nig."* The title, subtitles, and pseudonymous, authorial signatory, like the authorial posture, narrative tone and perspective, vacillate between representing direct social criticism and self-reflexive irony. The first subtitle—"Sketches from the Life of a Free Black, in a Two-Story White House, North"—references direct social criticism about white people's hypocritical refusal to extend constitutional law to black people by revising the idyllic plantation romance and by evoking an incomplete analogy between Our Nig's place of residence—white house, North—and its absent referent—the idealized plantation mansion, South. Possibly fearing that her audience might miss the point that racial oppression is not restricted to the South, Wilson added the additional subtitle: "Showing that Slavery's Shadows Fall Even There." This last subtitle implicates white abolitionists in the racial oppression of northern black people and complicates what had to have been at least an indirect appeal to the very people who had the financial means to assist her with her project by purchasing the book.

The lexical identity established between the novel's principal title—*Our Nig*—and its pseudonymous authorial signatory—"Our Nig"—inscribes a sophisticated mode of self-reflexive irony that extenuates direct public censure. The title and the signatory are locked in cyclic parody, like black people in tarface on the minstrel stage; as a result, the aspersion in the self-reflexive title circuitously finds its real target—the very people H.E.W. claimed she wished not to offend in her preface—"our good anti-slavery friends at home." Thus, the text calls attention to the fact that they were ultimately responsible for the quality of life for those free black people who lived among them. In other words, by displacing the well-known slave narrative signatory—Written by Him or Herself—with the diminutive form of a racist epithet—"Our Nig"—the text shifts northern readers' likely resentment of public censure to a deliberately constructed self-derisive humility. Hence, the text exhorts their verification of Frado's hardships and by implication those generally suffered by northern, free, black people by seeing herself from a white perspective. After all, as Wilson insisted with her title, Frado was *their* "nig." Inasmuch as national public opinion had relegated black people, free or slave, to white ownership, Wilson ironically referred to her re-created self as chattel in order to give her voice uncontested authority. As *their* "nig," she could tell her own story of racial abuse seemingly from their point of view and possibly arouse the sympathy of white readers as well as demonstrate that her life was not substantially different from those who were born in bondage. This authorial strategy would also allow her to abort much of the criticism from readers who might regard her story as atypical or exaggerated because technically she was not a slave. However, this epithet may have alienated potential black readers who might not have seen its doubly reflexive irony. The prominent inscription of so hated an epithet among black people may have given them cause to question the racial identity of the book's author, and they may have erroneously concluded that *Our Nig* was a masked white story about black inferiority.

Perhaps the most interesting aspect of *Our Nig* concerns Wilson's assumption of authorial authority at a time when it was customarily unavailable to white women and black people in general. Wilson's preface explains her motives for writing the novel by stating that she was not fulfilling an "erudite" ambition, but rather seeking "some experiment which shall aid [her] in maintaining [her]self and [her] child without extinguishing this feeble life." After explaining her motive, she makes a direct appeal to her "colored brethren universally for patronage." No doubt, Wilson was well aware of the economic condition of black people to whom she appealed; in fact, her own story suggests their common penury. (In 1850 Nancy Prince had made a similar prefactory claim in her autobiography, *The Life and Times of Nancy Prince,* but she directed her appeal for patronage to liberal white people.) Although the general economic condition of black people has continually improved, one hundred years later black women writers were still unable to support themselves (and their children) with full-time writing incomes. In fact until the recent marketing success of writers such as Toni Morrison and Alice Walker, that ambition remained a delightful fantasy. My question, then, is could Wilson realistically expect to rescue her son from a foster home with income from writing? Does this ambition speak to her utter desperation? Or does her so-called experiment to fulfill maternal love and obligation cloak yet another?

Nineteenth-century white women writers who wrote much of the popular literature of sentimentality, some at considerable financial reward, claimed to have done so not for fame or fortune but because they had infirmed husbands or were widows supporting their small children.[24] Moreover, they trivialized their work, claiming not to be professionals who took writing seriously in deference to Victorian social conventions demanding female self-effacement. In short, these white women claimed to have been driven to take up the pen not by the desire for personal satisfaction but by financial desperation. This too is Wilson's claim; however, her constituency was not in the position to support her enterprise.

I suggest that the novel, its preface, and appendix cloak the allegory of desired authorship, structured as the story of frustrated motherhood. *Our Nig* is the fulfillment of the desire to re-create oneself as a more enduring historical subject. Hence, the novel and appended texts form a maternal allegory about a black woman's desire to reproduce her life symbolically. If we read *Our Nig* in this way, her stated motives for writing, that is, her maternal obligation and her expressions of literary humility, achieve logical consistency. Wilson's expressed justification for the novel arises from her fulfilling the socially prescribed role of a mother. I am in no way questioning the integrity of her desire to fulfill this responsibility; that I accept as fact. I am, however, hypothesizing that Wilson's effort to fulfill her maternal obligations, a story that lies outside the text of the novel, inscribes a parallel story within the novel: the story of the mother-author's obligation to nurture a symbolic child—her text. In the prefatory remarks, she writes: "In offering to the public the following pages, the writer confesses her inability to minister to the refined and cultivated, the pleasure supplied by abler pens. . . . My humble position and frank confession of errors will, I hope, shield me from severe criticism. Indeed, defects are so apparent it requires no skilful hand to expose them." Jacobs's references to "errors," "abler pens," and "defects that are so apparent it requires no skilful hand to expose them" are inscriptions of conventional male models of prefatory effacement found in eighteenth-century sentimental texts, like Henry Fielding's *Tom Jones*, that both invite literary judgment and mask authorial ego. However, *Our Nig* deconventionalizes the male model of effacement by combining it with the nineteenth-century female metaphor of writing as

mothering the text.[25] In addition to evoking the male mode of authorial modesty and the metaphor of literary maternity, *Our Nig* masks
black authorial prerogative with the ironic assumption of presumed
racial inferiority like a form of literary blackface minstrelsey.[26] Given
the claims of impropriety routinely addressed to black men and white
women writers, as a black woman Wilson may have, indeed, felt the
need for even more complex forms of authorial effacement than those
usually found in the eighteenth- and nineteenth-century works of
white male, black male, and white female authority. These modes of
effacement allow *Our Nig* to fulfill the dominant nineteenth-century
society's prescriptives for black subservience and maternal obligation.
In addition, her revised text of mother, that is, the conflation of her
story of actual maternal obligation and female authorial propriety, en-
abled her to appropriate a mode of representation for re-creating herself in the semiotics of maternal love, to condemn racism, to fend off
likely attacks from those who regarded black and female authorship
doubly unnatural, to express sympathy for her white mother who
abandoned her, and possibly to retrieve her son from foster care.
Moreover, complex narration, subtle reflexive irony, well-chosen ep-
igrams from diverse English and American authors, and what Gates
calls "belabored erudition"[27] all demonstrate her intelligence at a time
when black people (and all women) were categorically presumed
mentally inferior. She hoped that her "colored brethren" would not
condemn her novel as an "attempt of their sister to be erudite"; nevertheless, the text demonstrates that she must have been an erudite sister
indeed. More important, though, motherhood both motivates and
justifies Wilson's authorship, and *Our Nig* appropriates the discourse
on motherhood as its mode of literary representation. The maternal
discourse is allegorical and historically factual; it is both sign and referent. Ironically, the death notice of the child who justified *Our Nig's*
existence was the scholarly key for rescuing this allegory of female
desire from oblivion.

Marrying the Revised Text of Husband

A century of events and changing attitudes separates nineteenth-
century black women from us; yet it is theoretically possible to recon-

struct, in this case, their feelings about the relationship between marriage and family life, on the one hand, and their historic desire for full racial equality signified generally as freedom, on the other, by examining their postbellum sentimental fiction. It provides a provocative frame for viewing how they mediated marriage as a political institution for their epoch. In this writing, the marriage story does not evolve from dramatizing the ideology of romantic love. The courtship is devoid of all ardent sentiment that does not arise from noble admiration. Respect kindles love, and mutual commitment to advancing the race engenders love, as Frances Harper explained in *Iola Leroy*: "In their desire to help the race their hearts beat in loving unison. One grand and noble purpose was giving tone and color to their lives and strengthening the bonds of affection between them." [28] Matrimony, in this context, is the very sign of social progress for black Americans; it provides the medium for expressing a people's affirmation of their civil liberty and for measuring their propensity for civilization. Thus, the works of Harper and her contemporaries instruct us not to regard marriage as simply an elaborately planned church ritual. In fact, the wedding ceremonies in black, female, postbellum sentimental fiction are extremely effaced. Seldom do we observe the bride in lace and satin, for as one of Harper's characters insists, "there is a great deal of misplaced sentiment at weddings" (277). Instead, we find that the emphasis falls on explaining how the couple plans to live out their married life actively engaged in working for racial progress.

Mrs. Nathan F. Mossell, a well-known nineteenth-century black intellectual and social reformer, expressed this viewpoint in *The Work of the Afro-American Woman* (1894) in which she wrote that "home is undoubtedly the cornerstone of our beloved Republic. . . . Marriage constitutes the basis for the home." Anna Julia Cooper, another well-known race woman of that day, similarly wrote, in *A Voice from the South* (1892), that "a race is but a total of families. The nation is the aggregate of its homes." [29] Marriage, then, was a central prerequisite for a civilized society.

Nineteenth-century black women's writing gives emphatic expression to this view; their exposition and fiction alike are deeply imbued with their desire to appropriate and revise confining Victorian gender codes, especially those about marriage, so as to qualify their feminine character and extend the feminine domain to black public enterprise.

On examining the title page of Mossell's *The Work,* for instance, we find that she effaces her female subjectivity by referring to herself as Mrs. N. F. Mossell rather than Mrs. Gertrude B. Mossell, while simultaneously assuming the public role of spokeswoman under the guise of designating appropriate work for black women. To further sanction the alignment of matrimony, motherhood, and social reformer, Mossell presented herself in a photograph flanked on each side by her daughters to whom she dedicated the volume: "To my two little daughters, Mary Campbell and Florence Alma Mossell, praying that they may grow into a pure and noble womanhood, this little volume is lovingly dedicated." The signs—Mrs., the picture, and the dedication with expressed diminution of the book's significance—all reference proper feminine posture for an upper-class black woman, while the text appropriates the entire world of Afro-American public and private affairs for her domain. Thus, carefully ensconced in the book's front matter is the conflation of two discursive fields that together revise the familiar black male discourse on protesting racial injustice. Here we find a black female discourse of desire for full social participation mediated through the political institutionalization of womanhood and the professionalization of the domestic sphere, both in the name of racial progress. This conflation is the staple of black women's postbellum sentimental fiction.

Harper's *Iola Leroy* (1892), mentioned above, and Hopkins's *Contending Forces* (1900), for example, dramatize the familiar racial discourse on racial and sexual abuse associated with slavery; however, the discourse is located in their respective prefatory antebellum stories. Harper's heroine Iola Leroy endures slavery, successfully preserves her sexual purity, and eventually selects a mate whose notions about male and female ambition are not fixed by convention. However, Hopkins's Sappho Clark is not so fortunate. Although she survives an encounter with racism that originates in slavery, she bears its scars. More importantly, though, she uses her scarred womanhood for heroic self-transformation, revising conventional notions of feminine respectability by asserting her virtue "on complex moral grounds," to use Jean Fagan Yellin's term (xxxi), rather than on the single issue of premarital virginity. Hence, Sappho transforms herself from a passive heroine, the object of male desire, into an active female-hero, the subject of her own desire. This act of heroic self-transformation is signaled with her change of name from Mabelle Beaubean to Sappho Clark, with the latter referencing the famous classical poet—Sappho—who wrote gynocentric verse.[30] Both novels employ the conventions of sentimentality to rewrite the antebellum racial discourse on protestation and thereby construct postbellum domestic idealism as the revised liberational discourse. Although idealized domesticity in these and other black female sentimental fictions probably reflects a desire to escape racism, a desire that black people still undoubtedly share, this idealism also minimally presumes interracial stability in the fictive world. Put simply, black domestic idealism in these novels is the direct consequence of successful racial protest. Hence, these texts make intraracial affirmation rather than interracial protestation their principal subject.

Integral to black women's postbellum sentimental fiction is the manner in which it revises the conventional gender conduct of husbands and wives for that period: first, by blurring the distinctions between male and female decorum; second, by inscribing the father's absence in the text; and third, by qualifying the heroine's husband with the attributes of her sibling. Each of these tactics revises the conventional patriarch (who is inscribed in the fiction of male sensibility) to varying degrees.

The first tactic redefines the patriarch's role by divesting him of the presumed rights to unquestioned authority over household management and absolute deference from women and children. For instance, the latter portion of *Iola Leroy* has Iola preparing to become a teacher, when Dr. Frank Latimer (her future husband) makes his intentions clear. He prescribes a "change of air, change of scene, and change of name" (270) for her. "Seating himself near her, he poured into her ears words eloquent with love and tenderness" (270). But his words, as Harper continued, "were more than a tender strain wooing her to love and happiness, they were a clarion call to a life of high and holy worth, a call which found a response in her heart" (271). Iola and Frank share a love woven of "kindred hopes and tastes" (271). Harper went on to explain that "grand and noble purposes were lighting up their lives; and they esteemed it a blessed privilege to stand on the threshold of a new era and labor for those who had passed from the old oligarchy of slavery into the new commonwealth of freedom" (271). Their love is not characterized as impassioned pronouncements of dedication to their mutual happiness; to the contrary, their love is buttressed against "the threshold of a new era and labor" for the advancement of black people.

From a postmodernist vantage point, Iola seems confined to the domestic sphere, inasmuch as "she quietly took her place in the Sunday-school as a teacher, and in the church as a helper" (278). However, we must be mindful that Iola's is not a marginal enterprise by nineteenth-century standards. At that time, the church and family formed the central sphere of civilized society. In pursuit of social advancement, men and women frequently blurred the boundaries between gendered spheres of influence. What nurtured civilization also strengthened the family and the church. What contributed to the decline of either was the enemy of every man, woman, and child. Linked to the common goal of beneficial advancement, church men and women each could ill afford to preserve absolute rigidity between boundaries of social influence.

Frank and Iola's honeymoon distracts our attention from the following modifications in the prescribed roles of husband and wife that permit Iola to retain her public ambitions. Believing that "no other woman of [her] race will suffer as [she] has done" (273), Iola abandons the familiar racial discourse on sexual outrage and literally embraces a new discursive mode of virtual sexual equality with her husband. This becomes evident when Iola's brother insists that Frank and Iola have begun to speak for one another, emphatically blurring the presumed distinctions between male and female epistemic systems and between public and private spheres of social influence: "I don't believe that there is a subject I could name to him from spinning a top to circumnavigating the globe, that he wouldn't somehow contrive to bring Iola in. And I don't believe you could talk ten minutes to Iola on any subject, from dressing a doll to the latest discovery in science, that she wouldn't manage to lug in Frank" (277). Whereas Frank immediately realizes his role as "a leader in every reform movement for the benefit of the community" (279), Iola is slower to fulfill her leadership role. Frank advises her to "write a good, strong book which would be helpful to them [black people]" (262), the ambition that Harper herself fulfilled; thus in a sense she became the heroine. Iola's ambition may appear as part of the discourse on matrimonial love because it follows the chapter entitled "Wooing and Wedding." However, in Harper's world, domesticity does not exist apart from the political, and her authorial note, following the final chapter, is a reminder that the novel's closure is not meant as a reflection of reality but as that of a visionary world. In Harper's words the novel's mission is to "awaken in the hearts of our countrymen a stronger sense of justice . . . [and] add to the solution of our unsolved American problem" (282).

The second tactic of inscribing the father's absence decenters the nuclear family, diminishes the importance of excessive patriarchal demands for feminine piety, purity, and propriety, as well as mitigates feminine prescriptives for absolute deference to male authority. This revised family discourse shifts narrative hegemony from racial protest to domestic ideality. Hence, ideal families evolve in the absence of what is conventionally known, in patriarchal societies, as the father's law. *Contending Forces* stands at the crossroads of this hegemonic shift because although this novel inscribes both the racial and domestic discourses, the former becomes increasingly reticent here, while the latter, which inscribes what I call the mother's law, is dominant. The mother's law centers a black gynocentric morality that metes out reward and punishment in direct proportion to the moral character of one's deeds and serves as the basis for redefining a virtuous woman.

Luke Sawyer and John Langley give expression to the father's law. In the chapter entitled "Sawyer Speaks to the League," Sawyer describes how he and Mabelle's father recovered her after she was kidnapped: "After *three weeks* of incessant searching we found her a prisoner in a house of the vilest character . . . [she was] a poor, ruined, half-crazed creature in whom it was almost impossible to trace a resemblance to the beautiful pet of our household." [31] Just in case there is any doubt in the reader's mind about what the word "ruined" means, Luke goes on to say that he left her at a convent, and *"there she died when her child was born"* (261; the emphasis is Hopkins's). Sawyer represents the father's law of patriarchal judgment, and it designates Mabelle as a ruined woman. Another character, John Langley, corroborates this judgment when he uses his knowledge of Sappho's history to force her into becoming his *"fille de joie"* (338). Sappho has struggled to cast off such designations until Langley's action makes her conclude that she cannot escape the father's law and that she is, indeed, unworthy of becoming Will's wife. In a note for him she writes, "[Langley] has made me realize how much such a marriage with me would injure you. Disgrace shall never touch you or yours through me" (329).

Mrs. Willis is the principal proponent for the law of the mother. In the chapter entitled "The Sewing Circle," she advises Sappho, on hearing her fictitious version of her personal history. Sappho recalls: "I once knew a woman who had sinned. . . . She married a man who would have despised her had he known her story; but as it is, she is looked upon as a pattern of virtue for all women. . . . Ought she not to have told her husband before marriage? Was it not her duty to have thrown herself upon his clemency?" (15). Mrs. Willis replies: "I am a practical woman of the world and I think your young woman builded wiser than she knew. I am of the opinion that most men are like the lower animals in many things—they don't always know what is for their best good" (156). Mrs. Willis's advice does not sanction the father's law; instead, she insists that man's view is finite, while God's judgment is infinite (157). She interprets God's infinity as "[Sappho's] duty . . . to be happy and bright for the good of those about [her]" (157). The preeminence of the mother's law also directs the lives of Will Smith and his sister, Dora. For them their father is a sacred memory, connecting them to a history of racial strength as well as oppression. However, his absence also mitigates the strength of patriarchal values on their immediate lives and permits their mother to become the authority figure who not only nurtures them but manages the household affairs. Although the text makes no explicit mention of her managerial skills, it informs us that she runs a comfortable rooming house, and has a son enrolled at Harvard and a daughter who does not work outside the home. These details represent Mrs. Smith's proficiency in financial management and encourages the characters (and us) to regard women not as masculine complements but as individuals in their own right, deserving respect. Equally important to the evolving plot, the absence of the father and his law permits Will to follow his own desire in selecting his wife, rather than institutionalized patriarchal desire for premarital virginity. As a result he is free to marry the so-called ruined woman and to father her child as if it were his own.

The fact that Mrs. Willis is also a widow is important because she and Mrs. Smith are the principal means for inscribing the absence of the black patriarch. Mrs. Smith is the ideal maternal figure, which the text underscores by repeatedly referring to her as Ma Smith. Her widowhood is idealized, while Mrs. Willis's widowhood is problematic. The text describes Mrs. Willis's deceased husband as "a bright Negro politician" (143) who had secured "a seat in the Legislature" (146). In addition, she had "loved [him] with a love ambitious for his advancement" (145). Despite "the always expected addition to [their] family" (146), she was the woman behind the man. However, at his death there was no trust fund to meet her financial needs and she has to work. For her the question becomes what line of work can fulfill both her financial needs and ambition. No longer able to represent her ambition as desire for her husband's advancement, Mrs. Willis has to find a cause. "The best opening, she decided after looking carefully about her, was in the great cause of the evolution of true womanhood in the work of the 'Woman Question' as embodied in marriage and suffrage" (146). Thus, Mrs. Willis comes to the Woman Question not out of a burning passion for women's rights but out of a desire to advance herself as well as black women and the race. In short, she is a professional, or, in her own words, "a practical woman of the world" (156) who has "succeeded well in her plans" (147), which the text continues to describe as "conceived in selfishness, they yet bore glorious fruit in the formation of clubs of colored women banded together . . . [to] better the condition of mankind" (147). To her audience she is a "brilliant widow" (143) who "could talk dashingly on many themes" (146). However, Mrs. Willis incites "a wave of repulsion" (155) in Sappho; yet "Sappho [is] impressed in spite of herself, by the woman's words" (157). Mrs. Willis is a model for the successful professional woman of that epoch who has stepped far into the public realm of political ambition. Sappho detects Mrs. Willis's conscious desire for power as well as the will to grasp it, and this detection excites her contradictory feelings about women's ambitions for power and conventional gender prescriptives designating it as inappropriate, which Hopkins's contemporaries no doubt also experienced.

Before I examine the third principal tactic for revising the text of husband, that of characterizing him as a virtual sibling equal, I address probably the most obvious way in which Johnson's *Clarence and Corinne* and Kelley's *Megda* differ from the above novels and, indeed, from what has become an Afro-American novelistic tradition: they present characters that are racially nonspecific. Traditional scholars have generally presumed that such characters are white,[32] and this presumption has produced serious misreadings that typify how these scholars have judged all literature of black authorship against the discursive standard of black phallocentric racial protest. To place these novels in a white milieu, as this scholarship does, erases the political statement of racelessness. Moreover, this view probably accounts for the mass obscurity of such works in literary history. Yet *Clarence and Corinne* and *Megda* are not nonpolitical, apolitical, or reactionary; to the contrary, each seeks to eliminate race as the absolute determinant for qualifying personal esteem, access to virtuosity, and social and financial success. In other words, by eliminating race and thus racial sterotypes and prejudices, these texts place human potential into the hands of the individual and qualify the concept of domestic idealism and public ambition without racial designation, restriction, or precondition.

Returning to the third tactic for deconventionalizing the patriarchal husband, we find that these works generally characterize the heroine's husband as a man who has been like her brother. Not only is he extremely virtuous, but this brotherly hero–husband is not superior to her because he is a man. In addition, because the heroine and her husband have virtual sibling status, she need not be deferential toward him. They can treat one another with the respect accorded to equals and effect a relationship that displays spontaneous expressions of honesty, loyalty, and geniality. *Clarence and Corinne* and *Megda* also provide poignant dramatizations of this particular tactic in operation.

In the first novel, Clarence and Corinne Burton endure the typical childhood hardship that sets most sentimental fiction in motion.[33] Virtue and hard work enable them to transcend early misfortune (Corinne becomes a teacher and Clarence becomes a doctor). Together they maintain the household of their adoptive parents and establish another for themselves based on sibling equality. This latter home is the idealized revision of their childhood home, as Clarence reminds his sister: "Corrie, do you remember going with me, one afternoon, to gather chips for our poor mother? . . . Well, this is the very house that was then being built, and where we got those chips."[34] What is particularly significant about this new home is that it houses two sets of male and female siblings: Clarence and Corinne as well as their childhood best friends Bebe and Charlie Reade. The story closes with the text insisting that "the sequel could be read without the book. But there was a marriage speedily, and the bride was BeBe Reade, while the groom was Dr. Burton. There was another, also, soon after. This time Corinne Burton and Charley Reade took the principal parts" (186–87). The hero and heroine literally marry their surrogate siblings, and the two sets of cross-sibling spouses set up an ideal household in which they are not merely husbands and wives; they are a collective of helpmates and mutual friends. Moreover, they are described as "our friends" (187), and together they emphatically revise the conventional notions about the nuclear household and the preeminence of the patriarch.

In addition to characterizing the brotherly hero-husband and inscribing the father's absence, *Megda* displays many other characteristics of black female sentimental revisionism. First, the heroine Megda Randall identifies a new model for female heroic character, for she sees, as she says, "no reason why a woman should not possess character as well as a man."[35] Second, the novel's luxurious household artifacts and clothing, like Meg's "new suit of navy-blue cashmere trimmed with chinchilla" (110), are the semiotics of rewarded virtue and evidence of participation in the dominant values of an emergent bourgeois-capitalistic society. And, third, particularly emphatic in this novel is the insistence that an ideal matrimonial union arises not only from long-term friendship, mutual respect, and piety but from a good sense of humor as well. Indeed, there is a considerable amount of laughter and good humor in this novel. Piety and humor are linked together quite early in the text, when we witness a hilarious scene with the Reverend tying his misshapen derby to his head with Meg's neck ribbon, much like a bonnet (23–26). This scene is not merely indicative of good humor; it also transposes gender traits and deconstructs traditional notions about masculine and feminine decorum, thus liberating men as well as women from artificial standards of behavior. Unlike Clarence and Corinne, Meg does not have to overcome physical hardship; that story is displaced onto another character—Ruth Dean. The central concern in *Megda* is the mediation of Meg's excessive independence, vanity, and ambition into a new feminine ideal characterized by spirit (or temper), pride, willfullness, and piety.

Thus in the midst of the excessive display of sentimentality, diminution, gentility, and luxury, Meg is freed from the role of the obsequious wife. No longer bound by notions of idealized wifehood, Meg is free to display her "little fault[s] . . . the little flashes of temper, the spirit of pride that shows itself now and then, the natural willfulness of her disposition" (376) without fear that her husband will withhold affection. As the text insists, "he loves them all; for, as he once laughingly said . . . 'Meg would not be Meg without [her faults]'" (376).

Domestic idealization—the trope of racial and sexual liberation for nineteenth-century texts of black female authority—is generally absent in similar texts of black male authority; here we find that the dominant discourse concerns protesting racial injustice. This difference in discursive dominance, I suggest, has been responsible for the marginality of early black women's texts in Afro-American literary scholarship. I suspect that when black female texts were judged by a scholarly tradition that was defensive about issues of race, the texts were at a serious disadvantage because the scholarship and the texts were mutually antagonistic. Protest-centered scholarship appears to have allowed its frustrated desire for racial equality to condition its practice. As a result, it has been vigilant in rewarding those texts that argue unabashedly for civil justice in an interracial context, while questioning both the social efficacy and aesthetic value of those works that neither overtly dramatize racism nor explicitly argue for civil justice. Unfortunately, this critical practice has missed the pedagogic intentionality of early black women's fiction. However, by historicizing this fiction, we can see that it does indeed inscribe liberational discourses; they are merely different. Moreover, a historically conditioned critique uncovers new historical and cultural significance for this large body of neglected fiction. Nineteenth-century black women's sentimental narratives symbolically represent the inalienable rights of black people as the consummated rights of families—thus their emphatic valorization of marriage and domestic idealism. For nineteenth-century black women writers, marriage and family life were not the culminating points of a woman's life but the pinnacles of a people's new beginning.

'The Permanent Obliquity of an In(pha)llibly Straight': In the Time of the Daughters and the Fathers

The title's reference to a passage from *Moby-Dick* is itself an obliquity in relationship to the theme of this essay. But I adopt it here as a kind of lookout on the subject as it concerns kinship and filiation among African-Americans cast as daughters and fathers. In short, the line of inheritance from a male parent to a female child is not straight. It is "oblique," since she, if everybody looks handsome, will one day shed his name, his law, and the effects of his household for another male's. In that regard, the patriarchal daughter remains suspended as a social positionality between already-established territories. Bearing a name that she carries by courtesy to legal fiction and bound toward one that she must acquire in order "to have" her own children, "daughter" maintains status only insofar as she succeeds in disappearing, in deconstructing into "wife" and "mother" of *his* children. This is the familiar law of high patriarchist culture in a heterosexual synthesis as the little girl imbibes it, and from then on she is a more or less willing agent in the text of a cultural conspiracy. Among African-Americans in the midst of violent historic intervention that, for all intents and purposes, has banished the father, if not in fact murdered him, the Father's law embodies still the guilt that hovers: one feels called on to "explain," make excuses, for his "absence." But the African-American-Father-Gone is the partial invention of sociologists, as the African-American female-as-daughter is consumed in their thematics of the "Black Matriarchate."[1]

This lopsided textual sociometry that eats up female difference and identity in notions of the ahistoric "Familius Aeternus" essentially reconfigures in fiction by black American writers as a puzzle, not a closure. This articulated problematic comes nearer the "truth" because it plants ambiguity at the heart of an interpretation of the Father's law. What secrets do these texts cover up? Maya Angelou's *I Know Why the Caged Bird Sings* (putative "autobiography"), Gayl Jones's *Corregidora,* James Baldwin's *Just Above My Head,* Ralph Ellison's *Invisible*

Man, Alice Walker's "The Child Who Favored Daughter" (from *In Love and Trouble*), and Walker's *Color Purple* all embody fictions concerned in part with fathers and daughters, and all of these works posit an incestuous link between them.[2] But of these selected texts, only Ellison's *Invisible Man* and Walker's "Child Who Favored Daughter" project a sufficient symbolic apparatus that renders bearable a sustained contemplation of the theme of father-daughter incest. Indeed, it seems that certain ideas, like the face of the Divine, can only be approached with a very wide-angle lens; intimations of incest are among them.

It seems that parent-child incest, in its various ramifications, remains the preeminent dream-thought that not only evades interpretation (or dreaming), but is so layered itself in avoidance and censorship that an interpretive project regarding it appears ludicrous and useless. On one level of imagination incest simply cannot occur and never does.[3] Under the auspices of denial, incest becomes the measure of an absolute negativity, the paradigm of the outright assertion *against*— the resounding no! But on the level of the symbolic, at which point the "metaevent" is sovereign, incest translates into the unsayable which is all the more sayable by very virtue of one's muteness before it. The fictions of incest therefore repose in the involuted interfaces between ephemeral event and interpretive context, but more than that, these fictions materialize that "other" and alien life that we cannot recognize or acknowledge (and it's probably a good thing!) as being for consciousness. In that regard, fictions about incest provide an enclosure, a sort of confessional space for and between postures of the absolute, and in a very real sense it is only in fiction—from the psychoanalytic session to the fictive rendering—that incest as dramatic enactment and sexual economy can take place at all. Whether or not father-daughter incest actually happens and with what frequency is not a problem for literary interpretation. For good or ill, it belongs to the precincts of the local police department (and the "cat" should go to jail.)

But before we attempt a reading of portions of Walker's and Ellison's work, we should make a handful of admissions that are permissible. I attempt this writing, in fact, as the trial of an interlocking interrogation that I am persuaded in by only 50 percent: Is the Freudian landscape an applicable text (to say nothing of appropriate) to social and historic situations that do not replicate moments of its own historic origins and involvements? The prestigious Oedipal dis-ease/ complex, which apparently subsumes the Electra myth, embeds in the heterosexual "nuclear family" that disperses its fruits in vertical array. The Father's law, the Father's name pass "down" in concentrated linearity and exclusion. Not only "one man, one woman," but these two—this law—in a specific locus of economic and cultural means. But how does this model, or does this model, suffice for occupied or captive persons and communities in which the rites and rights of gender function have been exploded historically into sexual neutralities?

The original captive status of African females and males in the context of American enslavement permitted none of the traditional rights of consanguinity. The laws of the North American Slave Code stipulated that the newborn would follow the status of its mother—the *partus sequitur ventrem*—but that stroke of legal genius, while assuring hegemony of the dominant class, did nothing to establish maternal prerogative for the African female.[4] The child, though flesh of her flesh, did not "belong" to her, as the separation of mothers and children becomes a primary social motif of the "Peculiar Institution." Exceptions to the gender rule intrude a note of the arbitrary, but this very arbitrariness, depending on individual instances of human kindness in slaveholders, throws in even bolder relief the subjugative arrangements of the "institution." For the African female, then, the various inflections of patriarchilized female gender—"mother," "daughter," "sister " "wife"—are not available in the historic instance.

If North American slavery in its laws outraged the classic status of motherhood in the African case, then it asymmetrically complicated notions of fatherhood. In effect, the African person was twice-fathered, but could not be claimed by the one and would not be claimed by the other. The person, following the "condition" of the mother, very often bore only a first name—Niger I, Niger II, Phoebe, Cassius, Jane, Sue, and so forth.[5] While the suppression of the patronymic engenders a radically different social and political economy for African-Americans, it involves us, relatedly, in nested semiotic readings: the African name is not only "lost" to cultural memory, but on that single ground the captive African is symbolically broken in two—ruptured along the fault of a "double consciousness"[6] in which the break with an indigenous African situation is complete, but one's cultural membership in the American one remains inchoate. A social subject in abeyance, in an absolute deferral that becomes itself a new synthesis, is born—the African-American, whose last name, for all intents and purposes, becomes historically X, the mark of his/her borrowed culture's profound "illiteracy."

In this fatal play of literally misplaced/displaced names, the African father is figuratively banished; fatherhood, at best a cultural courtesy, since only mother knows for sure, is not a social fiction into which he enters. Participation in the life of his children, indeed the rights of patriarchal privilege, is extended to him at someone else's behest. In this historic instance, the "unnatural" character of the reproductive process is rendered startlingly clear—reproduction is covered by culture, in culture, at every stage so that "free" sexuality remains the scandalous secret in the Father's house. Only by executive order and legislative edict does reproductive process gain cultural legitimacy for African-Americans as freed persons, which suggests the origins of the myth of "parenting" in sociopolitical consensus. In this calculus of motives, the "master" and his class—those subjects of an alternative fatherhood—cannot be said to be "fathers" of African-American children at all (without the benefit of quotation marks) since, by their own law, the newborn follows the "condition" of the mother. But in those instances where they were begetters of children, the puzzle of the father is fully elaborated. As "owners" of human "property," they offer impediment to the operations of kinship; by denial of kinship, they act out symbolically the ambiguous character of fatherhood itself, perpetuating it in this case as blank parody. In that regard, the notorious X, adopted by illiterate persons as the signatory mark and by literate black Muslims in the twentieth-century United States as the slash mark against a first offensive, comes to stand for the blank drawn by Father's "gun."

We situate ourselves, then, at the center of a mess, altogether convoluted in its crosshatch of historic purposes. There is no simple way to state the case, but crudely put, we might ask: to what extent do the texts of a psychoanalytic ahistoricism, out of which the report, the transactions of incest arise, abrade, or reveal against the historic scene and its subsequent drama? Does the Freudian text translate, in short (and here we would include the Freudian progeny Lévi-Strauss and Lacan among them)? This question in its various guises provides the background against which the hermeneutical enterprise unfolds to the black scholar-critic. We are a long way from specific acts of texts, but Every [Black] Reader shall be discomfited. Let that be a law, inasmuch as one is attempting to read not only a given text—Foucault's "parallelepiped"—and the vortices of subtexts spinning around it, but also this against and/or despite those pretexts that neither go away nor yield the secret.

The preeminent rule of incest is that Everybody has one.[7] This universal prohibition involves us in a democracy of ancient scandal that must be related in some sense to the architectonics of domesticity. If possible, children have their own bed in their own room, as do adults, or the circumstance (at least in the United States) is identified as "poverty." By six years old, the child, mysteriously, has already acquired a sexual consciousness and loses her place in the parental bed, between the lovers. The Lacanian "imaginary" has long ago dissipated into the "symbolic"—the realm of division, of father-sovereignty.[8] But how many layers of flesh, like so many blankets, are required to cover household carnality? The violation of this fundamental layering generates the drama of Ellison's Trueblood clan, and Houston Baker's interpretation of the incest scene in *Invisible Man* (1952) is solidly grounded in an economically determined reading.[9] The latter, however, seeks perspective with Baker's model of the black artist, grounded, in turn, in an American cultural situation. "Daughter," however, drops out of Baker's critical protocol into an elaboration of "Family." But in the sexual confusion engendered by incest, "Family" loses the delicate balance of sexual economy and hierarchization that makes "Father" father, "Daughter" daughter, and the entire household gender-distinctive. It would appear that the incest prohibition obtains to a symbolic function as well as an actual and historic one: to fix the male and female in specific cultural work, it is male sexuality that must be sealed off, impeded, by implication, in order to found female sexuality and its limits. It is not surprising, then, that the legends of incest are "male-identified," phallogocentrically determined.

But the excess inherent in the prohibitive nature of incest also leads us to suspect that it engages us (under wraps) with its opposite—the failure of potence as human possibility, which is the only way we could explain the unwritten father's law that surrounds and covers the nubile young female in his household. Alice Walker inscribes her story "The Child Who Favored Daughter" with this epigram: "that my daughter should/fancy herself in love/with *any* man!/How can this be?" (emphasis added). Why does Father need to pose to himself such an inquiry unless there is an element of too much protest? In other words, the drama of incest as it plays in fiction expresses the fatherly fear—on the level of the symbolic—that his "cargo" is hardly sufficient to bring under permanent rein the sexual impulses represented (in his own febrile imagination) by the silent and mighty sexuality of the females within his precincts. Why else would the father want to appropriate a lover's status (since, theoretically, all other women outside his "sphere of influence" are available to him) unless the very ground on which his sexuality is founded (the household) threatens to slide beneath him in the prohibitive mark itself? These counters of interdiction, then, do not ease the way to a phallic sovereignty, but open to even greater exposure the principle upon which a threatened male sexuality is said to turn.

The entire tale of incest in *Invisible Man* is told by Trueblood, who is also a singer of the blues, "a good tenor." For all intents and purposes, the wife/mother Kate and the daughter/surrogate lover Matty Lou are deprived of speech, of tongue, since what they said and did and when are reported/translated through the medium of Trueblood. These silent figures, like materialized vectors in a field of force, are curiously silent in the sense that incest fiction, even written by women, never, as far as I know, establishes the agency of the incestuous act inside the female character. This fiction in a fiction, central to the kind of symbolic content that the "I" must absorb in order to achieve the biographical uses of history, is articulated, appropriately, on the margins of the novel's society: In the approach to the Trueblood cabin, the driver of the car that bears Mr. Norton must turn off the highway "down a road that seemed unfamiliar. There were no trees and the air was brilliant. Far down the road the sun glared cruelly against a tin sign nailed to a barn. A lone figure bending over a hoe on the hillside raised up wearily and waved, more a shadow against the skyline than a man" (31). Further on we are told that, taking a hill, the occupants of the chauffered car are "swept by a wave of scorching air and it was as though we were approaching a desert"

(36). This abrupt fall into an alternative topographical center catches "invisible man" and his charge out on a radically different plain of human and symbolic activity wherein the play of signs between interlocutors focuses a mismatch of meanings and intentions. Because the road is "unfamiliar" to "invisible man," he both knows it and he doesn't, which suggests he has no idea where he is and every right to dread the undifferentiated and impulsive intimations hinted in the "crude, high, plaintively animal sounds Jim Trueblood made as he led [his] quartet" in song (36–37). "Out here," where time has ceased, attested in the parallelism and contrast between an ox team, sunlight on a tin sign, a lone figure bending over a hoe, and "a powerful motor purring" in the precise articulations of a measurable and oscillating mph, we are prepared, without even knowing it, for a venture into the marginal state; the suspension of rules; the cultural vestibularity that transports us to the region of "danger and power."[10] But danger and power for whom? In a traditional reading of this powerfully intruded narrative, Jim Trueblood emerges wealthier, healthier (because of "new wealth," we are led to suppose), and wise. But is it true?

In his marginality, Trueblood becomes a twice-marked figure: (1) by his literally peripheral status to the novel's college community from which he is set apart, as though "criminal" and contaminated (as he is, in fact, according to the rules of "civilization"), and (2) by the imaginably hideous, fly-swarmed ax mark that he will carry for a fictional eternity, inflicted by his wife Kate, who sides with civilization and determines, according to Trueblood's imitation of her, that he "done fouled." This terrible scar that designates him (until his "change comes") a mesmerized, agonized precultural inscription suggests that no man crosses the boundary of undifferentiated sexuality, even in a dream, unless he is prepared to pay the cost of a crucifixion/castration. Even though the evidence tells us no such thing about Trueblood, since wife and daughter are simultaneously pregnant, as though the promise of a twin birth, we might imagine that Ellison's narrator suggests—between the lines, where the actual sex act has indeed occurred—that Trueblood has not only copulated his last "blow," but will live to tell his privation (equal to the silence of the pregnant female) over and over again in a stunning repetition crisis, in a riveting narrative obsession that resembles in every way the awful preambulatory nightmare of Coleridge's ancient mariner. Trueblood tells his story because he cannot help himself, and he has no idea why white men in their exhibitionist urge need to pay him (somebody-anybody) to hear what they would love to perform. Trueblood becomes their whore/gal of dangerous, powerful entertainment, appointed to maintain their notions of the "civilized" (by refocusing marginality as a living space) as well as provide them the kicks they need—substituting his flesh for their distanced and protected bodies—that orality renders. This oral tale is articulated in a novel, a writing, as Trueblood enters the chain of signifiers as an item of syntax, albeit a powerful one. But the tale is essentially absorbed as an aspect of elixir with which invisible man returns to the world as a novelist, as one who has discarded rather more simplified narrative urges. Trueblood is the man who invisible man must slay, then reencounter, and make articulate, if he will comprehend the coeval period of African-American consciousness. Trueblood is, as Baker contends, the "true blood," and that is precisely the problem.

The violation of the incest taboo entangles Trueblood, it seems, in his own "blood lines" which merge inner and outer at the source of difference—the ahistoric, reified female. So trammeled, father/man, as such, disappears into an endless progression of enclosures that replicate the vaginal/uterine structure in which he has every right to fear that he will get lost and, quite correctly, fall bereft of his penal powers. I am not certain that this reading is right, but Ellison's narrator has so loaded the dream sequence—the major portion of the tale—with an invaginated symbolic plan that we seem justified in reading the breach of the incest taboo, as it is elaborated in this scene, as a symptom of an inverted castration complex. We could say, if this notion holds water, that the implanted fetus *is* the male-loss, as the vaginal vault swallows the thrust toward it. Taking the relevant text apart at this point might be helpful.

As Trueblood explains to an anxious, greedy-for-adventure Norton, the family, on the particular night of cold, huddles together for warmth—"me on one side and the ole lady on the other and the gal in the middle" (42). The daughter's intermediary posture here is highly suggestive. Since Matty Lou is pubescent, we might say she is made to effect a sexually competitive possibility between father and mother. In that sense, we are close to a marriage of three. From another point of view, the intervening child-body poses as a "cock-blocker," a strategy of contraception that is not necessarily recognized as such. In that sense, the male must penetrate layers of mediation in order to reach the target, and as unhappy fathers, unbedded by the presence of little-boy sons grudgingly admit, no man can get through all that. But the narrator plants a female body in this space for quite obviously practical narrative reasons. We might wonder to what extent, under the circumstances, "daughter," in this case, forms a collusive bond with "mother" in opposition to the wonted powers of the male organ. From this angle, the doubled female body becomes a frontier that offers resistance to assault: in order to "enter," Trueblood must first climb Brodnax Hill, as it were, and run the gauntlet of a scalding landscape before the awful climax of this tale can be reached.

Falling off to sleep in this "dark, plum black" atmosphere, Trueblood thinks his way back to Mobile and a particular young woman he knew then. Living in a two-story house on the river, Trueblood and his lover would listen to the sounds of the Mississippi and of boats moving along it. But sound modulates into visual synesthesia, translating into "young juicy melons split wide open a-layin all spread out and cool and sweet on top of all the striped green ones like it's waitin just for you, so you can see how red and ripe and juicy it is and all the shiny black seeds it's got and all" (43). These contiguous rhetorical properties that render sound visible not only suggest the loosening of coherence, as the liminal state between waking and dreaming induces, but also the lapse of distinctions that sustain the boundaries between parts of the family. Trueblood, at this point, transforms into the mercurial "boundary crosser," no longer conscious that it is his daughter sleeping beside him. But this loss of customary place that installs us on a frontier of danger and power has already been prepared for by the sort of sleeping arrangements that adhere and according to the absence of even a hint of light. As Trueblood tells it, the room is as "black as the middle of a bucket of tar" (42). Things turn elemental—"me, the old lady and the gal"—even though Trueblood discovers a plenitude of narrative turns to elaborate the event.

If the preceding sequence might be termed a narrative preplay, then what follows equals a full-dress opening night. Trueblood recalls, in the inauguration of the dream proper, that he is looking for "fat meat," but appropriate to the charged insinuations of nearly every line of his narrative, fat meat is exactly what we think it is—a full-grown watermelon. One thinks also of the strickoline, or "fat *back*" of a southern diet that garnishes a vegetable platter, or offers a bacon substitute with a cerealized rice dish, buttermilk biscuits, and sweetened coffee spiked with Old Grand Dad. Many a southern child remembers that bourbon in certain southern households is refrigerated. Trueblood, aptly, then, is looking for the grail of his environment, as it runs parallel to the symbolically inscribed female flesh. Because it is basic for him, it is holy, as one must risk his life, his sex, in order to have it. Yes, the "watermelons" are lying in wait for Jim Trueblood, but he mistakes the reasons why.

Because, we are told, we are not responsible in any ethical sense for what we dream, nor can we be held accountable for what we desire, Trueblood is, technically speaking, not blameworthy. In fact, he was not "there" when it happened, so he has committed no mistake, even though his "innocence" (de facto, or is his a guilt de jure?) provokes in him the sense of unconscionable error and the terrible consequence of guilty ignorance. Trueblood has prestigious precedent in this regard, as "invisible man" recalls a fictitious English professor named Woodridge, who assigned his class readings from Greek plays (31). But the single impenetrable element of the puzzle of fatherhood as Trueblood enacts it has to do with the manifestations of the feminine that appear across the dreamscape. It is as though another layer of intrusion is interculated between Trueblood and "his woman/ women," which introduces an Ellisonian boomerang into this otherwise "straight" Freudian Family Drama with an Electra twist. Brodnax holds the key to "fat meat," as Trueblood climbs to his place, but not finding the "master" at home, Trueblood enters anyway, and we appear to mix signals, momentarily, with Richard Wright's Bigger Thomas and the pervasive "whiteness" that surrounds Mary Dalton. Trueblood enters a door into a "big white bedroom"; as on an occasion with his Ma, Trueblood has gone to the "big house."

But is Ma in this instance a function of the gigolo between her boy and Miss Thang, so that, for him, carnality comes to rest in a surrogate female, the other woman, who initiates the young male into the ceremonies of the throbbing flesh? (In Faulkner's *Absalom, Absalom!* we are led to surmise that sexual license arises always *in* the "other" woman). In Ellison's case, it is a white woman who engenders

Trueblood's entré on the terrain of interdiction. A "white lady" steps out of a grandfather's clock, and she is robed in "white silky stuff and nothin else" (45). Clearly we are meant to understand a doubling of the prohibitive effect in this scene, as we already know, without Trueblood's having to tell us, that she is "holding" him and he is "scared to touch her cause she's white" (45). But this she is holding his fantasies as much as anything else his dream-body brings to bear on the scene, we could even say that Trueblood's body "perambulates" and materializes his fantasies so that the "real" world of scarcity, to which Trueblood is fixed like an object in protective coloration, has always historically translated into a potentially mutilated body. In that regard, this transactional scene ejects a body turned inside out, in which case the symbolic thrust of the passage does nothing to disguise or ameliorate the real situation of the dreaming body. The power and the danger that this moment projects apparently claim it under the auspices of pleasure, but the end—of the dream and of the tale—brings on Trueblood the truth of a severe disjuncture: the torn flesh of his face—the branding that establishes his deep knowledge of the forbidden female.

Frantz Fanon projects a white woman in the big house at the center of the displaced African male's prerevolutionary consciousness, but in the Fanonian scheme, the woman appears to be a familiar appurtenance of a politicocultural empowerment.[11] We expect from her (at this angle) an implacable muteness, just as Ellison's female bodies speak only through the embodied vocality of Jim Trueblood. But is it possible to retrieve from this representational cul de sac a different reading? How did this woman get in Trueblood's dream, and/or the other way around? In other words, what does this scene suggest about the daughter of this incestuous coupling, and does she, on the "lower frequencies"—which is exactly where *this* daughter occurs spatially in the dream, beneath the blond, speak also for the white woman?

Because Matty Lou, the ole lady, Ma, and the white woman— essentially appropriating the same function of the feminine, melding into a gigantically sexualized repertoire—all occupy the same semantic/symbolic fold, we have no business telling them apart, except that the intrusive markers of whiteness (and they fix this scene in obsessive repetition) signal the difference that we cannot overlook. But we assume that we know already what the *not overlooking* means. This shrouding detail not only offers an obstruction and evasion of what might have occurred—"that woman just seemed to sink outta sight, that there bed was so soft"—but also covers the identity of "daughter" so completely that she configures as an obscured aspect of landscape—a "dark tunnel . . . like the power plant they got up to the school":

> It's burnin' hot as iffen the house was caught on fire, and I starts to runnin', tryin' to get out. I runs and runs til I should be tired but ain't tired but feelin' more rested as I runs, and runnin' so good it's like flying' and I'm flyin' and sailin' and floatin' right up over the town. Only I'm still in the *tunnel*. Then way up ahead I sees a bright light like a jack-o-lantern over a graveyard. It gets brighter and brighter and I know I got to catch up with it or else. Then all at once I was right up with it and it burst like a great big electric light in my eyes and scalded me all over. Only it wasn't a scald, but like I was drowin' in a lake where the water was hot on the top and had cold numbin' currents down under it. Then all at once I'm through it and I'm relieved to be out and in the cool daylight agin. (45–46)

Since Trueblood's dream is literary, we have nothing, we assume, to discover that the narrator does not deliberately point. The symbol system of the dream apparatus appears to work, then, both transparently and symbolically as the consciously manipulated stuff of a waking intelligence, working through Trueblood as a mimetic device. We rightly assume that Matty Lou and Trueblood are already sexually entangled at this point and that the "scalding" stands for an ejaculation. When Trueblood wakes, he will try "to move without movin'," or having "flown" in, now "walk out" (46). But these contradictory signals point, in a deeper sense, to an even greater paradox, which I think the narrator does not foresee: The white woman becomes the symptom of a sexual desire that locates expression in the daughter so that the former is the term that drops out of sight, as the latter loses both human and social identity. We could say by way of these subtlelized displacements that sexuality, domesticated as a sacralized body and firmly inscribed within an enclosure that hides its "true" purposes in objects of evasion, escape, decor, can only be executed in the "underground" of sex—the actual confrontation between the genitalia. This basic situation, wherein subjectivity "thingifies," transposes into an unlocalized space that is neither here nor there. This "u-topic" suspension, brought on by a burning house, which mobilizes the droll and the dreadful (a "jack-o-lantern over a graveyard"), is appropriately undifferentiated, as the "dark tunnel" and the pit-dark in which the dreaming bodies sleep have already signaled. In this order of things, father runs, sails, floats as though rescued from the immediate situation that moors him even to a dream context, and daughter becomes the instrument of his release. In this dark of the oceanic, there are no fathers and daughters, but only children, whose being finds the perfectly magical formula that abandons them to the situation of a not-human other.

The scene splits wide open not only between a pair of female legs, but at the moment of juncture between houses—civilization, sexuality, and a feminine body identified as such, and the "lay of the land"— tunnels, graveyards, and the open air.[12] But each of these externalized interiorities that suggest freedom within a uterine enclosure translates marginality—the tunnel is nowhere yet, and the graveyard describes the largest future. We are here in passage, at the entrance to the forbidden currents of a civilized sexuality, under the auspices of a white man-not-at-home. That a woman guards the inner sanctum of Brodnax's big house poses blond and daughter in the way of a furious combat that neither can win, as such. But even before these faces of the feminine can be brought into contact, the intervened masculine must be moved aside as the teller of the tale. There is no simple leaping of this breach, and moreover, this sexual drama essentially poses a male and only one of the two females; if that is so, then sexuality also eludes the house of the father (or the circumstance of the true blood) as that boundary across which subject/subjectivity cannot go. The white woman in that regard is fixed as the "female body in the West"[13] in the first and last frontier of a "barred subject."[14] "Daughter," the stuff of which "she" is made, is established, relatedly, as a "barred subject," both plus and minus. That "she" bears the pregnant body shadows forth a fundamental economy of female signification: a body integrates and "hides" those layers of the flesh that give it identity and differentiation. There is at work in the white woman a different and informing femininity for which we yet have no name, except to call it "not woman." In this place of incestuous linkage, there is also "not man." In the fictional enactment of incest, then, black is not a color; it is a circumstance, wherein human becomes "thing," and thing turns "human" in an absolute lapse of a hierarchical movement.

We would go further: Wherever incest occurs as a fictional/symbolic motion, it takes place in the "dark, plum black . . . as the middle of a bucket of tar." The shape, the outline, melt down in an inexorable play of sameness, of identities misplaced and exchanged. One can no more find a "father" here as she can a "daughter," and the one thing we cannot account for is Trueblood's presence in the big house in the first place. The male body between female stuff, the forbidden presence on the run from the burning dream house renders a fugitive and an outlaw; this "father," in the twice-theft of the prohibited gift, forms an analogy on the band of the banished brothers. But it is not Trueblood's place to kill the fathers who have run him off, but the task of "invisible man" in the making of a fictionalized social order that resurrects history and steps into "culture"/differentiation. Here the theme of a fictional incest allows us to see closer up the failure of phallic signification, not its fulfillment.

Even though Alice Walker's "father" by implication, in "The Child Who Favored Daughter," executes "the judge, the giver of life" (35), his doing so impels him toward madness. In fact, the closural passage of the narrative, in its fierce immobilization of human and natural subjects, poses a sculptural stasis as (and in the place of a) dramatic immediacy: "Today" hardly registers a near-presence of chronology, but all the "nows" that possibly roll in upon the standing mastectomy inflicted on the "child, who favored Daughter," who is *his* daughter. These embodied surrogate motions, in which this "father" replays his father and this "daughter" replays his sister called Daughter, touch neither time nor "realism," but intrude themselves as an awful lyrical moment of eleven published pages between a "birth" (the tale's inauguration) and a "death" (its closure) in the subjunctive passivity of an aftermath, stylized by anaphora and the hint of a paradox of motion:

> Today he is slumped in the same chair facing the road. The yellow school bus sends up clouds of red dust on its way. If he

stirs it may be to Daughter shuffling lightly along the red dirt road, her dark hair down her back and her eyes looking intently at buttercups and stray black-eyed susans along the way. If he stirs it may be he will see his own child, a black-eyed Susan from the soil on which she walks. A slight, pretty flower that grows on any ground; and flowers pledge no allegiance to banners of any man. If he stirs he might see the *perfection of an ancient dream still whispered about, undefined*. If he stirs he might feel the energetic whirling of wasps about his head and think of ripe late summer days and time when scent makes a garden of the air. If he stirs he might wipe dust from the dirt daubers out of his jellied eyes. If he stirs he might take up the heavy empty shotgun and rock it back and forth on his knees, like a baby. (Emphasis mine; 45–46)

It is as though the narrator has not told us a tale at all, but a short-hand of one, an idea that lights across the mind and is gone. In that regard, "The Child Who Favored Daughter" renders a dream that actualizes a nightmare that reflects a "might have happened." But does this dreamer awake to discover that it is not so? Trueblood lives to talk; the father of daughter never did, except that in an unguarded moment of self-reflection the deepest layers of his pysche find a ventriloquist. This story does not read like a case history, but it seems to embody one.

The story has two beginnings, one of them seen through the lens of the character called child (35–36) and the other, over the same objective terrain of a given nature, filtered through the eyes of the character called he (37ff.). In the second segment, the narrator sketches in relevant psychological detail concerning his past—a beautiful and beloved sister, "impaled on one of the steel-spike fences near the house" (39). "Cut down" by a father dishonored and shamed by her liaison with "the lord of his own bondage," she has already recurred in the atavistic nightmare alluded in the opening line: "She knows he has read the letter," whose contents will crucify the child. In this deadlock grid of original sin (and incest is certainly a candidate for "it"), and on the terrain of the intramural and internecine that stages the family as a network of shared neuroses, fathers and sons link back to a common ancestry of "unnamable desire" that threatens every female alike—in these lines of poetry from the tale, sisters and spouses enjamb across run-on lines that do not stop:

> *Memories of Years*
> *Unknowable women—*
> *sisters*
> *spouses*
> *illusions of soul*
> (repeated twice on 38; emphasis is Walker's)

Because "he" has lost "daughter" and is never the same, "the women in his life faced a sullen barrier of distrust and hateful mockery. . . . His own wife, beaten into a cripple to prevent her from returning the imaginary overtures of the white landlord, killed herself while she was still young enough and strong enough to escape him" (40). But she leaves "a child, a girl, a daughter." Seizing on an absolutely striking narrative/descriptive detail that becomes a powerful lacuna in the Walker text, Harryette Mullen points out that Walker's female characters are often in search of mothers. Specifically addressing *The Color Purple* as a critique of patriarchy in the West, Mullen observes: "The story presupposes two things: a powerful black husband/father with the financial means to dominate his family; and a weak, dead, or otherwise absent or estranged mother who is unable to protect herself or her children from this man." [15] I would not necessarily agree with Mullen that this man is powerful, but in the case of *The Color Purple,* he is certainly powerful enough, and enough is as much as a feast. But the critical thematic of the missing/absent mother (who is always assumed) throws a different light on fictionalized father-daughter incest: recall that in James Baldwin's *Just Above My Head,* the mother of Julia Miller is deceased when Joel turns his daughter into more than his sporadic lover; the mother figure of Maya Angelou's *I Know Why the Caged Bird Sings* has either just abandoned her bed, with her daughter in it, beside Freeman, or just left the house, permitting him the space of isolation he needs to ostracize himself and the twice-abandoned girl-child still further. In the tale of Trueblood, Kate, who will raise very hell when the "dead" awakens, is asleep when her mate commits the mistake of his life. In Walker's *Color Purple,* Celie apparently takes on the function of a surrogate wife; as in

"The Child Who Favored Daughter," "daughter" becomes proto- or Ur-lover, who makes "wife" a superfluity, if not an outright impossibility. In effect, there can be no daughter without wife/mother, as this story lives and breathes the consequences of such absence. Appropriately, a girl-child springs up over a female's dead body, having none of the prerogatives extended "daughter" in the hierarchic, father-centered household. Exposed, therefore, to a child-man who is locked in powerful infantile memory that lives on into the moment, Walker's child reinscribes the surrogate motions of a man who wishes to sleep with his sister. Failing that, he invents a female body who essentially reinstitutes the sister's erotic reign that leads instead to daughter-murder.

There is an immediate cause of war in this male character's soul that offers an element of intrusion comparable to Trueblood's white woman of his dream. Daughter of the story, like the real daughter, loves a white man and has apparently written him a love letter, which becomes, in propinquity to the gun across his knees, a major dramatic prop of the tale. Armed with his evidence—"white man's slut!" (Would it have made a difference had the white man married her? I doubt it.)—he is determined to beat this hell out of her and to force her to deny that she wrote the letter, in short, to deny the erotic signature behind which she stands firmly ensconced, that fills him with a desire that agonizes. And kills. We could say that this occasion marks one of those rare fictional instances in which a woman's scribbling will bring on her literal castration. These marks on the page precisely time and measure the short distance between her life and death, and we nearly wish that she had not written it, or had not been discovered or betrayed, until we realize that this is not an avoidable tale of detection. It is Walker's version of an allegory in which race becomes the most pellucid, loud alibi for the male to act out a fundamental psychodrama: having had a sister whom he could not love in an open, consummated way, this father never finds love at all. Carnality knocks him down, and his response to it is typically penal, punitive: he flails and beats; his medium and his memory are guns, "steel-spiked fences," and great big butcher knives. In short, he is a perfect Sadeian sadist with none of the ostensible pleasures, so far as we can tell. I doubt that the sniff of white man's flesh makes a great deal of difference here, except that it breaks the law, and this male character knows only that—the heat, the rush, the dread, the domination of his enforced, ball-busting, back-breaking labor. He will not use his "gun" where it counts, but only against one who will whimper and drag her hair in the dirt ground before him. Because he will toss her castrated breasts to the dogs, yelping at his feet, we are led to suppose, he joins them, and no man can or should live as a dog. (Even though some of them have done remarkably well as cockroaches.) The ambiguous closure in which the male figure is either dead or as dead as we need him reminds us, however, that imputing blame and coming up with a moral are to render the story realistically. The narrator, I think, means anything but that, as we are called upon to observe, to inquire into a configuration of psychic forces, of imaginative possibilities that might/not be enacted, as fictionalized incest remains a negative drive in a field of force.

Inasmuch as incest in Walker's tale must be described between quotation marks twice (in fiction, and then not "really"), it probably goes even further than Trueblood's narrative to alert us to the familial economies of symbolic father-daughter incest. All the instruments of torture in this feminized space of the shed—are an unmistakable weaponry: a "harness from the stable" whose buckles draw blood, "curling into the dust of the floor" (42). They are wielded, unmistakably, in an attitude of maiming, but in the allegory it is either never clear or conflatedly transparent exactly what the father wants to murder and pulverize. Clearly, ambiguously, he loves her, as the lines from the letter, in his night-long vigil (it seems), refer to both her own writing and what runs through his mind in a wounding flash: "It is rainsoaked, but he can make out 'I love you' written in a firm hand across the blue face of the letter" (42). This is fairly remarkable because we are almost persuaded to say that the one thing that rushes him out of his father's closet, so to speak, is this female's writing— even rain-soaked, it is a firm hand "across the blue." Would she still have been a girl-child alive, riding on a yellow school bus, except for that act of inscription that affirms beyond guess her powers of desire? To choose, to say who and when she wants? Her crime has been her desire. The daughter cannot want, and so far as this one is concerned, "no amount of churchgoing changed her ways" (43). It is a patent contradiction to the Father's law that the young nubile female in his midst should desire. (The wishes of wife, even an adulterous one, do not matter, since she has already been had.) He is flummoxed, however, in the face of the daughter's vast and untried sexual possibilities, and we suspect why: he, essentially, drew his woman out of another man's familial/sexual integrity, which move kills the Father, if the Law works, throughout all the generations; I suppose we could say that not until a man marries—which, humorously, depends on a woman's consent—does he complete his Oedipal mission and gain, thusly, brotherhood in the status of a patrimonial destiny.

Does the incestuous instinct become, then, in the fictional text the fatherly plea that the young woman not "disgrace" her father, not "cut him loose" in the transfer of unspoken sexual allegiance? We are accustomed to think that men exchange women, as the fundamental reason of property behind the prohibition, but is it possible that the female figure, the woman, simply by looking at what she wants, fixing it at eye level, effects the point of transfer and transit that must be blocked off at all costs? Does this vast and fundamental negation, then, cover this muted place at which the father gains insight into his own limitations of body and flesh? Perhaps it is not by accident that the unwed daughter, especially in the house of a dead father, is viciously referred to in heterosexist language and tradition as the old maid, the aged female "stuff" whom Father needn't marry?

Because this daughter writes her wish, she assumes the proportions of a monstrosity (the narrator has also given her school books off whose sight the father's eyes glide down to the point of promise), as she becomes, exactly, "in the shed"—rain-soaked, hair-draggled, immured in the blood of her flesh. He sees her blouse, "wet and slippery from the rain," sliding off her shoulders, "and her high young breasts are bare":

> He gathers their fullness in his fingers and begins a slow twisting. The barking of the dogs create a frenzy in his ears and he is suddenly burning with unnamable desire. In his agony he draws the girl away from him as one pulling off his own arm and with quick slashes of his knife leaves two bleeding craters the size of grapefruits on her bare bronze breast and flings what he finds in his hands to the yelping dogs. (45)

Any woman reader of this paragraph is convinced by now, if not by anything that precedes it, that this swift, matter-of-fact, single, choreographed verbal gesture does not qualify as the imitation of any conceivable action. We must be somewhere else in a region of imagined revenge. There is no apparent and immediate aftermath that the text records: No noise? No hysterical motion? No drowning? And no Divinity comes down here now? And how could a woman write this, without self-(or "other"?) intervention? We read it again and decide that it is comparable with a female body "impaled on a steel-spiked fence *near the house*" (emphasis mine). And it remains unbearable. No act of criticism that I could perform on the text at this point would retrieve the passage for me as a usable text, since it transgresses every sexual/sexually discursive aspect of a cultural code that I have received from Father/Mother (the most immediate and evident sexual "origin") as a plausible carnality and therefore a potential mimesis/representation of a sort. But that point at which my own readerly sensibilities switch off, at which my own aesthetic rules go in revolt, at which, in *this* case, I, in an empathetic gesture that has no business intruding itself between the "clean" text and me, may well demarcate precisely that moment at which I should hang on. It possibly signalizes the "quick slash marks" that divide "me"—violently—from the peace and "piece" of self-imputed w(hole)ness. "This sex which is not one" [16] not only inscribes the symbolic outcome of the female's divided labial economy, but offers this configuration as the groundwork of a different system of signification altogether. If this is so, then "daughter" in Walker's text not only escapes the patriarchal household of this tale (by death?), but also, consequently, the unitary implications of the phallic by which she is adjudged an other.

If "daughter" escapes patriarchy by mutilation and effacement only, then the victory is hardly worth the father's cost, since this fictionalized circuit of desire has shorted out, as it were. If the incestuous impulse leads, by a detour, to a "more or less manifest endogamy," then the "realization of incest is not only possible, it is necessary, albeit through a third party, lest any form of relationship between human beings become exhausted." [17] According to this theory, Father-Daughter incest must occur on the symbolic level and therefore in its manifestations as the incest taboo, in order to bring about "differences in cases where identity threatens to block the functioning of some fixed culture." Roustang goes so far as to contend that

> Incestuous desire is operative for the individual only if it actually remains a possibility, but that possibility, to remain valid, must

be the effective deviation, the actual derivation of incest. If incest is unrecognized, rejected, repressed, the individual will be left with nothing but the arid, closed field of some abandonment or deadly depression. If incest is overtly practiced and the individual has eyes, ears, and sex only for those closest to him or their surrogates, then he will always be on the verge of fragmentation and breakdown.[18]

The father of Walker's text cannot recognize the ground of his own "unnameable desire," or else he recognizes it all to well. Having "eyes, ears, and sex only for those closest to him"—in this instance, a ruse or surrogate for "Daughter"—he actually carries out, on the level of an inverted dream, the motions of breakdown and falling apart that the text displaces through the daughter's dismemberment. We are left, I believe, with a stunning excision, pointing in two directions at once. The text both engenders and conceals these oppositional vectors by circumvention. The slumping figure that we encounter in the closural scene of the tale cradles a "heavy empty shotgun" that might be read as a deflated tumescence. But the essential stillness of the passage, as though time will not cease in an eternity of undifferentiated movement, also claims it for a death at the level of vegetal growth: the dirt daubers have seized this body, jellied its eyes, as the choreographed effects of the natural overwhelm names, identities, and genders in a democratic rage for sameness. This reduction to the fundamental, brought on by an oversupply of the domestic phallus (the one "near the house"), not only parodies a "return of the repressed," but also mocks the Father's law as a basic castration fear.

But what might it mean for this daughter to "underwrite" this father? In other words, how is it that we know daughter only through father? Indeed, it seems that "he" marks the founding auspices of a female representation and that we have no way out. I maintain, however, that the loss of difference—which occurs in an actualized fictitious outcome of incest, as in the tale of Trueblood, or in a surrogate fictitious outcome, as in "The Child Who Favored Daughter"—abolishes those very sexual distinctions that hold the Father-daughter relationship in a delicate balance. Its violation, in at least two contemporary fictional instances, brings about "castration," or its equivalent: in the case of Trueblood, the daughter's pregnancy and a sexual future from which Trueblood has been barred; in Walker's father's case, a future rolling backward and ahead toward unlocalized human origins. In either instance, sexual life or human-as-sexed-subject stalls at the moment of penetration so that the penis, in this speaking, actually lops itself off. If this is so, then the suspension of the taboo generates the deepest division, if to signify here is to break up into layers of fragmentation. A sort of magic pervades this economy: Fathers and Daughters are called upon to divide without division, to acquire that difference that no one ever "thought" was other than difference in the first place; since this is true, father can save himself only in bypassing the daughter's sex, which is also anatomically inscribed, but it is the difference within that he must only guess. Have we, then, done nothing more than point out that even in fiction, especially in fiction, the incest taboo prevails and prevails for very good reason?

It seems that we have arrived at the household of the African-American Daughter and Father by a kind of detour of our own. This arriving possibly demarcates a text running parallel to that of a Euro-centric psychomythology, and I would concede that by way of it we land also on the ground of pure (fictional?) speculation: the Freudian/Lacanian text of incest and phallic signification might apply to this community of texts—both fictional and historic—only by accident, which the writers sense more palpably than the sociologists. The Father *and* the Daughter of this social configuration are "missing" historically because the laws and practices of enslavement did not recognize, as a rule, the vertical arrangements of their family. From this angle, fathers, daughters, mothers, sons, sisters, brothers spread across the social terrain in horizontal display, which exactly occurred in the dispersal of the historic African-American domestic unit. In this movement outward from a nuclear centrality, "family" becomes an extension and inclusion—anyone who preserves life and its callings becomes a member of the family, whose patterns of kinship and resemblance fall into disguise. In other words, the "romance" of African-American fiction is a tale of origins that brings together once again children lost, stolen, or strayed from their mothers. We pursue these thematics in works by Frances E. W. Harper, Pauline Hopkins, and Charles W. Chesnutt, among others, who wrote late in the nineteenth century and early into the twentieth.[19] We also encounter the changeling, the orphaned, or lost child in other fictions, certainly, but I am not acquainted with any other cluster of fictional texts based in historic experience that seems designed to sever the maternal bond, shrouding the paternal connection in redoubled uncertainty. On this basis, it is fair to say that one aspect of the liberational urge for freed persons is not so much the right to achieve the nuclear family as it is the wish to rescue African-Americans from flight, to arrest their wandering away from . . . toward—essentially, to bring the present into view rather than the past. We could go so far as to say that African-Americans in historic flight perfectly inscribe the "body in pain,"[20] on a contracted world ground, whose sole concern becomes the protection of the corporeal body, and it is the corporeal, carnal body that incest brings brazenly into relief precisely because it is prohibited.

If "family," on this historic occasion, describes, for all intents and purposes, a site of interdiction and denial, we could go so far as to say that the mark of incestuous desire and enactment—a concentrated carnality—speaks for its losses, confusions, and, above all else, its imposed abeyance of order and degree. We might tentatively look at the situation this way: moments of African-American fiction show Father-Daughter incest or its surrogate motions as an absence, not an overdetermination. Something is wrong, precisely because fathers and daughters, in a cultural marginality, fictively inscribed, are impeded in their movement toward culture/difference/division. The urge here compels characters to get out of incest, out of the carnal body, whose only means of expression remains the flesh, as Trueblood's branding makes evident, into the "clean" blood. If this is true, then the prohibition must be embraced (in order to cancel out the other interdiction) not only in Father's interest, but that the Daughters might know the appropriate lover and the future. In this case, the origins of the incest taboo are not at all shrouded in mystery, nor are they longer-going than the history of the United States, for example: Wherever human society wishes to move into an articulation, the Father must discover and humbly observe his limit. In that regard and at least from the viewpoint of a couple of writers, Father-Daughter incestuous desire and taboo possesses no originary moment, but arises each day, as a precise diachronic unfolding, in a situation of blindness and overcoming.

Living on the Line: Audre Lorde and *Our Dead Behind Us*

In Audre Lorde's poem "A Meeting of Minds," a woman who "stands/in a crystal" is not permitted to dream ("the agent of control is/a zoning bee") or to speak ("her lips are wired to explode/at the slightest conversation"), although around her, "other women are chatting."

> the walls are written in honey
> in the dream
> she is not allowed
> to kiss her own mother
> the agent of control
> is   a white pencil
> that writes
> alone.[1] (36)

Denied access to her sleeping consciousness, this heroine cannot see her past or future, nor can she fully know and constitute herself. Prohibited conversation, she cannot connect with other women except in what feels like one-way visual separation, rendered even more cruel by her observing of their verbal sharing with each other around the honeyed walls. Crystal, a gem used by women for vision, protection, and the transmission of healing energy, becomes here cold, imprisoning stone whose properties only enhance her torment and isolation. Kissing her mother, her own and not a stepmother, would reinstate the first and most basic contact in a touch that embraces and validates the self. But even this simple bloodright/rite is not allowed.

As bad as the zoning bee and explosives undoubtedly are, Lorde's climactic and pointed placement of the "white pencil/that writes/ alone" (note the spatial pause between "is" and "a white pencil") signals its overall importance. This pencil which signs the woman's ultimate alienation is, first of all, white and, second, self-contained and -propelled. Its color is the blank neutrality of the dominant world, and there is no visible agent-author to own its powerful interdictions. It has the deterministic force of Khayyam-FitzGerald's "moving finger" (which having writ, moves on), plus a disembodied horror impossible to efface.

Lorde has spent her entire career as a black lesbian feminist poet writing against this white, Western, phallocentric pencil. She has placed a colored pen within the woman's grasp and authorized her to inscribe her own law—an order that valorizes dreaming, speaking, and kissing the mother and, above all, does not seek to hide its hand in a transparently cloaked objectivity. Honesty and responsibility—even in the midst of difficult saying—are premier goals and motivations. Lorde's poem "Learning to Write" (53) begins with a question:

> Is the alphabet responsible
> for the book
> in which it is written
> that makes me peevish and nasty
> and wish I were dumb   again?

This present-tense outburst against someone's vexing use of language triggers a childhood memory of practicing the drawing of letters, and then concludes with a resolution obviously generated in response to what has irritated her:

> I am a bleak heroism of words
> that refuse
> to be buried alive
> with the liars.

Time and again she asserts her position, comparing her honesty (in "A Question of Climate") to her "powerful breast stroke"/"a declaration of war" which she developed by being "dropped into the inevitable" (39).

Identity is no meaningless accident. Thus, writing honestly requires acknowledging the particulars that construct the self. This seems to be the message of "To the Poet Who Happens to Be Black/ and the Black Poet Who/Happens to Be a Woman," a title that places sarcastic weight on the word *happens* and a heavy disapproval on those poets who discount their race and gender. Part one of the poem records her first birth "in the gut of Blackness/from between my mother's particular thighs." The second stanza recounts the first sister touch, a joyous woman birth which wrote into her body a "welcome home." Black and woman born, she survives all the attempts in part three of the poem to cancel her out "like an unpleasant appointment/ postage due." The movement ends:

> I cannot recall the words of my first poem
> but I remember a promise
> I made my pen
> never to leave it
> lying
> in somebody else's blood. (7)

There is always the pitfall of lying, which is accentuated in these lines by the obvious pun. Writing with the ink of her own precisely claimed blood keeps Lorde from using her pen—like a ghostly white pencil—to spill the blood of others.

Of course, saying honestly is not especially easy. Having worked through inner pressures and prohibitions, the poet still must face the unspeakable in experience and language. When "cadences of dead flesh/obscure the vowels," there can be "no honest poems about dead women."[2] Likewise, in "This Urn Contains Earth from/German Concentration Camps" (24–25), Lorde contemplates the well-trimmed order of a West Berlin memorial, its

> Neatness
> wiping memories   payment
> from the air.

She contrasts this scene with a summer picnic, where "rough precisions of earth" marked her "rump" and a smashed water bug oozed eggs into a bowl of corn. It is this latter which is

> Earth
> not the unremarkable ash
> of fussy thin-boned infants

and adolescent Jewish girls
liming the Ravensbruck potatoes

This realization forces the sobering knowledge that

careful and monsterless
this urn makes nothing
easy to say.

Here, by juxtaposing the abstract "mythization" of the Holocaust horror with concrete corporeality, Lorde makes her project clear. She is rescuing meaning from immateriality, from the sanitized wipeout of traditional history's magic pencil. Unburying the bones and rotting flesh of what has been covered up may not be pretty, but, for her, the unthinkable alternative is muteness, a condition she ascribes to bottles and wood and interdicted women encased in stone.

Lorde began her published work in 1968—twenty years ago—with *The First Cities*.[3] When she arrived via five volumes of verse and a growing reputation at *Between Our Selves* (1976) and *The Black Unicorn* (1978), she had gone from merely writing poetry to casting wise and incantatory magic. A *Choice* reviewer put it quite sensitively when s/he wrote:

Audre Lorde has always been a good poet. . . . But now, with the arrival of *The black unicorn,* these previous books [of hers] have an added value; for they show, in a unique way, how a black poet has changed over a decade, in response to the poetic styles and to her own deepening sensibilities. . . . As a woman, mother, teacher, lover, she has been a strong lyrical figure in Afro-American Life. Now she has added another self—the spirit that has gone to Africa. . . . Here is poetry that is rich, startling in its speed and fervor. The personal experience still startles her, as in her previous work, but the stark, ironic, almost taunting poems of her earlier years have given place to words of acceptance and transcendence.[4]

The Black Unicorn is a majestic voicing of statements and propositions whose applications are further worked out in her later book, *Our Dead*

Behind Us (1986). Much of the struggle of defining and instating herself was done in the earlier volume, so that now she can simply put herself in motion, acting and being who she is. And because we know—and she knows that we know—where she is coming from, there is no need for her to repeat herself. At this hard-earned point, we can read Audre Lorde in her own light.

When Lorde names herself "sister outsider," she is claiming the extremes of a difficult identity. I think we tend to read the two terms with a diacritical slash between them—in an attempt to make some separate, though conjoining, space. But Lorde has placed herself on that line between the either/or and both/and of "sister outsider"—and then erased her chance for rest or mediation. However, the charged field between the two energies remains strong, constantly suggested by the frequency with which edges, lines, borders, margins, boundaries, and the like appear as significant figures in her work. One of the more striking uses begins her famous poem "A Litany for Survival":

> For those of us who live at the shoreline
> standing upon the constant edges of decision
> crucial and alone[5]

Those for whom she chants this survival song are outsiders who exist between their versions of life and the conflicting hegemonic scheme, who occupy the moment between a precarious present and a better future, "looking inward and outward/at once before and after." This margin, their place—if a space this untenable can be so concretely designated—is for marginal, that is, expendable beings. Lorde celebrates their "instant" and their "triumph," stating: "We were never meant to survive."

Two contiguous poems in *Our Dead Behind Us* further explore limits. After venturing past the easy spots where men catch proven trout in calm, knee-deep water, the speaker in "Fishing the White Water" (28) confesses that she "never intended to press beyond/the sharp lines set as boundary." Yet she finds herself laboring in rapids back to back with her lover, choosing her partner's "dear face" over "the prism light makes/along my line." "On the Edge" (30) contemplates relationship possibilities in terms of slicing blades and dangerous knives, leaving the speaker dreaming "I am precious rock/touching the edge of you."

Yet, it is not simply lines which attract Lorde. She is almost equally fascinated by what happens as they cross and recross, touch, and intersect with one another. Hence the "grids" and "crostics" of her poems (and also the bridges, which I do not discuss here). Her lover's face is "distorted into grids/of magnified complaint." Life in New York City forms "the complex/double-crostic of this moment's culture." A couple's two names become "a crostic for touch." [6] These puzzling, intersecting lines that posit communication also attempt to pattern a map that can both locate and guide one through difficult geographies. Place is central in Lorde's work. Ethiopia, Berlin, Florida, Soho, and Vermont appear in her titles as a sampling of all the hot and troubled spots which engage her—Amsterdam Avenue, Mississippi, Grenville, Grenada, 830 Broadway, Santiago de Chile, Bleecker Street, Vieques, St. Georges, Johannesburg, White River Junction, Southampton, Maiden Lane, Pretoria, Alabama, Eau Claire, Tashkent, Gugeleto, and on and on—all place-names marking the wide area of her political and personal concerns. Lorde's vision encompasses the world, although she often approaches it from inside the woods, a garden, the next room, on a trail or a path to the deeper and broader meanings which glue the grid together. The bottom line is drawn clearly in the conclusion to "Outlines":

> We have chosen each other
> and the edge of each other's battles
> the war is the same
> if we lose
> someday women's blood will
> congeal
> upon a dead planet
> if we win
> there is no telling.

Lorde's seemingly essentialist definitions of herself as black/lesbian/mother/woman are not simple, fixed terms. Rather, they represent her ceaseless negotiations of a positionality from which she can speak. Almost as soon as she achieves a place of connection, she becomes uneasy at the comfortableness (which is, to her, a signal that something critical is being glossed over) and proceeds to rub athwart the smooth grain to find the roughness and the slant she needs to maintain her difference-defined, complexly constructed self. *Our Dead Behind Us* is constant motion, with poem after poem enacting a series of displacements. The geographical shifts are paralleled by temporal shifting in a "time-tension" which Mary J. Carruthers sees as characteristic of lesbian poetry: "the unspoken Lesbian past and the ineffable Lesbian future bearing continuously upon the present."[7] The ubiquitous leave-takings are not surprising—"Out to the Hard Road" ("I never told you how much it hurt   leaving"), "Every Traveler Has One Vermont Poem" ("Spikes of lavender aster under Route 91/ . . . I am a stranger/making a living choice"), "Diaspora" ("grenades held dry in a calabash/leaving"). Yet even more telling is the way Lorde brackets "home."

A poem with that title begins:

> We arrived at my mother's island
> to find your mother's name in the stone
> we did not need   to go to the graveyard
> for affirmation
> our own genealogies
> the language of childhood wars.

Ostensibly, these lines confirm a beautiful sisterhood between the two travelers which goes beyond the need for external documentation. And well it does—for none of the conventional "proof" of origin and kinship is forthcoming. At the outset, another mother's name occupies the space where the speaker expected to find her own matrilineage. Nor does proof come from the "two old dark women" in the second stanza who blessed them, greeting

> Eh Dou-Dou you look *too* familiar
> to you   to me
> it no longer mattered. (49)

Has this woman arrived at home, the place where her particular face is recognized?

"On My Way Out I Passed over You/and the Verrazano Bridge" (54) is a mediated suspension between leave-taking and home. In fact, the poet is literally hanging in the midair of an airplane flight, "leaving

leaving." Beneath is water, sand, "silhouette houses sliding off the horizon," her and her lover's house, too, which "slips under these wings/shuttle between nightmare and the possible." The home which "drew us" because of space for a growing green garden now holds "anger" in a "landscape of trials," comparable to the way sulfur fuels burned in New Jersey have turned the Staten Island earth bright yellow. So what is to be done?

> we live on the edge
> of manufacturing
> tomorrow or the unthinkable
> made common as plantain-weed
> by our act of not thinking
> of taking
> only what is given.

Their domestic conflict is encompassed by global pain and injustice which render home/place tenuous and terrifying for people all over the world—from Poland to Soweto, the Bay Street Women's Shelter, and the altars of El Salvador. Winnie Mandela's steps and her blood are slowing "in a banned and waterless living." Thus, when Lorde says

> I am writing these words as a route map
> an artifact for survival
> a chronicle of buried treasure
> a mourning
> for this place we are about to be leaving

all of this madness is what she wants to put behind.

The penultimate movement of the poem telescopes ordinary, heroic women at war, some of them "burning their houses behind them" or being "driven out of Crossroads/perched on the corrugated walls of her uprooted life." This unkind history necessitates

> articulation
> of want   without having
> or even the promise of getting.

So permitted, the poet—returning to her immediate conversation with her lover—can

> dream of our coming together
> encircled   driven
> not only by love
> but by lust for a working tomorrow
> the flights of this journey
> mapless   uncertain
> and necessary as water.

Despite its long and torturous charting of this farewell gesture, the poem ends as it began, suspended in moving uncertainty. Home is continually deferred in a world which, as Matthew Arnold put it, "hath really neither joy, nor love, nor light,/nor certitude, nor peace, nor help for pain."[8] Lorde herself had told us earlier, in *The Black Unicorn,* that

> for the embattled
> there is no place
> that cannot be
> home
> nor is.[9]

Lorde's inability to rest—in place, time, or consciousness—is reflected in a technique she frequently uses of playing meaning along lines that shift both backward and forward. In the first excerpt from "Home" quoted above, the clause "we did not need" stands as its own declarative, but it also modifies "stone" in a completion of "the stone we did not need," as well as begins the new sentence of "we did not need to go to the graveyard." The next phrase, "for affirmation," is likewise shared, as prepositional closure for the "graveyard" behind it and as introduction for the forwarding statement of "for affirmation, [we had] our own genealogies." The "to you   to me" of the second quote is also doubly constructed. In the first "On My Way Out" passage, the reader pauses after "of manufacturing"—only to have to pick up the burden of the line to make an object of "tomorrow or the unthinkable," which then becomes the subject of "made common"—if one has not already read "we" as that phrase's nominative designation.

The poet is not (only) playing games; she is also writing political poetry. We need to think about the industrial pollution that neighbors us *and* the way we determine our future tomorrows. We need to realize that willfully not thinking makes both ourselves and the worst world we can imagine "common" (also meaning vulgar) and acceptable. Amitai F. Avi-ram has published a study of Lorde's use of this technique which in rhetoric is termed *apo koinou,* a Greek phrase meaning "in common." She has this to say about its thematic and formal functions in Lorde's poetry:

> *apo koinou* seems to be a controlling method in Audre Lorde's art. It enables her to suspend the ordinary pressures of sentence-closure, to reveal the suspect "nature" of such closure and its ideological consequences, and to reveal the hidden possibilities of meaning in words, especially in their ideological dimensions. It also enables her to form a new language that both criticizes reality and pursues the articulation of feeling as the satisfaction of a kind of erotic demand. In so doing, finally, *apo koinou* affords Lorde a technique for an alternative constitution of the subject in poetry as one that makes contact and has intense feelings in common with others, but preserves its ability to experience and to mean by observing its own differences in a world fraught with difference.[10]

Employing this stratagem, she is pressing further

> the sharpened edge
> where day and night shall meet
> and not be
> one.[11]

Lorde's tricky positionality—as exemplified by her relationship to home and poetic lines—also extends to community, which she likewise desires, but problematizes and finds problematic. An early poem, "And What About the Children," alludes to the "dire predictions" and "grim speculations" that accompanied her interracial

marriage and mixed-race offspring. She takes defiant comfort in the
fact that if her son's head "is on straight,"

> he won't care
> about his
> hair
> nor give a damn
> whose wife
> I am.[12]

"Between Ourselves" recalls her former habit of walking into a room
seeking the "one or two black faces" which would reassure her that
she was not alone; but

> now walking into rooms full of black faces
> that would destroy me for any difference
> where shall my eyes look?
> Once it was easy to know
> who were my people.[13]

Caught during a women's rally between a racially deferent black
counterman at Nedick's restaurant and a group of white companions
discussing their problems with their maids, Lorde learns afresh that

> I who am bound by my mirror
> as well as my bed
> see causes in color
> as well as sex[14]

In "Scar," having "no sister no mother no children" is juxtaposed
with what is "left": "only a tideless ocean of moonlit women/in all
shades of loving." [15]

These communal displacements are not so critically prominent in
Our Dead Behind Us—perhaps because, by now, they are so familiar.
Instead, we find glyphs of female connection—the "large solid
women" who "walk the parapets beside me"; the "corn woman bird
girl sister" who "calls from the edge of a desert" telling her story of
survival; the "Judith" and "Blanche" with whom she hangs out; the

"warm pool/of dark women's faces" at a Gainesville, Florida, lecture.[16] At this point, Lorde has achieved spiritual bonding with an ancestral and mythic past. The Amazons and warrior queens of Dahomey and the orisha of the Yoruba religious pantheon have given her a family that cannot fail:

> It was in Abomey that I felt
> the full blood of my fathers' wars
> and where I found my mother
> Seboulisa[17]

Even on 125th Street in New York City,

> Head bent, walking through snow
> I see you Seboulisa
> printed inside the back of my head
> like marks of the newly wrapped akai [braids]
> that kept my sleep fruitful in Dahomey[18]

The cover of *Our Dead Behind Us* consists of "a snapshot of the last Dahomean Amazons," "three old Black women in draped cloths," superimposed upon a sea of dark and passionate South Africans at a protest demonstration. This image projects Lorde's membership in a community of struggle which stretches from ancient to modern times. In "Call" she invokes "Oya Seboulisa Mawu Afrekete," "Rosa Parks and Fannie Lou Hamer/Assata Shakur and Yaa Asantewa/my mother and Winnie Mandela" (75), speaking into exclusionary spaces a transcendent black woman power "released/from the prism of dreaming." [19]

However uneasy her identity may be, it is imperative for Lorde that she read the world as a meaningful text and not as a series of interesting and elusive propositions. For her, to "read" is (1) to decipher—like the musician Prince—the signs of the times, (2) to decode—as the lesbian/gay community does—the submerged signification of the visible signs, and (3) to sound out clearly and "to your face" uncompromising truth as she sees it, in that foot-up, hands-on-hip loudness that is self-authorized black female jeremiad, sermon, and song. From the beginning, her vatic voice has defined her moral and didactic arena—in the same way that her presence claims its territory on the stage or in a photographic frame. She and Adrienne Rich, especially, have been criticized for their heavy seriousness. However, with so many dead behind her, Lorde is too busy pulling the bodies from bars and doorways, jungle tracks and trenches to find time for unrestricted poetic laughter. Her task is to foreground the carnage in a valiant effort to make such senseless dying truly a thing of the past.

From the first poem in her first book, "Memorial II," Lorde has decried society's chewing up of young girl-women like "Martha" (in *Cables to Rage*) and "Genevieve." She begs, "Genevieve tell me where dead girls/Wander after their summer," and asks, in "Suffer the Children," "But who shall dis-inter these girls/To love the women they were to become/Or read the legends written beneath their skin?" [20] Their spirits still shadow her lines—as she yearns each spring "to braid the hair of a girl long dead" ("Beams," 70), or as they reincarnate as the liminal "dark girls" of her haunted lyrics (for example, in "Diaspora").

These readings are gentle, compared to the devastating fury that drives poems such as "Equal Opportunity" (16) and "For the Record" (63). In the latter, it is the poet herself who "counts" the big fleshy women like black grandmother Eleanor Bumpers who was brutally murdered by police while defending her home and then ignominiously carried out "dress torn up around her waist/uncovered." The next day Indira Gandhi, another sixty-seven-year-old "colored girl," is shot down in her garden, and the two women—who are now perhaps talking to each other—"weren't even sisters." The first poem is scathing satire of the black female "american deputy assistant secretary of defense/for Equal Opportunity" who preens in her crisp uniform and defends the department's "record/of equal opportunity for our women"—while United States troops invade Grenada, terrorizing "Imelda young Black in a tattered headcloth" whose empty cooking pots are overturned and garden trampled, whose husband was "buried without his legs," and who stands carefully before these trigger-nervous men asking for water for herself and her child. In "Soho Cinema" (19), she takes to task a well-off white woman for her complacently liberal nonresponse to the world's problems.

Irony blasts in these poems as explosively as it does, laughter-tinged, in "A Question of *Essence*," where Lorde repeats that magazine's query, "Is Your Hair Still Political?" and quips "tell me/when it starts to burn." This is her kind of humor—piercing wit in the service of a serious cause. "The Art of Response" reads:

> The first answer was incorrect
> the second was
> sorry   the third trimmed its toenails
> on the Vatican steps
> . . . .
> the sixth   wrote a book about it
> the seventh
> argued a case before the Supreme Court
> against taxation on Girl Scout Cookies
> the eighth held a new conference
> while four Black babies
> and one other   picketed New York City
> for a hospital bed to die in
> . . . .
> the thirteenth
> refused
> the fourteenth sold cocaine and
> shamrocks
> near a toilet in the Big Apple circus
> the fifteenth
> changed the question. (37)

The cataloged responses are wildly comic, but the point is that the problem of how to live in this mad world—the unstated "question"—is usually posed in terms that make meaningful, efficacious response impossible; thus the only valid move is for one to change the "question." Similarly, the "some women" in "Stations" who love to wait at various spots "for life   for a ring/in the June light   for a touch/of the sun to heal them," for "their right/train   in the wrong station," for love "to rise up," for visions, "that do not return/where they were not welcome," for themselves "around the next corner," are contrasted with the women in the final stanza who wait for something

> to change   and nothing
> does change
> so they change
> themselves. (15)

Both "Stations" and "The Art of Response" carry a lilt and tone different from most of Lorde's work.

Her way is to paint social and political injustice in intimate and familiar forms. She "outlines" the difficulties faced by an interracial lesbian couple in a racist-sexist-homophobic culture "with not only our enemies' hands/raised against us": dog shit dumped on the front porch, brass wind chimes stolen, a burning cross ten blocks away, and the "despair offerings of the 8 A.M. News" reminding them that they are "still at war/and not with each other" (11–12). This union is as charged with significance as the play of language and power which structures an exchange between the poet and an almost extinct Russian Chukwu woman in "Political Relations." Their warm words to each other must be spoken across the thin lips of dominance, white Moscow girls who translated for them "smirking at each other" (51).

"Sisters in Arms," the brilliant poem that begins *Our Dead Behind Us,* starts with:

> The edge of our bed was a wide grid
> where your fifteen-year-old daughter was hanging
> gut-sprung on police wheels

Instantly, the poet and the black South African woman in bed beside her are catapulted through space and time into the embattled Western Reserve where the girl's body needs burying:

> so I bought you a ticket to Durban
> on my American Express
> and we lay together
> in the first light of a new season.

The "now" of the poem is the speaker clearing roughage from her autumn garden and reaching for "the taste of today" in embittering *New York Times* news stories that obscure the massacre of black children. Another shift occurs with "we were two Black women touching our flame/and we left our dead behind us/I hovered   you rose the last ritual of healing." These lines show traces of the deep, joyous, authenticating eroticism Lorde describes in another of her poems as "the greed of a poet/or an empty woman/trying to touch/ what matters." [21]

These two women's loving is flecked with the cold and salt rage of death, the necessity of war: "Someday you will come to *my* country/and we will fight side by side?" When keys jingle, threatening, in "the door ajar," the poet's desperate reaching for "sweetness" "explodes like a pregnant belly," like the nine-year-old Joyce mentioned earlier who tried to crawl to her bleeding brother after being shot during a raid, "shitting through her [own] navel." The closing section of the poem looks backward on the grid to the only comfort in sight—a vision of warrior queen Mmanthatisi nursing her baby, then mapping the next day's battle as she

> dreams of Durban   sometimes
> visions the deep wry song of beach pebbles
> running after the sea

—in final lines whose rich referentiality links all the "Sisters" together in an enduring tradition of nurturance and hopeful struggle.

The oracular voice that powers—at different frequencies—Lorde's work can best be heard full force in the majestic orality of "Call," a spiritual offering of praise and supplication that is chilling, especially when she reads it. Aido Hwedo is, a note tells us, "The Rainbow Serpent; also a representation of all ancient divinities who must be worshipped but whose names and faces have been lost in time." Stanza one summons this

> Holy ghost woman
> Stolen out of your name
> Rainbow Serpent
> whose faces have been forgotten
> Mother - loosen my tongue or adorn me
> with a lighter burden
> Aido Hwedo is coming.

She invokes this deity in the name of herself and her sisters who, "on worn kitchen stools and tables," are piecing their "weapons together/ scraps of different histories":

> Rainbow Serpent who must not go
> unspoken
> I have offered up the safety of separations
> sung the spirals of power
> and what fills the spaces
> before power unfolds or flounders
> in desirable nonessentials
> I am a Black woman   stripped down
> and praying
> my whole life has been an altar
> worth its ending
> and I say Aido Hwedo is coming.

She brings her best while asking for continuing power to do her work as a woman/poet. And she is blessed to become not only the collective voice of her sisters, but Aido Hwedo's fiery tongue, "the holy ghosts' linguist."

Critic Robert Stepto pronounced *The Black Unicorn* "an event in contemporary letters" because of its author's "voice or an *idea* of a voice that is essentially African in that it is communal, historiographical, archival, and prophetic *as well as* personal in ways that we commonly associate with the African *griot, dyēli,* and tellers of *nganos* and other oral tales." This voice holds in her later volume, which continues to "explore the modulations within that voice between feminine and feminist timbres" and also to chart "history and geography as well as voice." [22]

Lorde's moral and political vision combined with her demanding style make her difficult for many readers. Her aggressive exploration of her own alterity (she is a repository of "others" personified) is strategic defiance. Reviewing *Our Dead Behind Us* in the *Los Angeles Times,* Ted C. Simmons even uses that word: "What further animates Lorde's work beyond this ore vein of contrapuntal interplay is her defiance. She seems to live defiance, thrive on it, delight in it. She is up-front, a feminist and militant, an activist juju-word woman." [23]

Her stance impels commentators to approach her writings in terms of sympathy/guilt and the likeness/unlikeness of potential readers to the poet herself. A particularly exaggerated version of this tack occurs in the *Village Voice* review of her essay collection *Sister Outsider:* "the

more you resemble her target of white, -male, -thin, -young, -hetero-
sexual, Christian, and financially secure, the more you'll squirm under her verbal guns. . . . If you're black, gay, or left-wing, it's easier
to identify with Lorde because we can never join the patriarchy, even
if we're tempted." [24] The same theme sounds in remarks such as the
following about her poetry: "[*Chosen Poems—Old and New*] has an
enormous appeal for those who share the author's feelings and would
like to see their own feelings and experiences confirmed in print."
"The *content* [of *Our Dead Behind Us*] is laudable; at least if you agree
with her. But . . . there's more than a little of the disingenuous about
her approach, which seems bent on instilling guilt in the reader as
much as offering enlightenment." [25] Those who squirm the most
seem to be those who are most uncomfortable with their own privileged identities, and a great deal of the "guilt" is unacknowledged
responsibility inappropriately reversed.

The wide divergence of opinion regarding the worth of Audre
Lorde's poetry is striking. At one extreme rests the critic who believes
that, in *The Black Unicorn*, "ugliness predominates" and that "most
of the poems are simply bad; they don't work as organic wholes and
leave the reader surprised that a piece continues on the next page." [26]
The renowned Hayden Carruth begins his assessment of the book
with negative judgment and ends in a confusion of praise. "The truth
is, I don't care much for her writing, which seems far too close to the
commonplace. . . . Yet few poets are better equipped than Lorde to
drive their passion through the gauzy softness of commonplace dic-
tion and prosody. One can't help being absorbed in it. Her best poems
move me deeply." [27]

Many critics pinpoint what they perceive to be her weaknesses, and
credit their discoveries of beauty and strength: "If I have a complaint,
it is that lines sometimes tend to be prosaic . . . yet the musicality and
the self-assurance make it work as poetry." "Audre Lorde is a brilliant
and honest poet, and while no poem in this volume touches me as the
earlier Lorde poems do, *The Black Unicorn* should be read for its own
wit, wisdom, and incandescence." [28] Others are even more unstinting
in their admiration. The *Library Journal's* reviewer consistently describes Lorde as "an excellent craftsman: her voice is lyrical and her
eye is sharp" and pronounces her poems "hard-edged, compelling,
and vital." Stepto concluded his discussion of Lorde with "*The Black*

Unicorn offers contemporary poetry of a high order, and in doing so may be a smoldering renaissance and revolution unto itself." Paula Giddings begins her review of *Our Dead Behind Us:* "Each new volume published by Audre Lorde confirms the fact that she is one of America's finest poets." [29] On the dust jacket of *The Black Unicorn,* Adrienne Rich elevates Lorde's "poems of elemental wildness and healing, nightmare and lucidity" which "blaze and pulse on the page, beneath the reader's eye."

Readers who—by whatever means of experience, empathy, imagination, or intelligence—are best able to approximate Lorde's own positionality most appreciate her work. For instance, it is clearly Siconolfi's ethnocentric ignorance of African traditions and their importance to Afro-Americans which leads him to arrogantly dismiss Lorde's "surprising" ("for a resident of Staten Island") "dragging in" of "a plethora of African mythology (a handy glossary is mercifully provided)" as a "purple Dashiki patch"—while black American critics Stepto and Andrea Rushing see this same material as a creative use of important African sources. [30] Yet readers who also have "radically-situated subjectivities" [31] still find themselves challenged by Lorde's poetry. Sandra Squire Fluck, a self-described "educator, poet/writer, and peace and social justice activist," writes the following in her review of *Our Dead Behind Us:* "As uncomfortable as Lorde makes me feel here about the world situation, I do not have to relive my own righteous anger, brimming with angst and isolation, as it used to [be]. But I do have to accept Lorde on her terms, because she challenges me to see history her way as a Black lesbian woman." Only Lorde's recognition of "the limits of righteous anger" allows Fluck to "say yes" to her "without being threatened or overwhelmed." [32] As I write this, I recall that my own "Poem for Audre" of a few years ago begins with the words

> What you said
> keeps bothering me
> keeps needling, grinding
> like toothache
> or a bad conscience[33]

Clearly, Lorde keeps her reader—as she does herself—unsettled.

Viewed stylistically, Lorde's poetry is not transparent. Understanding her texts requires attention, effort, energy, hard work. Even a sympathetic reviewer like Fahamisha Shariat admits that Lorde "may not be totally clear on a first, or even a second reading—sometimes her language approaches the surreal," but that "her poems are rich enough to send us back for new discoveries with each reading."[34] *Our Dead Behind Us* is simpler in language and reference than *Coal* or *The Black Unicorn,* the poems less coded and more straightforward. Nevertheless, today's literary marketplace seems to be filled with customers looking for an easy "read" (usually fiction) and setting aside most of what cannot be conveniently discussed as narrative/narrativity.

Taking up Lorde reminds us of the still-unique nature of poetic discourse, the essence of which is a submerged textuality that, like Nietzsche's truth, remains an army of metaphors. Lorde's own poetry is basically a traditional kind of modernist free verse—laced with equivocation and, to use an old-fashioned concept, allegory. Only in her black Broadside Press–published books does she employ to any significant extent a recognizable ethnic idiom. Thus, who we hear with her foot up, specifying, does not sound to our ears like Zora, or Bessie, or, among the contemporaries, Sonia or Nikki, Pat or June.[35]

Trying to read Lorde's more veiled texts can leave one foundering in her wake. These poems, I think, derive from a more vulnerable, unprocessed self, or from the poet's desire to keep some secrets partially hidden. "Berlin Is Hard on Colored Girls" comes across as a private joke about personal deprivation in a strange city and some kind of (dream?) encounter. Even read in the light of its two predecessors, "Generation III" remains densely impenetrable, except to suggest something emotionally strenuous related to mother-family and child-children. A handful of these private poems touches haltingly on Lorde's protracted fight with cancer and the idea of impending death—"Mawu" (which ends with the line "insisting/death is not a disease"), "From the Cave" perhaps, and "Never to Dream of Spiders" (with its glimpses of hospital surgery, recovery, a fiftieth birthday in 1984, and its concluding phrase, "a burst of light," which became the title for her second book about her health and illness).

Finally, Lorde's stylistic challenges are probably related to the manner in which she came into language/poetry.[36] An inarticulate, left-handed child who had been forced to use her right hand, Lorde did

GLORIA T. HULL

not talk until she was five years old. Screaming in a four-year-old tantrum on the floor of the Harlem library (caused, I am sure, by the frustration of not being able to otherwise communicate), she was taken up by an impressive librarian who sat down and read her some stories. Audre knew instantly that that was "something I was going to do," and went on from there to read, then talk, then write—in that unusual order.

Words became for her "live entities." As a child she would take them "apart and fragment them like colors." She possessed a vocabulary which she had never heard spoken and did not know how to pronounce. These words such as *legend, frigate,* and *monster* "had an energy and power and I came to respect that power early. Pronouns, nouns, and verbs were citizens of different countries, who really got together to make a new world." During this period, she charmed away nightmares by choosing words which most terrified her and then "stripped them of anything but the sound—and put myself to sleep with the rhythms of them." This sense of words as sound full of both malevolent and joyful possibility is captured in her early poem "Coal" (which contains the lines, "how sound comes into a word, coloured/by who pays what for speaking").[37]

Lorde's first language was, literally, poetry. When someone asked her "How do you feel?" "What do you think?" or any other direct question, she "would recite a poem, and somewhere in that poem would be the feeling, the vital piece of information. It might be a line. It might be an image. The poem was my response." Since she was hit if she stuttered, "writing was the next best thing." At this point, Audre was well on her way to becoming schizophrenic, living in "a totally separate world of words." She got "stoned on," retreated into poetry when life became too difficult. As miscellaneous poems no longer served to answer questions from herself and others, she began to write her own. These she did not commit to paper, but memorized and kept as a "long fund" in her head. Poems were "a secret way" of expressing feelings she was "still too afraid to deal with." She would know that she "finally had it" when she spoke her work aloud and it struck alive, became real.

Audre's bizarre mode of communication must surely have meant frequently tangential conversations, and certainly placed on her listeners the burden of having to "read" her words in order to connect her second-level discourse with the direct matter at hand. At any rate, her answer to "How do you feel?" or "Do you want to go to the store with me?" could rarely be a simple "fine" or a univocal yes or no.

In high school, she tried not to "think in poems." She saw in amazement how other people thought, "step by step," and "not in bubbles up from chaos that you had to anchor with words"—a kind of "nonverbal communication, beneath language" the value of which she had learned intuitively from her mother. After an early, pseudonymously published story, Lorde did not write another piece of prose until her 1977 essay "Poetry Is Not a Luxury." Even though she had begun to speak in full sentences when she was nineteen and had also acquired compositional skills, "communicating deep feeling in linear, solid blocks of print felt arcane, a method beyond me." She "could not focus on a thought long enough to have it from start to finish," but she could "ponder a poem for days." Lorde possessed an admirable, innate resistance to the phallogocentric "white pencil," to being, as she put it, "locked into the mouth of the dragon." She had seen the many errors committed in the name of "thought/thinking," and, furthermore, had formed some precious convictions about her own life that "defied thought." She seems always to have been seeking what she calls, in *Our Dead Behind Us,* "an emotional language/in which to abbreviate time." [38]

Lorde had not connected words with a reality outside her individual head until she stood on a hill in Mexico one breathtaking morning, also when she was nineteen, and realized that she could "infuse words directly with what I was feeling," that "I didn't have to create the world I wrote about," that "words could tell." She found that the "trees" and "forest" she used to dream and fantasize about could indeed "be a reality" that words can "match" and "re-create." With this, Lorde had taken the final step of a journey that had begun when, extremely nearsighted and legally blind, she had put on her first pair of spectacles at four and saw that trees were not "green clouds."

This remarkable story inescapably suggests what the French poststructuralist critic Julia Kristeva posits about language and subjectivity—her locating of meaning in the unconscious, chaotic, preverbal, infant *chora,* in the rhythmic pulsing of semiotic sound, the drives and tides of a maternal body. According to Kristeva, this locus (which appears most strongly in poetry and which Kristeva even calls at one

GLORIA T. HULL

point poetic language) dynamically charges and interacts subversively with the symbolic, thetic world where rational, conceptual language and communication are situated.[39] Lorde's is a living experience of that about which Kristeva theorizes.

Viewing Lorde's poetry in the light of Kristeva's theory reminds us that finding new, more provocative ways to discuss black women's poetry is a project that could claim more attention than is currently focused in that direction and, further, that these ways might well evolve from sensitive digging in the soil of diverse traditions.

I Shop Therefore I Am:
Is There a Place for Afro-American Culture
in Commodity Culture?

> Adults, older girls, shops, magazines, newspapers, window
> signs—all the world had agreed that a blue-eyed, yellow-haired,
> pink-skinned doll was what every girl child treasured.
>
> —Toni Morrison,
> *The Bluest Eye*

In her powerfully compressed first novel, *The Bluest Eye,* Toni Morrison scrutinizes the influence of the white-dominated culture industry
on the lives and identities of black Americans. She tells the story of
three young girls: Claudia and Frieda, who are sisters, and Pecola,
who comes to stay with them during a period when her own brawling
parents are cast out of their storefront home. The book's setting is a
working-class urban black neighborhood during the 1930s and 1940s,
a time when it is already clear that American culture means white
culture, and this in turn is synonymous with mass media culture.
Morrison singles out the apparently innocuous—or as Frieda and Pecola put it, "cu-ute"[1]—Shirley Temple, her dimpled face reproduced
on cups, saucers, and baby dolls, to show how the icons of mass culture subtly and insidiously intervene in the daily lives of Afro-
Americans.

Of the three girls, Claudia is the renegade. She hates Shirley Temple and seethes with anger when she sees the blue-eyed, curly haired
child actress dancing alongside the culture hero that Claudia claims
for herself—Bojangles. As she sees it, "Bojangles is [her] friend, [her]
uncle, [her] daddy, [and he] ought to have been soft-shoeing it and
chuckling with [her]" (19). Claudia's intractable hostility toward Shirley Temple originates in her realization that in our society, she, like
all racial "others," participates in dominant culture as a consumer, but
not as a producer. In rejecting Shirley Temple and wanting to be the
one dancing with Bojangles, Claudia refuses the two modes of accom-

modation that white culture holds out to black consumers. She neither accepts that white is somehow superior, which would enable her to see Shirley Temple as a proper dancing partner for Bojangles; nor does she imagine herself miraculously translated into the body of Shirley Temple so as to vicariously live white experience as a negation of blackness. Instead, Claudia questions the basis for white cultural domination. This she does most dramatically by dismembering and tearing open the vapid blue-eyed baby dolls her parents and relatives give her for Christmas presents. Claudia's hostility is not blind, but motivated by the keen desire to get at the roots of white domination, "to see of what it was made, to discover the dearness, to find the beauty, the desirability that had escaped [her], but only [her]" (20).

Claudia's unmitigated rage against white culture, its dolls and movie stars, is equaled only by her realization that she could ax little white girls made of flesh and blood as readily as she rips open their plaster and sawdust replicas. The only thing that restrains Claudia from committing mayhem is her recognition that the acts of violence she imagines would be "disinterested violence" (22). This is an important point in Morrison's development of Claudia as the representation of a stance that Afro-Americans in general might take against white domination. By demonstrating that violence against whites runs the risk of being "disinterested violence," Morrison suggests that white people are little more than abstractions. As the living embodiments of their culture, all white people partake of the Shirley Temple icon. To some extent, all are reified subjects, against whom it is impossible for blacks to mount passionate, self-affirming resistance or retaliation. In defining Claudia as someone who learns "how repulsive disinterested violence [is]" (22), Morrison affirms the fullness of her character's humanity.

Being Different

Morrison's treatment of Claudia explores the radical potential inherent in the position of being "other" to dominant society. The critical nature of *The Bluest Eye* may be best appreciated when apprehended in relation to efforts by Edward Said and Frantz Fanon to expose the emotionally crippling aspects of colonialism. Morrison's genius as a writer of fiction is to develop the experience of "otherness" and its denunciation in ways that were not open to either Said in *Orientalism* or Fanon in *Black Skin White Masks*. This is because Morrison's fictional characters, while they articulate history, are not themselves bound by historical events and social structures as were Fanon's patients whose case histories are the narrative raw material of his book. Morrison's portrayal of Pecola is the most horrifying example of the mental distortion produced by being "other" to white culture. She transforms the Fanonian model of a little black girl caught behind a white mask into a little black girl whose white mask becomes her face. Pecola's dialectical antithesis is, then, Claudia who tears to shreds the white mask society wants her to wear.

However, Claudia's critical reversal of "otherness" is short lived. Indeed, she later learned to "worship" Shirley Temple, knowing even as she did "that the change was adjustment without improvement" (22). In this, Morrison suggests that white cultural domination is far too complex to be addressed only in a retaliatory manner. A simple, straightforward response to cultural domination cannot be mounted, let alone imagined, because domination is bound up with the media, and this with commodity gratification. Claudia's desire to dance with Bojangles raises a question so crucial as to put all of American culture to the test. That is, can we conceive of mass culture as black culture? Or is mass culture by its very definition white culture with a few blacks in it? Can we even begin to imagine the media as a form capable of expressing Afro-American cultural identity?

Morrison addresses these questions by way of a parable. She tells the story of how Claudia and her sister plant a bed of marigolds and believe that the health and vigor of their seeds will ensure the health and vigor of their friend's incestuously conceived child. Morrison makes the parallel explicit; "We had dropped our seeds in our own little plot of black dirt just as Pecola's father had dropped his seeds in his own plot of black dirt" (9). But there were no marigolds. The seeds "shriveled and died" (9) as did Pecola's baby. The parable of the flower garden resonates with more meaning than the mere procreation and survival of black people. In its fullest sense, the parable asks if we can conceive of an Afro-American cultural garden capable of bringing all its people to fruition. In the absence of a whole and sustaining Afro-American culture, Morrison shows black people making "adjustments" to mass white culture. Claudia preserves more integrity than her sister, Frieda, but both finally learn to love the white icon. Pecola magically attains the bluest eyes and with them the madness of assimilation to the white icon. Maureen, the "high-yellow dream child with long brown hair," mimics the white icon with rich displays of fashion: "patent-leather shoes with buckles," "colored knee socks," and a "brown velvet coat trimmed in white rabbit fur and a matching muff" (52–53). Taken together, the four young girls represent varying degrees of distortion and denial of self produced in relation to a culture they and their parents do not make, but cannot help but consume. Can we, then, conceive of Afro-American culture capable of sustaining all four young girls, individually and collectively? And can such a culture take a mass form? To open up these questions, I move into the present, out of literature and into advertising, where mass media culture has made black its "other" most frequently viewed population as compared to the less visible Asian-Americans and all but invisible Hispanics.

Shop till You Drop

I don't want to know! I just want that magical moment when I go into a store and get what I want with my credit card. I don't even want to know I'll have to pay for it.—Comment made by a white male student when I explained that commodity fetishism denies knowledge of the work that goes into the things we buy.

There is a photograph by Barbara Kruger that devastatingly sums up the abstraction of self and reality in consumer society. The photo shows no more than a white hand whose thumb and forefinger grasp a red credit-card-like card, whose motto reads "I Shop Therefore I am." [2] Kruger's photo captures the double nature of commodity fetishism as it informs both self and activity. The reduction of being to consumption coincides with the abstraction of shopping as well. This is because "using plastic" represents a deepening of the already abstract character of exchange based on money as the general equivalent.

If shopping equals mere existence, then the purchase of brand names is the individual's means for designating a specific identity.

I SHOP THEREFORE I AM

Consumer society has produced a population of wearers of such corporate logos as Esprit, Benetton, Calvin Klein, Jordache, and the latest on the fashion scene, McDonald's McKids. The stitched or printed logo is a visible detail of fashion not unlike the stickers on a banana peel. In the eyes of the corporate fashion industry, our function is to bring advertising into our daily lives. We may well ask if we are any different from the old-time sandwich board advertisers who once patroled city streets with signs recommending "Eat at Joe's."

Until recently it was clear in the way fashion featured white models that buying a brand name designer label meant buying a white identity. The workers who produce brand name clothing today are predominantly Chinese, Filipino, and Mexican; or, closer to home, they are Hispanics and Asian Americans, but the corporations are as white as the interests and culture of the ruling class they maintain. The introduction of black fashion models in major fashion magazines like *Vogue, Harper's Bazaar,* and *Glamour* may have at one time represented a potential loosening of white cultural hegemony. But this was never fully realized because high fashion circumscribes ethnic and racial identity by portraying people of color as exotic. Today, blacks appear in all forms of advertising, most often as deracinated, deculturated black integers in a white equation. This is even true in many of the ads one finds in such black magazines as *Ebony* and *Essence,* where the format, models, and slogans are black mirror images of the same ads one sees month by month in the white magazines. For instance, in February 1988, Virginia Slims ran a magazine and billboard ad that featured a white model in a red and black flamenco dancing dress. Black magazines and billboards in black neighborhoods ran the same ad, same dress. The only difference was the black model inside the dress.

Whether black people can affirm identity by way of a brand name is nowhere more acutely posed than by Michael Jordan's association with Air Nike. Michael Jordan *is* Air Nike. He is not just shown wearing the shoes like some other champion might be shown eating "the breakfast of champions." Rather, his name and the brand form a single unified logo-refrain. No other sports star, white or black, has ever attained such an intimate relationship between self and commodity. However, the personal connection between product and star does not suggest a more personalized product, rather it speaks for the commodification of Jordan himself. Moreover, the intimate oneness between the black basketball player and the white sneaker does not represent an inroad on the white corporation, but it does ensure that thousands of black youths from sixteen to twenty-five will have a good reason for wanting hundred-dollar shoes.

A decade before Michael Jordan made black synonymous with a brand name, Toni Morrison used another of her novels to demonstrate the futility of affirming blackness with a white label. In *Song of Solomon,* Morrison depicts the anguish of Hagar, who wakes one morning to the realization that the reason for her boyfriend's lack of interest is her looks. "Look at how I look. I look awful. No wonder he didn't want me. I look terrible." [3] Hagar's "look" is black urban, northern, working class, with a still strong attachment to the rural South. What little connection she has to the larger white culture has been fashioned out of her mother's sweepstakes prizes and her grandmother's impulse purchases. There is nothing contrived or premeditated about Hagar and the way she spontaneously defines herself and her love for Milkman. Her boyfriend, on the other hand, is the progeny of the urban black middle class whose forbears conquered the professions and gained access to private property. Not as fully assimilated to the brand name as Michael Jordan, Milkman nevertheless is a walking collection of commodities from his "cordovan leather" shoes (255) to his "good cut of suit" (256).

In rationalizing her boyfriend's rejection of her as a fault of her "looks," Hagar assimilates race to style. She had previously been devastated by Milkman's flirtation with a woman with "penny-colored hair" and "lemon-colored skin" (319), and decides that in order to hold on to her boyfriend she must make herself into a less-black woman. What Hagar does not grasp is that Milkman's uncaring regard for her is an expression of his primary sexism as well as his internalized acceptance of the larger society's racist measure of blacks in terms of how closely an individual's skin and hair approximate the white model. Hagar lives her rejection as a personal affront and turns to the only means our society holds out to individuals to improve their lot and solve their problems: consumption. Hagar embodies all the pain and anxiety produced when racism and sexism permeate an intimate relationship; she is the living articulation of consumer society's solution to racism and sexism. This is, buy a new you. Transform yourself by piling on as many brand name styles and scents as your pocketbook will allow. The solution to a racist society is a "pretty little black skinned girl" (310) "who dresses herself up in the white-with-a-band-of-color skirt and matching bolero, the Maidenform brassiere, the Fruit of the Loom panties, the no color hose, the Playtex garter belt and the Joyce con brios" (318); who does her face in "sunny glow" and "mango tango"; and who puts "baby clear sky light to outwit the day light on her eyelids" (318).

Morrison reveals her sensitive understanding of how commodity consumption mutilates black personhood when she has Hagar appear before her mother and grandmother newly decked out in the clothes and cosmetics she hauled home through a driving rainstorm: her "wet ripped hose, the soiled white dress, the sticky, lumpy face powder, the streaked rouge, and the wild wet shoals of hair" (318). If Hagar had indeed achieved the "look" she so desperately sought, she would only have been a black mimicry of a white cultural model. Instead, as the sodden, pitiful child who finally sees how grotesque she has made herself look, Hagar is the sublime manifestation of the contradiction between the ideology of consumer society that would have everyone believe we all trade equally in commodities, and the reality of all marginalized people for whom translation into the dominant white model is impossible.

Morrison's condemnation of commodity consumption as a hollow solution to the problems of race, class, and gender is as final and absolute as are Hagar's subsequent delirium and death. Unable to find let alone affirm herself, unable to bridge the contradiction in her life by way of a shopping spree and a Cinderella transformation, Hagar falls into a fever and eventually perishes.

If consumer society were to erect a tombstone for Hagar, it would read "Shop till you drop." This is clearly the ugliest expression ever coined by shopping mall publicity people. Yet it is currently proclaimed with pride and glee by compulsive shoppers from coast to coast. Emblazoned on T-shirts, bumper stickers, and flashy advertising layouts, "shop till you drop" attests the ultimate degradation of the consumer. How often have you heard a young woman remark, such as the one I saw on the "Newlywed Game," "Whenever I feel low, I just shop till I drop!"? This is exactly what Hagar did. The difference between Morrison's portrayal of Hagar and the relish with which the "Newlywed" contestant characterizes her shopping orgies is Morrison's incisive revelation of the victimization and dehumanization inherent in mass consumption. "Shop till you drop" is a message aimed at and accepted largely by women. (I have yet to hear a male shopper characterize himself in such a way.) The extreme sexism of the retail and advertising industries could not be more abusively stated. However, the victimization, the sexism, the degradation and dehumanization—all go unnoticed because the notion of consumption is synonymous with gratification. To demonstrate the fundamental impossibility of realizing gratification in commodity consumption, we have only to shift the focus from consumption to production. Now I ask you, would anyone wear a T-shirt proclaiming "Work till you drop"? The cold fact of capitalism is that much of the work force is expendable. Are we to assume that a fair number of consumers are also expendable provided they set high consumption standards on the way out?

From Black Replicants to Michael Jackson

Toni Morrison's blatant condemnation of the fetishizing quality of white-dominated commodity culture is by no means unique to the tradition of black women writers. In her novel *Meridian,* Alice Walker creates a caricature of the reification of white society that is even more grotesque than Morrison's frozen-faced white baby dolls. This is the dead white woman whose mummified body is carted about from town to town and displayed as a side-show attraction by her money-grubbing husband. In death, as was probably the case in her life, the white woman's labor power is the basis for her husband's livelihood. As a dead body, she is literally the embodiment of the congealed labor that exemplifies the commodity form. What Morrison and Walker are documenting in their portrayals of reified white characters is the consequence of the longer and deeper association with the commodity form that whites in our society have had as opposed to racial minorities. In reacting so strongly against the fetishizing power of the commodity, contemporary black women's fiction stands aghast at the level of commodity consumption that Hagar attempts in *Song of Solomon,* and suggests that total immersion in commodities is a fairly recent historical phenomenon for the broad mass of Afro-Americans. Indeed, one way to read *Song of Solomon* is as a parable of black peoples' integration with the commodity form that is depicted across the book's three female generations, from Pilate who trades and barters for daily needs and very seldom makes a commodity purchase, to her daughter, Reba, who gets and gives a vast array of commodities that she wins rather than purchases, to Hagar, who desperately yearns for and dies because of commodities. The larger implications of Morrison's parable suggest that while the commodity form has been dominant throughout the twentieth century, daily-life economics may have been only partially commodified owing to the many social groups that, until recently, did not fully participate as consumers.

While Morrison rejects out of hand the possibility of creating a positive, affirming black cultural identity out of "sunny glow" and "mango tango," Kobena Mercer, the British film and art critic, dramatically affirms the contrary. In considering the politics of black hairstyles, Mercer defines an approach to consumer society that sees commodities giving new forms of access to black people's self-expression.[4] Mercer contrasts the social meanings associated with the Afro, a hairstyle popular among black radicals in the sixties and the general cultural movement that promoted "black is beautiful" on into the seventies, with the conk, a hairstyle contrived during the late thirties and early forties by urban black males. Mercer sees the popular interpretation of these two hairstyles wholly influenced by the way Western culture has, ever since romanticism, validated the natural as opposed to the artificial. The "Fro" was read culturally as making a strong positive statement because it was taken to represent the natural. Then, because Western mythology equates the natural with the primitive—and primitive with Africa—the "Fro" was seen as truly African, hence, the most valid form of Afro-American cultural expression. Mercer deflates all the myths by pointing out that the "Fro" was not natural but had to be specially cut and combed with a pik to produce the uniform rounded look. Moreover, the cultural map of African hairstyles reveals a complex geography of complicated plaits and cuts that are anything but natural. Mercer's final point is that if the "Fro" was seen as natural, it was defined as such by dominant white society for whom the longer hairstyles of the late sixties meant hippies and their version of a communal back-to-nature movement. In this way, dominant white culture assimilated the "Fro" to its meanings, including its countercultural meanings.

By comparison, Mercer sees the conk allowing a form of Afro-American cultural expression that was not possible with the "Fro" precisely because the conk was seen as artificial. At the time of its popularity and even on into the present, the conk has been condemned as an attempt by black men to "whiten" their appearance. Mercer gives the prevailing line of thought by citing Malcolm X on his own first conk: "on top of my head was this thick, smooth sheen of red hair—real red—as straight as any white man's. . . . [The conk was] my first really big step towards self-degradation." In contrast, Mercer's opinion of the conk is very different. As he sees it, if black men were trying to make themselves look more white and more acceptable to white ideals of style, they would not have chosen the conk. The hair was straightened by what he calls a "violent technology" and treated to produce a tight cap of glistening red to orange hair. For its artificiality, the conk made a radical cultural statement that cannot be inscribed in dominant racialized interpretations of culture.

> Far from an attempted simulation of whiteness I think the dye was used as a stylized means of defying the "natural" colour codes of conventionality in order to highlight artificiality and hence exaggerate a sense of difference. Like the purple and green wigs worn by the black women, which Malcolm mentions in disgust, the use of red dye seems trivial: but by flouting convention with varying degrees of artifice such techniques of black stylization participated in a defiant "dandyism," fronting-out oppression by the artful manipulation of appearances.[5]

Mercer's point is finally that black culture has at its disposal and can manipulate all the signs and artifacts produced by the larger culture. The fact that these are already inscribed with meanings inherited through centuries of domination does not inhibit the production of viable culture statements, even though it influences the way such statements are read. The readings may vary depending on the historical period as well as the class, race, and gender of the reader. Mercer's own reading of the conk is facilitated by current theories in popular culture that see the commodity form as the raw material for the meanings that people produce. From this point of view, the most recognizable commodity (what is seen as wholly "artificial") is somehow freer of past associations and more capable of giving access to alternative meanings.

There is, however, an important consideration that is not addressed either by Morrison in her condemnation of commodity culture or by Mercer in his delight over the possibilities of manipulating cultural meanings. This is the way the dominant white culture industry produces consumable images of blacks. Considerable effort in Afro-American criticism has been devoted toward revealing racism in the images of blacks on television and in film, but little has been written about more mundane areas such as advertising and the mass toy market. I suggest a hypothesis that will help us understand consumer society in a more complex way than to simply point out its racism. That is, in mass culture many of the social contradictions of capitalism appear to us as if those very contradictions had been resolved. The mass cultural object articulates the contradiction and its imaginary resolution. Witness the way mass culture suggests the resolution of racism.

In contrast to Morrison's Claudia, who circa 1940 was made to play with white baby dolls, black mothers in the late sixties could buy their little girls Barbie's black equivalent: Christie. Mattel marketed Christie as Barbie's friend, and in so doing, cashed in on the civil rights movement and black upward social mobility. With Christie, Mattel also set an important precedent in the toy industry for the creation of black replicants of white cultural models. The invention of Christie is not wholly unlike the inception of a black Shirley Temple doll. If the notion of a black simulacrum of Shirley Temple is difficult to imagine, this is because only recent trends in mass marketing have taught us to accept black replicants as "separate but equal" expressions of the white world. In the 1930s a black Shirley Temple would not have been possible, but if she were a five-year-old dancing princess today, Mattel would make a doll of her in black and white and no one would consider it strange. I say this because as soon as we started to see those grotesque, sunken-chinned white Cabbage Patch dolls, we started to see black ones as well. Similarly, the more appealing, but curiously furry-skinned My Child dolls are now available in black or white and boy or girl models. Clearly, in the 1980s, race and gender have become equal integers on the toy store shelf. I know many white girls who own mass-marketed black baby dolls such as these, but I have yet to see a single little black girl with a black Cabbage Patch doll. What these dolls mean to little girls, both black and white, is a problem no adult should presume to fully understand, particularly as the dolls raise questions of mothering and adoption along with race. I mention these dolls because they sum up for me the crucial question of whether it is possible to give egalitarian expression to cultural diversity in a society where the white middle class is the norm against which all else is judged. This is another way to focus the problem I raised earlier when I asked whether it is possible for Afro-American culture to find expression in a mass cultural form.

In an essay inaugurating her participation in the new magazine *Zeta,* bell hooks develops the important distinction between white supremacy and older forms of racism. Hooks sees white supremacy as "the most useful term to denote exploitation of people of color in this society"[6] both in relation to liberal politics and liberal feminism. I would add that white supremacy is the only way to begin to understand the exploitation of black people as consumers. In contrast to racism which bars people of color from dominant modes of production and consumption, white supremacy suggests the equalization of the races at the level of consumption. This is possible only because all the models are white. As replicants, black versions of white cultural models are of necessity secondary and devoid of cultural integrity. The black replicant ensures, rather than subverts, domination. The notion of "otherness," or unassimilable marginality, is in the replicant attenuated by its mirroring of the white model. Finally the proliferation of black replicants, in toys, fashion, and advertising smothers the possibility for creating black cultural alternatives.

While the production of blacks as replicants of whites has been the dominant mass-market strategy for some twenty years, there are indications that this formula is itself in the process of being replaced by a newer mode of representation that in turn suggests a different approach to racism in society. I am referring to the look of racial homogeneity that is currently prevalent in high-fashion marketing. Such a look depicts race as no more meaningful than a blend of paint. For example, the March 1988 issue of *Elle* magazine featured a beige woman on its cover. Many more fashion magazines have since followed suit in marketing what is now called "the new ethnicity." The ethnic model who appeared on *Elle* is clearly not "a high yellow dream child," Morrison's version of a black approximation to whiteness circa 1940. Rather, she is a woman whose features, skin tone, and hair suggest no one race, or even the fusion of social contraries. She is, instead, all races in one. A skimming perusal of *Elle*'s fashion pages reveals more beige women and a great number of white women who have been photographed in beige tones. The use of beige fashion models is the industry's metaphor for the magical erasure of race as a problem in our society. It underscores white supremacy without directly invoking the dominant race. To understand how this is achieved we have only to compare the look of racial homogeneity to the look of gender homogeneity. For some time now the fashion industry has suggested that all women, whether they are photographed in Maidenform or denim, whether they are twelve years old or forty-five, are equally gendered. Dominant male-defined notions about female gender, such as appear in fashion advertising, have inured many women to the possibility of gender heterogeneity. Now the suggestion is that women with the proper "look" are equally "raced." Such a look denies the possibility for articulating cultural diversity precisely because it demonstrates that difference is only a matter of fashion. It is the new fall colors, the latest style, and the corporate logo or label—a discrete emblematic representation of the otherwise invisible white corporate godfather.

I mention *Elle*'s beige women because the fashion industry's portrayal of racial homogeneity provides an initial means for interpreting Michael Jackson who in this context emerges as the quintessential mass cultural commodity.[7] Nowhere do we see so many apparent resolutions of social contradiction as we apprehend in Michael Jackson. If youth culture and expanding youth markets belie a society whose senior members are growing more numerous, more impoverished, more marginal every day, then Michael Jackson as the ageless child of thirty represents a solution to aging. If ours is a sexist society, then Michael Jackson, who expresses both femininity and masculinity but fails to generate the threat or fear generally associated with androgeny, supplies a resolution to society's sexual inequality. If ours is a racist society, then Michael Jackson, who articulates whiteness and blackness as surgical rather than cultural identities, offers an easy solution to racial conflict.

SUSAN WILLIS

Recently I was struck when Benson on the television show by the same name remarked that Michael Jackson looked like Diana Ross. The show confirmed what popular opinion has been saying for some time. The comparison of Michael Jackson to Diana Ross is particularly astute when we see Jackson as both a "look" and a music statement. Rather than defining Michael Jackson in relation to the black male music tradition, I think it makes more sense to evaluate his music with respect to black women singers—and to go much further back than Diana Ross to the great blues singers like "Ma" Rainey, Bessie Smith, and Ethel Waters. Diana Ross and the Motown sound is in many ways the mass cultural cancellation of the threatening remembrance of "ladies who really did sing the blues." In a path-breaking essay on the sexual politics of the blues, Hazel Carby shows how the black women blues singers attacked patriarchy by affirming women's right to mobility and sexual independence.[8] Getting out of town and out from under a misbehaving man, refusing to be cooped up in the house, and taking the initiative in sexual relations—these are the oft-repeated themes of the black female blues tradition. By comparison, the incessant chant style developed by Diana Ross and the Supremes features refrains aimed at the containment of women's desire and the acceptance of victimization. Background percussion that delivers a chainlike sound reminiscent of slavery is an apt instrumental metaphor for lyrics such as "My world is empty without you, Babe," "I need your love, oh, how I need your love." By physically transforming himself into a Diana Ross look-alike, Michael Jackson situates himself in the tradition of black women's blues. The thematic concerns of his music often take up the question and consequences of being sexually a renegade, that is, "bad"; however, Jackson ultimately represents the black male reversal of all that was threatening to patriarchy in black women's blues music. Where the black women singers affirmed the right to self-determination, both economically and sexually, Jackson taunts that he is "bad" but asks for punishment. Jackson toys with the hostility associated with sexual oppression, but rather than unleashing it, he calls for the reassertion of a patriarchal form of authority.

This does not, however, exhaust the question of Michael Jackson. As the most successful Afro-American in the mass culture industry, Jackson begs us to consider whether he represents a successful expression of Afro-American culture in mass form. To begin to answer this question we need to go back to the notion of the commodity and recognize that above all else Michael Jackson is the consummate expression of the commodity form. Fredric Jameson offers one way of understanding Michael Jackson as a commodity when he defines the contradictory function of repetition. On the one hand, repetition evokes the endlessly reproducible and degraded commodity form itself. Jameson demonstrates how mass culture, through the production of numerous genres, forms, and styles, attempts to create the notion of newness, uniqueness, or originality. What is contradictory about repetition is that while we shun it for the haunting reminder of commodity seriality, we also seek it out. This, Jameson sees, is especially the case in popular music, where a single piece of music hardly means anything to us the first time we hear it, but comes to be associated with enjoyment and to take on personal meanings through subsequent listenings. This is because "the pop single, by means of repetition, insensibly becomes part of the existential fabric of our own lives, so that what we listen to is ourselves, our own previous auditions."[9]

From this point of view, we might be tempted to interpret Michael Jackson's numerous physical transformations as analogous to Ford's yearly production of its "new" models. Jackson produces a new version of himself for each concert tour or album release. The notion of a new identity is certainly not original with Jackson. However, the mode of his transformations and its implications define a striking difference between Michael Jackson and any previous performer's use of identity change. This is particularly true with respect to David Bowie, whose transformation from Ziggy Stardust to The Thin White Duke were enacted as artiface. Concocted out of makeup and fashion, Bowie's identities enjoyed the precarious reality of mask and costume. The inconcrete nature of Bowie's identities, coupled with their theatricality, were, then, the bases for generating disconcerting social commentary. For Jackson, on the other hand, each new identity is the result of surgical technology. Rather than a progressively developing and maturing public figure who erupts into the social fabric newly made up to make a new statement, Jackson produces each new Jackson as a simulacrum of himself whose moment of appearance signals the immediate denial of the previous Michael Jackson. Rather than making a social statement, Jackson states himself as a commodity. As a final observation, and this is in line with Jameson's thoughts on repetition, I would say that the "original" Michael Jackson, the small boy who sang with the Jackson Five, also becomes a commodified identity with respect to the subsequent Michael Jacksons. In Jameson's words, "the first time event is by definition not a repetition of anything: it is then reconverted into repetition the second time around." [10] The Michael Jackson of the Jackson Five becomes "retroactively" a simulacrum once the chain of Jackson simulacra comes into being. Such a reading is a devasting cancellation of the desire for black expression in mass culture which Toni Morrison set in motion when she asked us to imagine Claudia dancing in the movies with Bojangles. This interpretation sees the commodity form as the denial of difference. All moments and modes are merely incorporated in its infinite seriality.

Commodity seriality negates the explosive potential inherent in transformation, but transformation, as it is represented culturally, need not only be seen as an expression of commodity seriality. In the black American entertainment tradition, the original metaphor for transformation, which is also a source for Michael Jackson's use of identity change, is the blackface worn by nineteenth-century minstrel performers. When, in 1829, Thomas Dartmouth Rice, a white man, blackened his face and jumped "Jim Crow" for the first time, he set in motion one of the most popular entertainment forms of the nineteenth century. By the late 1840s, the Christy Minstrels had defined many of the standard routines and characters, including the cakewalk and the Tambo and Bones figures that are synonymous with minstrelsy. In the 1850s and 1860s, hundreds of minstrel troupes were touring the states, generally on a New York–Ohio axis. Some even journeyed to London where they were equally successful. By the 1880s and 1890s there were far fewer troupes, but the shows put on by the few remaining companies expanded into mammoth extravaganzas, such as those mounted by the Mastodon Minstrels.

Broadly speaking, the minstrel shows portrayed blacks as the "folk," a population wholly formed under a paternalistic southern plantation system. They were shown to be backward and downright simpleminded; they were lazy, fun loving, and foolish, given to philandering, gambling, and dancing; they were victimized, made the brunt of slapstick humor and lewd jokes. The men were "pussy whipped" and the women were liars, cheats, and flirts. No wonder the minstrel shows have been so roundly condemned by Afro-American intellectuals, including Nathan Huggins, for whom the most crippling aspect of minstrelsy is the way its popularity prevented the formation of an alternative "Negro ethnic theater." [11] Nevertheless, a few critics have advanced the notion that minstrelsy represents a nascent form of people's culture, whose oblique—albeit distorted—reference to real plantation culture cannot be denied. [12] What is interesting is that neither position in this debate seems adequate to explain why blacks performed in minstrel shows, and why, when they did so, they too blackened their faces with burnt cork and exaggerated the shape of their lips and eyes. If the shows promoted the debasement of blacks, can black participation in them be explained by their immense popularity, or the opportunity the shows provided to blacks in entertainment, or the money a performer might make? If the shows were an early form of people's theater, was it, then, necessary for blacks in them to reiterate the racist stereotyping that blackface signified?

An initial response to those questions is provided by Bert Williams, one of the most famous black actors of this century, who joined the Ziegfeld Follies against the protests of the entire white cast. Williams proved incredibly successful, earning up to $2,500 a week. Nevertheless, he chose throughout his career to perform in blackface. In their anthology of black theater, James Hatch and Ted Shine suggest that blackface was for Bert Williams "a badge of his trade, a disguise from which to work, and a positive reminder to his audience that he was a black man." [13] These explanations get at the motives behind Bert Williams's choice, but I suggest we consider blackface as something more than a disguise or mask and apprehend it, instead, as a metaphor that functions in two systems of meanings. On the one hand, it is the overt embodiment of the southern racist stereotyping of blacks; but as a theatrical form, blackface is a metaphor for the commodity. It is the sign of what people paid to see. It is the image consumed, and it is the site of the actor's estrangement from self into role. Blackface is a trademark, and as such it can be either full or empty of meaning.

In his comprehensive study on minstrelsy, Eric Lott interprets blackface in terms of race and gender relations. He describes it as the site where all sorts of dissimulations and transformations take place that have their origin in social tensions. In blackface, white men portrayed black men; black men portrayed white men portraying black men; and men, both black and white, became female impersonators and acted the "wench." Audiences enjoyed flirting with the notion of actually seeing a black man perform on stage, when such was generally not allowed. And they enjoyed the implications of seeing men put themselves in the bodies of women so as to enact sexual affairs with other men. Blackface allowed the transgression of sexual roles and gender definition even while it disavowed its occurrence. As Eric Lott points out, minstrelsy was highly inflected with the desire to assume the power of the "other," even while such power was being denigrated and denied. As he puts it, minstrelsy was "a derisive celebration of the power of blacks"[14] (and I would add, of women, too) which is contained within the authority of the white male performer. So, on the one hand, blackface is heavily laden with overt racist and sexist messages; on the other hand, it is hollowed of social meanings and restraints. This makes blackface a site where the fear of miscegenation can be both expressed and managed, where misogyny can be affirmed and denied, and where race and gender can be stereotyped and transgressed.

The contradictory meanings of minstrelsy offer another way of looking at Michael Jackson, who from this perspective emerges as the embodiment of blackface. His physical transformations are his trademark—a means for bringing all the sexual tensions and social contradictions present in blackface into a contemporary form. From this perspective, Jackson's artistic antecedent is not Diana Ross or even Bert Williams, but the great black dancer Juba, who electrified white audiences with his kinetic skill which had people seeing his body turned back to front, his legs turned left to right. While Juba performed in blackface, his body was for him yet a more personal means of generating parody and ironic self-dissimulation. Juba's "Imitation Dance" offered his highly perfected rendition of each of the blackfaced white actors who had defined a particular breakdown dance, as well as an imitation of himself dancing his own consumate version of breakdown. This is the tradition that best defines Michael Jackson's 1989 feature-length video, *Moonwalker*. Here, Jackson includes video versions of himself as a child singing and dancing the Motown equivalent of breakdown, then ricochets this "real" image of himself off the image of a contemporary child impersonator who imitates Jackson in dress, face, song, and dance, and finally, bounces these versions off a dozen or so other memorable Jackson images—his teen years, Captain EO—which are preserved on video and appear like so many Jackson personae or masks. In fading from one version of Jackson to the next, or splicing one Jackson against another, *Moonwalker* represents transformation as formalized content. Not surprisingly, most of the stories on the video are about transformation—a theme stunningly aided by the magic of every cinematic special effect currently available.

In opening her analysis of the sambo and minstrel figures, Sylvia Wynter states that the "imperative task" of black culture is "transformation." Wynter's optimistic account of the power of stigmatized black and popular culture to create a system of subversive countermeanings leads her to see minstrelsy as the place where black culture "began the cultural subversion of the normative bourgeois American reality." [15] Michael Jackson's *Moonwalker* opens with the desire for equally sweeping social change. The initial piece, "Man in the Mirror," surveys the faces of the world's disinherited, vanquished, and famished people, along with their often martyrized benefactors—Gandhi, Sister Teresa, the Kennedy brothers, Martin Luther King, Jr.—against whom are counterposed the images of fascist oppressors from Hitler to the Klan. The message of the song, hammered home to the beat of the refrain, is that if you want to change the world, begin with the Man in the Mirror. That the desire for social change is deflected into multitudenous self-transformations is to varying degrees the substance of all the video narratives assembled in *Moonwalker*. Two of these specifically demonstrate how blackface is redefined in the rubric of contemporary commodity culture.

In "Smooth Criminal," the grease and burnt cork that turned the minstrel artist into Jim Crow or Zip Coon are replaced by the metallic shell and electronic circuitry that turn Michael Jackson into a larger-than-life transformer robot. The story has Michael Jackson pitted against a depraved white drug lord bent on taking over the world by turning all young children (white and black; boys and girls) into addicts. The drug lord is aided by an army of gestapo troops, reminiscent of the stormtroopers from *Star Wars*. At the story's climactic moment, the army encircles Jackson, trapping him in the depths of their drug factory hideaway. Writhing on the floor under a relentless spotlight, completely surrounded by the faceless army, Michael Jackson is caught in a setting that dramatically summons up a parallel image: the rock star, alone on the stage in an immense stadium where he is beseiged by a wall of faceless fans. The emblematic similarity between the story of persecution and subjugation and the experience of rock stardom establishes a connection to the minstrel tradition where the theater was the site for enacting the forms of domination and their potential transformation.

Jackson's submission to the forces of domination is broken when the drug lord begins to beat a little girl whom he has kidnapped and whose cries push Jackson to the brink of superhuman action. Suddenly, Jackson's face, already tightly stretched over surgically sculpted bones, becomes even more taut—indeed, metallic. His eyes lose their pupils, glow, and become lasers. Jackson rises, and a control box pops out of his stomach. His feet and arms sprout weapons. Michael Jackson is a robot. The transformation makes a stunning commentary on all Jackson's real-life physical transformation that *Moonwalker* cites and suggests that robotics is the logical next step in medical technology's reshaping of the human body.

However, the most powerful implication of Jackson's transformation—one that every child will grasp—is that Michael Jackson has made himself into a commodity. He is not a generic robot, but specifically a transformer. This Jackson demonstrates when he subsequently transforms himself from robot warrior into an armed space vehicle. In this shape, he ultimately vanquishes the drug lord. In another essay, I developed the significance of transformers as metaphors of gendering under capitalism.[16] Jackson's assimilation to transformer includes the erasure of gender traits simultaneous with the assumption of absolute male sexual potency. The transformer represents industrial technology in commodity form. If in this country, industry and the market are controlled by a largely white male hierarchy, then Jackson's transformation figurally raises the question of social power relationships. The question is whether Jackson, in becoming a transformer, appropriates an image associated with white male economic and sexual domination or whether he has been assimilated to the image. Is this a case of usurping power, or has Jackson, as "other," merely been absorbed? Another way to look at this question is to ask if the appropriation of the commodity form is in any way analogous to previous instances where blacks have appropriated white cultural forms. We might substitute religion for the commodity and ask some of the same questions. Has religion, commencing with colonization and the slave trade, functioned as an ideological arm of white domination, or does the appropriation of religion by the black church represent the reverse of colonization, where blacks denied salvation claimed God for their own? We are back to the dilemma I initially posed with reference to Toni Morrison, who might well argue that the transformer represents a form of colonization even more dehumanizing than that embodied by the blue-eyed Pecola because in it race and gender are wholly erased. In contrast, Kobena Mercer might be tempted to see the transformer as today's equivalent of the conk.

As if in response, and to consider the commodity from yet another angle, Michael Jackson enacts another parable of transformation. In "Speed Demon," the video wizards employ the magic of claymation to turn Michael Jackson into a Brer Rabbit figure, whose invisible popular culture referent is, of course, Gumby. "He was once a little green blob of clay, but you should see what Gumby can do today." This is a refrain familiar to children's television audiences of the early seventies. The song is about transformation from blob of clay to boy, making Gumby a proto-transformer. Indeed, Gumby's boyish degendering corresponds with the erasure of gender traits that we see in the transformers. His body absolutely smooth and malleable, Gumby's only noticeable features are his big eyes and rubbery mouth. If gender is deemphasized, Gumby's green hue suggests possible racial otherness. This is not a farfetched interpretation, as Gumby coincides with the advent of "Sesame Street," where multiracial and multicultural neighborhoods are depicted by collections of multicolored humans, monsters, and animals. Purple, yellow, green, and blue are the colors of "Sesame Street's" Rainbow Coalition.

"Speed Demon" reworks the themes of pursuit and entrapment in a theatrical setting that parallels, although in a more lighthearted way, the portrayal of these themes in the transformer script. In this case Michael Jackson is pursued by overly zealous fans, who, during the course of a movie studio tour, recognize Michael Jackson and chase him through various lots and sound stages. The fans are grotesquely depicted as clay animations with horribly gesticulating faces and lumpy bodies. At one point Jackson appears to be cornered by a host of frenzied fans, but manages to slip into a vast wardrobe building where he discovers a full head mask of a rather goofy, but sly-looking rabbit. At this point, Jackson undergoes claymation transformation. This completely redefines the terms of his relationship to his pursuers. Claymation turns Michael Jackson into a motorcycle-riding Brer Rabbit, the trickster of the Afro-American folk tradition who toys with the oppressors, outsmarts them, outmaneuvers them—and with glee! The Speed Demon is Gumby, he is Brer Rabbit, and he is also most definitely Michael Jackson, whose "wet curl" look caps the clay head of the rabbit, and whose trademark dance, the moonwalk, is the rabbit's particular forte.

At the tale's conclusion, Michael, having eluded his pursuers, greets the sunrise in the California desert. Here he removes the rabbit disguise, which at this point is not the claymation body double but a simple mask and costume that Jackson unzips and steps out of. But lo and behold, the discarded costume takes on a life of its own and becomes a man-sized moonwalking rabbit who challenges Jackson to a dancing duel. In a video rife with transformations and doublings, this is the defining instance. In dance, the vernacular of black cultural expression, the conflict between the artist and his exaggerated, folksy, blackface alter ego is enacted.[17] Like Juba dancing an imitation of himself, Michael Jackson separates himself from his blackface and out-moonwalks the commodity form of himself.

In posing transformation as the site where the desire for black cultural autonomy coincides with the fetishization of commodity capitalism, *Moonwalker* denies commodity serialty. Instead, it defines the commodity form in the tradition of blackface as the nexus of struggle. The cultural commodity is not neutral, but instead defines a zone of contention where the terms of cultural definition have been largely determined by the white male–dominated system of capitalist production and reified by the fetishizing nature of the commodity itself.

In my accounts of "Smooth Criminal" and "Speed Demon," I suggest that some commodity manifestations provide more room for counterstatements than others. The transformers are so closely associated with high-tech capitalism that they offer little opening other than the ambiguity over appropriation versus assimilation. By comparison, the complex relationship between Gumby, Brer Rabbit, and Michael Jackson creates a space where the collision between black vernacular and mass media forms suggests the subversion of domination. "Speed Demon" deconstructs the commodity form, and with it, Michael Jackson as well, who, by the end of the video, emerges as a multiple subject reflected back from a dozen commodified mirror images. *Moonwalker* engages commodity fetishism and opens up the commodity form, but does it provide a platform for the emergence of what Stuart Hall calls the "concrete historical subject"?[18] Is there a *Meridian* in this text, capable of discovering a self out of the social fragments and conflicts? Can anything approaching the autonomous subject be discerned in this text? *Moonwalker* suggests a split between contemporary black women's fiction, which strives to create images of social wholeness based on the rejection of commodity capitalism, and what seems to be a black male position which sees the commodity as something that can be played with and enjoyed or subverted. Where Michael Jackson tricks the commodity form, and is able to do so precisely because its meanings are fetishized and therefore not culturally specific, Alice Walker refuses commodity fetishism and, in *The Color Purple,* imagines a form of cottage industry that has Celie organizing the collective production of customized pants for her extended community of family and friends. Jackson reaches back into the culture industry to minstrelsy and seizes blackface, updates it in contemporary forms, and unites himself with the history of black male actors who were made and unmade by their relationship to the commodity. Contrariwise, Alice Walker looks back upon commodity production, sees its earliest manifestation in the "slops" produced for slaves,[19] its continuation in the fashion industry that destroyed Morrison's Hagar, and summarily denies the possibility of the mass-produced commodity as having anything to offer Afro-Americans.

What Is Your Nation?: Reconnecting Africa and Her Diaspora through Paule Marshall's *Praisesong for the Widow*

In "Lave Tete," the third book of *Praisesong for the Widow*,[1] old Lebert Joseph accosts Avey Johnson with the question, "And what you is? What's your nation?"; both the question and the passionate manner of its asking throw Avey into confusion. Yet in its answer lies the key to her self-understanding. What follows is a reading of this novel to unearth the many cultural signs the widow needs to recognize or acknowledge, in order to answer that central question. Paule Marshall's project in this deceptively simple novel is a remarkably bold one. This novel becomes a journey not only for Avey, but for her readers, for to appreciate the widow's experiences fully, the reader must journey with her in the same active process of recognizing and reassembling cultural signs.

When the novel opens, the heroine, Avey Johnson, is about to interrupt a luxury cruise through the Caribbean Islands to return home to North White Plains, New York. But the journey she eventually takes instead is one she could never have anticipated. Both the interrupted journey and the unexpected journey take on great significance as metaphors of the progress of her life, a life whose meaning she no longer understands. By the end of the journey, that life has taken on new meaning, and it becomes a representative journey for all New World diaspora children.

In speaking of this work as a diaspora novel, I read it alongside such novels as Alice Walker's *The Color Purple*, Ama Ata Aidoo's *Our Sister Killjoy*, Michelle Cliff's *Abeng*, and Maryse Conde's *Heremakhonon*, among many others—novels by black women throughout Africa and the African diaspora which tackle questions about women reclaiming their stories in a context in which storytelling becomes part of a larger project of self-revalidation.

Storytelling is here one of a wealth of nonwritten cultural forms that must be reinvested with meaning. The validation of such forms within the work is a part of that lifelong process in Marshall's writing which led Edward Brathwaite to celebrate her, as many as fifteen years ago, as a novelist of the "African Reconnection." [2] The meaning of Africa in this (con)text is vital for Marshall, for whom reconnecting the scattered peoples, on the shared foundation of their African heritage, has been a continuing theme. In this work she gives her most thorough examination to date of the dynamics of this relationship. Along with the inheritance of stories, such elements as the efficacy of dreams and the ritual of song, dance, and drama are all delicately woven into the fabric of the tale, as Avey examines the tapestry of her life, to piece together again those parts that were becoming unraveled.

Marshall's concern is to take us through a journey of self-recognition and healing. Her text requires of us that we have a knowledge of "diaspora literacy," [3] an ability to read a variety of cultural signs of the lives of Africa's children at home and in the New World. Marshall articulates the scattering of the African peoples as a trauma—a trauma that is constantly repeated anew in the lives of her lost children. The life of the modern world and the conditions under which Afro-Americans have to live, the sacrifices they must make to succeed on the terms of American society, invariably mean a severing from their cultural roots, and, as Avey learns to her cost, this is tantamount to a repetition, in her private life, of that original historical separation. This is a sacrifice too high. But to understand the nature of the journey and the magnitude of the sacrifice, it is necessary not simply to mark the passage of Avey's journey but to become fellow travelers with her. It is not only Marshall's heroine, but Marshall's readers as well who need to acquire "diaspora literacy." For to do so is to be able to see again the fragments that make up the whole, not as isolated individual and even redundant fragments, but as part of a creative and sustaining whole.

Thus the first task for the reader is to learn, like the widow whose journey we experience, to recognize the cultural signs of a past left littered along our roads of doubtful progress. The crucial factor about *Praisesong* is that it is a novel about the dispossession of the scattered African peoples from their past and their original homeland and, in the present, from their communities and from each other. The boldness of Marshall's project here is to take us through a private history of material acquisition and cultural dispossession, which becomes a metaphor for the history of the group, the history of the African in the New World. The challenge therefore is not to look at literacy or cultural artifact as abstraction, but as a concrete aspect of our lives, where our meaning—our story—becomes what we can read and what we can no longer, or never could, read about ourselves and our lives. The act of reading becomes an exercise in identifications—to recognize life experiences and historic transformations that point the way toward a celebration, a coming together attainable only through an understanding and acceptance of the demands of the past, which are transformed into a gift for the future.

This project is undertaken by giving us a text full of signs and allusion which each reader responds to differently and thus reflects, each in his or her own way, the experience of the widow. For example, an Afro-American reader who recognizes lines from the songs of Nina Simone,[4] but for whom the Carriacou Tramp has no meaning or resonance, will experience the journey differently from a West African such as myself, for whom the opposite is true;[5] the ceremonies for the dead on Carriacou may resonate with meaning while references to specific blues songs go unremarked. The experience of the widow's journey is relived differently, depending on how many, and which, of the many cultural icons and codes within the text the reader can register.

These gestures of significance that need to be registered begin, even before the first word of the novel had been read, with the words of title, *Praisesong for the Widow*. For Africans, a praisesong is a particular kind of traditional heroic poem. Sung in various communities over the entire continent, praisesongs embrace all manner of elaborate poetic form, but are always specifically ceremonial social poems, intended to be recited or sung in public at anniversaries and other celebrations, including the funerals of the great. Praisesongs may embrace the history, myths, and legends of a whole people or their representative and can be used to celebrate communal triumph or the greatness of rulers, and the nobility of the valiant and brave, whether in life or death. Important for its use here, they can also be sung to mark social transition. Sung as a part of rites of passage, they mark the upward movement of a person from one group to the next. This novel therefore celebrates for the widow her coming to terms with her widowhood—a reconciliation that has greater implications than a coming to terms with the loss of an individual husband only. The whole narrative in itself acts as a "praisesong" for the widow, with the narrator as the griot. Specifically also the title refers to the communal song and the dance of the "beg pardon" at the end of the novel, which themselves become a praisesong for the widow in homage to her homecoming.

Praisesong for the Widow is a tribute in praise of the homecoming of a woman who succeeds in making an awesome physical and spiritual odyssey. Avey's epiphany is presented to us as an arduous progress through a partially familiar landscape littered with cultural artifacts as clues. The widow's narrative becomes a map, with music, song, dance, dress, and ritual as the cultural registers we need to decode to follow her across the terrain to journey's end. But journey's end is Africa. By the end of her journey, Avey has symbolically reversed the diasporic journey and recrossed that wrenching middle passage. Through Avey's life Africa is once more reinvested with worth, the continent is no longer fractured from human history but restored to consciousness with valid meaning. Through the healing of one of Africa's lost daughters, a scattered people are made whole again, and the question "What is your nation?" is no longer a bewildering and devastating mystery.

By the time Avey understands the meaning of that mystery, she also knows that years before, as a child, she was given the key to answering it through a story told by her Great-Aunt Cuney. In this work, storytelling is not only a metaphor for cultural self-possession and wholeness, it is a literal injunction. The quest the widow is embarked on culminates in her taking upon herself the mantle, bequeathed by her Great-Aunt Cuney, to tell the story of the African slaves at Ibo Landing. This story, though it plays a complex symbolic part within the text, is itself a simple one: Avatara's Great-Aunt Cuney takes her to the landing and narrates that the Ibo slaves had arrived at that very point on the river, by boat from the offshore slave ships, but as soon as they set foot on shore had stopped. Without a word they had studied the place and, with deep vision, had seen the whole history of slavery and suffering that awaited them all there, and had stepped out, shackles and all, and walked firmly upon the water with nothing to stop them, heading back home again to Africa. This story serves in the text as the representation of spiritual understanding and the will to survive and triumph. In taking it upon herself as her legacy, the widow finds a meaning to her own personal journey, which then also transcends the self and the family. She becomes a griot for the collective whole, recounting the story which represents the saving history of the group, and thus finds a way to look to the future without rendering the past valueless.

However, the journey to inherit this story is in itself, within the text, made up of more than the recognition of the importance of the story of the slaves at Ibo Landing. For the widow, storytelling, including the telling of her own story which we see in process, must be undertaken within a cultural context, a context that includes, as indexes in the composition of her story, aspects such as dress, food, dance, and formal and informal ritual, in addition to words themselves. It is not only the story itself which has meaning, but the circumstances of its telling, a form of ritual acculturation for the seven-year-old Avey:

> At least twice a week, in the late afternoon, . . . her great-aunt would take the field hat down from its nail on the door and solemnly place it over her headtie and braids. With equal ceremony she would then draw around her the two belts she and the other women her age in Tatem always put on when going out: one belt at the waist of their plain, long-skirted dresses, and the other (this one worn in the belief that it gave them extra strength) strapped low around their hips like the belt of a sword or a gun holster.
> "Avatara"
> There was never any need to call her, because Avey, keeping out of sight behind the old woman, would have already followed suit, girding her non-existent hips with a second belt (an imaginary one) and placing—with the same studied ceremony—a smaller version of the field hat (which was real) on her head. (32)

At the end of her journey Avey resolves to return to Tatem to tell the story her aunt had taught her, with the same words and gestures each time over the years, which Avey had learned in the exact manner her aunt had told it—the way griots inherit through oral transmission the sacred histories of the people. The *form* of their story is what helps

memory carry the message, so as a true griot, Avatara learns her in-
cantation and passes it on to her own grandchildren, physical and spiritual, in the same way her great-aunt had learned it from that
grandmother whose name she bears. It is the acceptance of the significance of all these factors, which she has spent three decades layering
over with the accoutrements of affluence, which she needs to reclaim—to return to the self beneath the expensive clothes Great-Aunt
Cuney strips off her with such violence in her dream.

At the point in the narrative at which Avey Johnson is posed the
question concerning me here, she is like a postulant being prepared
for consecration, and the living Lebert Joseph replaces dreams and
memories of Great-Aunt Cuney as the initiate who is to guide her
through the final stages of her rituals. The placing of the encounter
itself is crucial: it is situated in the book entitled "Lave Tete," with
the widow at a moment of crisis; she is fleeing a ship that for her has
become an emblem of burning hell, trying to get back to her house
in North White Plains. But that house too is under assault as, in her
memory, it has become "the museum at the foot of Mount Pelee in
the wake of the eruption that had taken place during her absence"
(181). That those days in her life which have driven her into Lebert
Joseph's presence should be seen as cataclysmic is further emphasized
by her reference to the dream of her Great-Aunt Cuney, who "had
stood there large as life in the middle of her dream, and as a result
there was a hole the size of a crater where her life of the past three
decades had been" (196). Essentially, although Avey cannot articulate
it, she feels she has nothing to return to, nothing at least to which she
can attach any viable meaning. She is in limbo, waiting.

Before Avey can return home she is taken to the farthest reaches
of her physical journey, off course, as she sees it, to the island of Carriacou, even called the "out island" by the people of Grenada, which is
one of the most easterly of the Caribbean Islands. That is, it is closest,
physically, to the home continent of Africa. This physical closeness is
simply a physical representation of the spiritual proximity that the
widow is to see manifest.

Everything about the placing of that question by Lebert Joseph is
important. The widow's journey has been littered with icons of significance which it is incumbent on the widow as postulant, and us as
readers and fellow travelers, to recognize. She has come to this

moment from the long reflection on what she has lost on the way from Halsey Street to North White Plains, and it is those remembrances that lead her to formulate for herself an intense series of questions. In being visited by the angry ghost of Jerome, Avey is forced to ask herself the central question of her life: Was the price paid for their material success and security truly necessary?

> They had behaved, she and Jay, as if there had been nothing about themselves worth honoring! Couldn't they have done differently? Hadn't there perhaps been another way? Questions which scarcely had any shape to them flooded her mind, and she struggled to give them form. Would it have been possible to have done both? That is, to have wrested, as they had done over all those years, the means needed to rescue them from Halsey Street and to see the children through, while preserving, safeguarding, treasuring those things that had come down to them over the generations, which had defined them in a particular way. The most vivid, the most valuable part of themselves! . . . What would it have taken? What would it have called for? The answers were as formless as the questions inundating her mind. They swept through her in the same bewildering flood of disconnected words and images. (139)

There are in a sense two sets of loss: one set she herself knows as loss; the other she does not even realize she once possessed. For Avey the meaning of loss and the essential spirit of themselves as family and as community are signified for her in the small things she has missed:

> They were things which would have counted for little in the world's eye. To an outsider, some of them would even appear ridiculous, childish, *cullud*. Two grown people holding a pretend dance in their living room! And spending their Sunday mornings listening to gospels and reciting fragments of old poems while eating coffee cake! A ride on a Jim Crow bus each summer to visit the site of an unrecorded, uncanonized miracle!
> Such things would matter little to the world. They had nonetheless been of utmost importance. . . . Not important in themselves so much as in the larger meaning they held in the qualities which imbued them. . . . Something vivid and affirming and

charged with feeling had been present in the small rituals that had once shaped their lives. . . . Moreover, something in those small rites, an ethos held in common, had reached back beyond her life and beyond Jay's to join them to the vast unknown lineage that made their being possible. And this link, these connections, heard in the music and in the praise songs of a Sunday had protected them and put them in possession of a kind of power. (136–137)

These memories trouble her spirit now because she has killed the joy that was in them, distanced herself from them, without knowing how, and with no reason why. They no longer are a living aspect of her life, but exist only as treasured memories. When she recollects them, they are still lifes, emblems of those dancing selves long disappeared. In this respect they bear the same relationship to her life as the dances Lebert Joseph speaks of bear to the Afro-American and Afro-Caribbean community at large. The acknowledgment of their importance is dramatized through the steps of a different, more ancient, dance.

Avey's journey, which is to end in the first steps of this ancient dance, had started years before, on that same walk to Ibo Landing, which would always take her past the small church, filled with the elders taking part in the Ring Shout:

Through the open door the handful of elderly men and women still left, and who still held to the old ways, could be seen slowly circling the room in a loose ring.

They were propelling themselves forward at a curious gliding shuffle which did not permit the soles of the heavy work shoes they had on to ever once lift from the floor. Only their heels rose and fell with each step, striking the worn pineboard with a beat that was as precise and intricate as a drum's. . . . They allowed their failing bodies every liberty, yet their feet never once left the floor or, worse yet, crossed each other in a dance step. (34)

By the end of her journey, Avey is to find herself dancing such a dance, and her journey is a carefully worked out reincorporation of song, dance, and ritual, specifically as it relates to the recognition of continuing African traditions. It is for this reason that Avey's physical journeying ends with her participation in the sacred excursion to Carriacou, a ritual that only those who share in it appreciate. Her guide on this trip, and central to her understanding of the meaning of her private journey, is the old man Lebert Joseph.

Lebert Joseph recognizes the vital importance of those traditions that carry history and meaning—the nation dances and the songs associated with them. It is these cultural forms which are sacred, for, as he demonstrates to Avey with the Bongo song about Ti-Walker and Zabette, they carry the myths and legends of the origins of the people and their histories of pain, triumph, and survival. It is the festival, its rituals and the oral culture surrounding it, which keeps the sacred unity of the group. And their significance is beyond any contemporary "reality"; thus for Lebert Joseph the word *Juba* still resonates of a once great imperial seat "from memories that had come down to him in the blood" rather than the "forgotten backwater that it has become" (178).

However, it is important to recognize Lebert Joseph himself as an iconographic figure. Old Lebert Joseph in this text performs the role of the deity Legba.[6] The name given in Ewe religious practice to the god of households and thresholds, and to the Yoruba god of crossroads who is the messenger of the gods, is, in Afro-Caribbean practice also, the lame god of crossroads. It is he who acts as the widow's guide, leading her back, at this crossroads in her life, to those ancestors whose spirits she has neglected or sacrificed, in order to move her onward. The association with the ancestors, and of him as guide, is made very clear. After his initial taciturn reception, in indignation over her ignorance of his origins, he starts chanting his lineage "like some Old Testament prophet chronicling the lineage of his tribe" (163). Furthermore, like the Ibos of the landing, he is farsighted and can read spiritual histories. Avey knows when she meets him that his penetrating look "marked him as someone who possessed ways of seeing that went beyond mere sight and ways of knowing that outstripped ordinary intelligence and thus had no need for words" (172). When they eventually arrive in Carriacou for the festival, even the physical description of this lame old man serves to underscore his relationship to the gods. The widow sees him almost as an apparition just at that moment when his function is to guide her into the realm that is going to reunite her with her past; like all gods of crossroads he walks before her into the unfamiliar realms through which she must travel. When she has made this last crossing of her journey, over the threshold into the ancestral home where the Beg Pardon takes place, she will then be able to tell of her origins.

It is this ability to tell her own story which is the final end of the tale, and when she meets Lebert Joseph and first asks him for shelter, she cannot answer his question about her self. In mythic terms, Avey is the traveler who must first find the answer to the question of origins before she can return home. It is the memory of Great-Aunt Cuney and the presence of Lebert Joseph which are to serve as her compassionate, but relentless, guides to this mystery. Lebert Joseph recognizes how hard a thing it is not to be able to name one's true nation and, like Great-Aunt Cuney, recognizes that Avey needs to learn to do this to be restored. Therefore, as Great-Aunt Cuney had waylaid her in her dream and forced her back to Ibo Landing, so Lebert Joseph hijacks her to Carriacou.

Before she arrives there, however, on her journey out, she has a series of important recollections of other journeys—childhood journeys to Tatem as commanded by Cuney, to spend her summers making that most central of journeys, the walk to Ibo Landing, to hear narrated the story of those slaves who walked on the waters back to Africa. She also recalls, while standing on the wharf:

> Boat rides up the Hudson! Sometimes, standing with her family amid the growing crowd on the pier, waiting for the Robert Fulton to heave into sight, she would have the same strange sensation as when she stood beside her great-aunt outside the church in Tatem watching the elderly folk inside perform the Ring Shout. As more people arrived to throng the area beside the river and the cool morning air warmed to the greetings and talk, she would feel what seemed to be hundreds of slender threads streaming out from her navel and from the place where her heart was to enter those around her. . . . Then it would seem to her that she had it all wrong, and the threads didn't come from her, but from them, from everyone on the pier, issuing out of their navels and hearts to stream into her as she stood there. . . . She visualized the threads as being silken, like those

used in the embroidery on a summer dress, and of a hundred different colors, and although they were thin to the point of invisibility, they felt as strong entering her as the lifelines of woven hemp that trailed out into the water at Coney Island. If she cared to she could dog-paddle (she couldn't swim) out to where the Hudson was deepest and not worry. The moment she began to founder those on the shore would simply pull in the silken threads and haul her in.

While the impression lasted she would cease being herself; instead, for those moments, she became part of, indeed the center of a huge wide confraternity. (190–191)

In fact her first recollection is not of this journey, but of the film presentation given by her daughter and spiritual sister, Marion, of a trip she had made to Ghana. The colors, sounds, and "pageantry of umbrellas" of the milling tide of people beside her reminded her of Marion's home movie. It is this recollection of Ghana that first makes the scene on the wharf so familiar and subsequently reminds her of that boat ride up the Hudson River to Bear Mountain. The triple link of communal history is thus complete, from Ghana to the Hudson River of her childhood, to Carriacou, through Tatem—because Tatem also is associated with the feeling of unity symbolized by her image of the silken threads, when standing with her great-aunt watching the worshipers at the Ring Shout. It is important that all the locations, both the north and the south of the United States, the Caribbean Islands, and Africa, the home continent, are embraced in this memory of the connections made by the silken threads.

But the reconnection is not only in this symbolic perception. That the widow is on a physical journey which ends in a dance is a fundamental part of her restoration, and this journey of restoration to the homeland of Africa is as painful as that of initial separation. There is a deliberate sudden and abrupt evocation of the middle passage as the widow from the United States crosses to Carriacou and remembers Africa:

It was nearing dusk and the *Emanuel C* was almost to port when the pall over Avey Johnson's mind lifted momentarily and she became dimly conscious. She was alone in the deck house.

That much she was certain of. Yet she had the impression as her
mind flickered on briefly of other bodies lying crowded in with
her in the hot, airless dark. A multitude it felt like lay packed
around her in the filth and stench of themselves, just as she was.
Their moans, rising and falling with each rise and plunge of the
schooner, enlarged upon the one filling her head. Their suffering—the depth of it, the weight of it in the cramped space—
made hers of no consequence. (209)

That is, on her spiritual journey from the New World back to Africa,
she reverses the middle passage and very specifically relives the original journey from Africa to the Americas. In doing this she also, in
meaning, reverses the location of the promised land, which now,
rather than being the United States as represented in the prosperity of
the plantations or, today, the Fulton Street of Jerome's success, becomes Africa as represented by Carriacou.

On the day she meets the old man who is to take her to Carriacou,
he is closing shop to go to the annual festival at Carriacou to hold the
"Big Drum" for the "Old Parents," as he calls the ancestors. Each
time he goes home, he goes to give them their remembrance, to feed
them, and to beg pardon and ask their care for all of them, present
and absent, including those who, like Avey, do not know they belong. When Lebert speaks, Avey thinks he has lost his mind, but these
are recognizable ceremonies. Such supplications to the ancestors are
still done to ensure the safe return of loved ones and to celebrate and
give thanks for their safe arrival when the ancestors and the gods
comply.

Furthermore, in her remembrance of Marion's talk about Ghana,
she recollected Marion speaking of a New Yam Festival and of feeding
the ancestors. This ritual, when Lebert Joseph mentions it to her,
seems strange to Avey. Yet when it actually happens, this too seems
quite normal, as it reminds her of a burial in Tatem where the old
man's favorite foods had been prepared and laid beside the coffin.
Thus these seemingly meaningless rituals from Ghana and fragmented
memories from her childhood in Tatem are reconnected here in Carriacou; in Lebert Joseph's festival we have the link made—the survival
of a festival that is culturally both religious and social in origins and
purpose. It keeps the whole community of the living and the dead

united, and keeps all the forces of life in harmony for another season. The ancestors must be remembered for their continuing protection, and failing to keep their memory alive leads to the destruction of the community.

Yet these rituals of remembrance are not simply idiotic romance on the part of the old man. The significance of his passion comes to Avey when she finally arrives at the feast itself and sees what a small, pathetic-seeming gathering it is:

> The bare bones. The Big Drum—Lebert Joseph's much vaunted Big Drum—was the bare bones of a fete. . . . To her surprise though she felt neither disappointment nor anger. Rather she found herself as the time passed being drawn more and more to the scene in the yard. The restraint and understatement of the dancing, which was not really dancing, the deflected emotion in the voices were somehow right. *It was the essence of something rather than the thing itself she was witnessing.* (240)

Everything that has happened to the widow since her meeting with Lebert Joseph has been a ritual preparation for this moment: she has been prepared spiritually through the ordeals of her two dreams, of Jerome and Great-Aunt Cuney, and her recognition of her spiritual orphanage; she has been prepared physically by being purged on the sea voyage, by vomiting and excreting everything inside her; and she has been prepared ritually and reminded of the essential unity of the body and the soul by being bathed for absolution like a supplicant by Lebert Joseph's daughter Rosalie Parvay.

It is at the festival that we perceive the significance of all the various folk motifs that have run through the text, as the opening "Padone Mwe" movingly gathers in the scattered of the families for whom prayers must be said. Culminating in this familiar festival, the folk elements show the survivals as across the diaspora and are the physical representation of those metaphysical silken threads that the child Avey sees on the boat trip up the Hudson. This is a festival of music and dance, and in the instruments too we have clear reference to the traditional music of parts of the African continent, as they have been reformed and adapted to the Caribbean landscape and lifestyle. The use of the drums and instruments of iron, in their adapted form, serves

the same function and purpose as their still extant African counterparts; thus rum kegs covered with goatskin replace Onyame's duru-
wood and hide, but the instrument is played the same way, and to the
same purpose. Similarly, the cowbells and hoe blades, instruments of
iron for Ogun—"Iron calling for its namesake and Creator." But it is
the occasional plaintive note of the drum, interrupting its own rhythmic beat, which reminds them why they are all there:

> The theme of separation and loss the note embodied, the unac-
> knowledged longing it conveyed summed up feelings that were
> beyond words, feelings and a host of subliminal memories that
> over the years had proven more durable and trustworthy than
> the history with its trauma and pain out of which they had
> come. After centuries of forgetfulness and even denial, they re-
> fused to go away. The note was a lamentation that could hardly
> have come from the rum keg of a drum. Its source had to be the
> collective heart, the bruised still-bleeding innermost chamber of
> the collective heart. (245)

And in recognition of keeping this collective heart in memory, the
festival begins with the nation dances, as each people dances their at-
tendance and recalls their own names in memory of who they are and
have been.

But for Avey it is when she joins the old people in their movement
counterclockwise round the group of young dancers in the Carriacou
Tramp, "the step which was something more than just walking," that
the telling moment comes.

> Because it was a score of hot August nights again in her mem-
> ory, and she was standing beside her great-aunt on the dark road
> across from the church that doubled as a school. And under
> cover of the darkness she was performing that dance that wasn't
> supposed to be dancing, in imitation of the old folk shuffling in
> a loose ring inside the church. And she was singing with them
> under her breath: "Who's that ridin' the chariot/Well well well
> . . ." The Ring Shout. Standing there she used to long to give
> her great-aunt the slip and join those across the road.

> She had finally after all these decades made it across. The el-
> derly Shouters in the person of the out-islanders had reached out
> their arms like one great arm and drawn her into their midst.
> (248)

The recognition of the origins of the Ring Shout, and its role in her
private life as well as in the life of the community, restores to wholeness the fragmented communities and makes the link across waters
and boundaries of generation and time. When Avey dances, the out-
islanders pay her the homage of recognition, and this time when she
is asked who she is, she can reply by saying her correct, given name,
Avatara.

The widow's name is Avatara, a name given her by her father's
Great-Aunt Cuney in memory of Cuney's own grandmother, whose
name it was. Great-Aunt Cuney had dreamed months before Avatara
was born that she would be a girl and sent word that she should be
called Avatara because "it's my gran' done sent her. She's her little
girl." The name, therefore, which has at its root a word meaning a
passing over or a human manifestation of a continuing concept or
entity, is of great symbolic importance; it was the name of the woman
from whom Great-Aunt Cuney learned, at Tatem, the story of Ibo
Landing, which carries the spiritual burden of the tale, and it is the
name given by her to the woman who finally understands that tale
and accepts the mission to pass it on.

The homage of the old people is for her a kind of homecoming,
and in fact the following day they inform her that they think they can
tell her nation by the way she danced the Carriacou Tramp. The question she was asked barely twenty-four hours before she can now answer. The festival may only have been "the bare bones of the feast,"
but it is the dance, and not how it may be described, which proves
truly vital. Avey Johnson must learn the reason to dance the restor-
ative ritual dance of Beg Pardon. And having remembered her own
steps from the Ring Shout of her childhood, she is then able to retell
the story of Ibo Landing. This story, about the miracle of survival,
liberty, and the will to live, is the story whose continued existence in
and of itself represents that same spirit of survival and cultural inheritance passed down through the ages. Storytelling, like song singing,
becomes cultural metaphor and the carrier of cultural meaning. This

is Avatara's true inheritance. But she must remember the dance and do that first, before she comprehends the necessity of her heritage of speech.

And she begins to dance, with the passion with which she had once danced for her young husband Jay, but, like the old people at Tatem, without once ever letting the soles of her feet leave the ground; she remembered the ancient rule still observed on the mainland continent for such dances, and danced a dance that was sacred, "the shuffle designed to stay the course of history."

Introduction

1. The epigraphs are taken from Toni Morrison, "Unspeakable Things Unspoken: The Afro-American Presence in American Literature," *Michigan Quarterly Review* 38, 1 (Winter 1989): 9, and Zora Neale Hurston, *Jonah's Gourd Vine* (1934; rpt., Philadelphia: Lippincott, 1971), 17; Hortense Spillers, "Cross-Currents, Discontinuities: Black Women's Fiction," in Marjorie Pryse and Hortense Spillers, eds., *Conjuring: Black Women, Fiction, and Literary Tradition* (Bloomington: Indiana University Press, 1985), 245.

2. Examples would include Houston Baker on Harriet Jacobs, Melvin Dixon on Gayl Jones, William Andrews on Jarena Lee, and Robert Hemenway on Zora Neale Hurston.

3. Toni Cade, "Preface," in *The Black Woman* (New York: New American Library, 1970), 11.

4. Robert Hemenway, "Zora Neale Hurston and the Eatonville Anthropology," in Arna Bontemps, ed., *The Harlem Renaissance Remembered* (New York: Dodd, Mead, 1972), 190.

5. In addition to the titles cited, works published by black women in 1970 include: Nikki Giovanni, *Re:Creation* (Detroit: Broadside Press, 1970); Louise Meriwether, *Daddy Was a Number Runner* (Englewood Cliffs, N.J.: Prentice Hall, 1970); Sonia Sanchez, *We a Badd People* (Detroit: Broadside Press, 1970); and Margaret Walker, *Prophets for a New Day* (Detroit: Broadside Press, 1970).

6. Reprinted in Audre Lorde, *Chosen Poems: Old and New* (New York: Norton, 1982), 49–50.

7. Mary Helen Washington, *Black World*, August 1972, 68–75; idem, *Black World*, August 1974, 10–18; idem, *Black-Eyed Susans* (New York: Anchor Books, 1975), 10.

8. Barbara Smith, "Toward a Black Feminist Criticism," reprinted in Elaine Showalter, ed., *The New Feminist Criticism* (New York: Pantheon, 1985), 170.

9. Ibid., 174.

10. Deborah McDowell, "New Directions for Black Feminist Criticism," in Showalter, *New Feminist Criticism*, 190–93.

11. Alice Walker, "In Search of Our Mothers' Gardens," in *In Search of Our Mothers' Gardens* (New York: Harcourt, 1983), 233. The "generations" Walker evokes are both a chronology and what Kristeva terms "a signifying space."

12. Ibid., 241.

13. Toni Morrison, "Rootedness: The Ancestor as Foundation," in Mari

Evans, ed., *Black Women Writers, 1950–1980: A Critical Evaluation* (New York: Anchor Press, 1984), 339–345; Paule Marshall, "The Poets in the Kitchen," in *Reena and Other Stories* (New York: Feminist Press, 1983), 3–12.

14. In addition to those already cited, monographs and critical anthologies that contribute to this effort include Barbara Christian, *Black Feminist Criticism* (New York: Pergamon Press, 1985) and idem, *Black Women Writers: The Development of a Tradition (Westport, Conn: Greenwood Press,* 1980); Roseann Bell, Bettye Parker, and Beverly Guy-Sheftall, eds., *Sturdy Black Bridges: Visions of Black Women in Literature* (New York: Anchor Press, 1979); Cherrie Moraga and Gloria Anzaldua, eds., *This Bridge Called My Back: Writings by Radical Women of Color* (Watertown , Mass.: Persephone Press, 1981); Mari Evans, ed., *Black Women Writers, 1950–1980: A Critical Evaluation* (New York: Anchor Press, 1984); Gloria Hull, Patricia Bell Scott, and Barbara Smith, eds., *But Some of Us Are Brave* (Old Westbury, N.Y.: Feminist Press, 1982); Barbara Smith, ed., *Home Girls: A Black Feminist Anthology* (New York: Kitchen Table: Women of Color Press, 1983); Gloria Wades Gayles, *No Crystal Stair* (New York: Pilgrim Press, 1984); Mary Helen Washington, *Invented Lives: Narratives of Black Women, 1860–1960* (New York: Anchor Press, 1987); Susan Willis, *Specifying: Black Women Writing the American Experience* (Madison: University of Wisconsin Press, 1987).

15. Washington, *Invented Lives,* xvii; Spillers, "Cross-Currents, Discontinuities," 251; Hazel Carby, *Reconstructing Womanhood: The Emergence of the Afro-American Woman Novelist* (New York: Oxford University Press, 1987), 15.

16. Bruss cites these factors among many others in *Beautiful Theories: The Spectacle of Discourse in Contemporary Criticism* (Baltimore: Johns Hopkins University Press, 1982), 15–22.

17. Barbara Christian, "The Race for Theory," *Cultural Critique* (1987): 51. The utility of poststructuralist theory has of course been hotly debated among feminist and Afro-Americanist literary critics. See, for example, the dialogue between Peggy Kamuf, "Replacing Feminist Criticism," and Nancy Miller, "The Text's Heroine: A Feminist Critic and Her Fictions," both in *Diacritics* 12 (1982): 42–47 and 48–53. See also the discussion among Joyce A. Joyce, Henry Louis Gates, and Houston Baker in the following essays in *New Literary History* 18 (Winter 1987): Joyce Joyce, "The Black Canon: Reconstructing Black American Literary Criticism," 335–344; and idem, "Who the Cap Fit," 371–383; Henry Gates, " 'What's Love Got to Do With It?': Critical Theory, Integrity, and the Black Idiom," 345–362; and Houston Baker, "In Dubious Battle," 363–369. Michael Awkward contextualizes the issues for black feminist criticism in "Race, Gender, and the Politics of Reading," *Black American Literature Forum* 22 (Spring 1988): 5–27.

18. Christian, "Race for Theory," 53.

19. Jonathan Culler, *The Pursuit of Signs* (Ithaca, N.Y.: Cornell University Press, 1981), 12.

20. Gayatri Chakravorty Spivak, "Reading the World: Literary Studies in the Eighties," *In Other Words: Essays in Cultural Politics* (New York: Routledge, 1988), 102.

21. Hortense Spillers, "Interstices: A Small Drama of Words," in Carole S. Vance, ed., *Pleasure and Danger: Exploring Female Sexuality* (Boston: Routledge and Kegan Paul, 1984), 73–100. Like Christian, who argues that black people have theorized in such forms as narrative, riddles, and proverbs, Spillers overlooks the fact that black women have historically written in the now privileged mode of the nonfictional feminist text. Examples include Anna Julia Cooper, *A Voice from the South* (1892); Victoria Earle Mathews, "The Value of Race Literature" (1895); and Zora Neale Hurston, whose "Characteristics of Negro Expression" (1934) develops an illuminating theory of Afro-American aesthetics.

22. Morrison, "Unspeakable Things Unspoken," 9. In the epigraph Morrison's reference is not limited to black women, but refers to Afro-Americans in general. Teresa de Lauretis, "Feminist Studies/Critical Studies: Issues, Terms, and Contexts," in Teresa de Lauretis, ed., *Feminist Studies Critical Studies* (Bloomington: Indiana University Press, 1986), 9. A conceptualization of a multiple and shifting identity as a literary strategy may be found in Rachel Blau DuPlessis, *Writing beyond the Ending: Narrative Strategies of Twentieth-Century Women Writers* (Bloomington: Indiana University Press, 1985), 142–161.

23. All of the contributors were invited to participate in the symposium, but Barbara Christian and Valerie Smith could not attend; Gloria Hull declined to present a paper, but was an active participant. Houston Baker, Hazel Carby, and Mary Helen Washington also presented papers at the symposium, but were unable to make them available for publication in this volume.

24. Zora Neale Hurston, *Jonah's Gourd Vine* (1934; rpt., Philadelphia: Lippincott, 1971), 17.

25. bell hooks, *Talking Back* (Boston: South End Press, 1989), 9.

26. Toni Morrison, *The Bluest Eye* (New York: Holt, Rineheart and Winston, 1970), 16.

27. Henry L. Gates, *Figures in Black: Words, Signs, and the "Racial" Self* (New York: Oxford University Press, 1987), xxi.

Speaking in Tongues

1. Gloria Hull, Patricia Bell Scott, and Barbara Smith, eds., *All the Women Are White, All the Blacks Are Men, But Some of Us Are Brave* (Old Westbury, N.Y.: Feminist Press, 1982).

2. Fredric Jameson, *The Political Unconscious: Narrative as a Socially Symbolic Act* (Ithaca N.Y.: Cornell University Press, 1981), 53.

3. The phrase "gender subtext" is used by Nancy Fraser (and attributed to Dorothy Smith) in Fraser's critique of Habermas in Nancy Fraser, "What's Critical about Critical Theory?" in Seyla Benehabib and Drucilla Cornell, eds. *Feminism as Critique* (Minneapolis: University of Minnesota Press, 1987), 42.

4. See Barbara Smith, ed., *Home Girls: A Black Feminist Anthology* (New York: Kitchen Table: Women of Color Press, 1983), xxxii.

5. John Carlos Rowe, "To Live Outside the Law, You Must Be Honest: The Authority of the Margin in Contemporary Theory," *Cultural Critique* 1 (2): 67–68.

6. Mikhail Bakhtin, "Discourse in the Novel," reprinted in Michael Holquist, ed., *The Dialogic Imagination: Four Essays by M. M. Bakhtin* (Austin: University of Texas Press, 1981), 292. Bakhtin's social groups are designated according to class, religion, generation, region, and profession. The interpretative model I propose extends and rereads Bakhtin's theory from the standpoint of race and gender, categories absent in Bakhtin's original system of social and linguistic stratification.

7. V. N. Volosinov [Mikhail Bakhtin], *Marxism and the Philosophy of Language* (New York: Seminar Press, 1973), 11, 29, 38. Originally published in Russian as *Marksizm I Filosofija Jazyka* (Leningrad, 1930). Notably, this concept of the "subjective psyche" constituted primarily as a "social entity" distinguishes the Bakhtinian notion of self from the Freudian notion of identity.

8. Bakhtin, "Discourse in the Novel," 292.

9. According to Bakhtin, "The processes that basically define the content of the psyche occur not inside but outside the individual organism. . . . Moreover, the psyche "enjoys extraterritorial status . . . [as] a social entity that penetrates inside the organism of the individual personal" (*Marxism and Philosophy of Language* 25, 39). Explicating Caryl Emerson's position on Bakhtin, Gary Saul Morson argues that selfhood "derives from an internalization of the voices a person has heard, and each of these voices is saturated with social and ideological values." "Thought itself," he writes, "is but 'inner speech,' and inner speech is outer speech that we have learned to 'speak' in our heads while retaining the full register of conflicting social values." See Gary Saul Morson, "Dialogue, Monologue, and the Social: A Reply to Ken Hirshkop," in Morson, ed., *Bakhtin: Essays and Dialogues on His Work* (Chicago: University of Chicago Press, 1986), 85.

10. Teresa de Lauretis, *Technologies of Gender* (Bloomington: Indiana University Press, 1987), 2.

11. Audre Lorde, "Eye to Eye," included in *Sister Outsider* (Tramansburg, N.Y.: Crossing Press, 1984), 147.

12. Barbara Christian, "The Dynamics of Difference: Book Review of Audre Lorde's *Sister Outsider,*" in *Black Feminist Criticism: Perspectives in Black Women Writers* (New York: Pergamon Press, 1985), 209.

13. While acknowledging the importance of historicism, I can only agree with Frank Lentricchia's conclusion that in some respects Gadamer's "historicist argument begs more questions than it answers. If we can applaud the generous intention, virtually unknown in structuralist quarters, of recapturing history for textual interpetation, then we can only be stunned by the implication of what he has uncritically to say about authority, the power of tradition, knowledge, our institutions, and our attitudes." See Frank Lentricchia, *After the New Criticism* (Chicago: University of Chicago Press, 1980), 153. Certainly, Gadamer's model privileges the individual's relation to history and tradition in a way that might seem problematic in formulating a discursive model for the "noncanonical" or marginalized writer. However, just as the above model of dialogics is meant to extend Bakhtin's notion of class difference to encompass gender and race, so the present model revises and limits Gadamer's notion of tradition. See Hans-Georg Gadamer, *Truth and Method* (New York: Seabury Press, 1975), 321–325. My introduction to the significance of Gadamer's work for my own reading of black women writers was first suggested by Don Bialostosky's excellent paper entitled "Dialectic and Anti-Dialectic: A Bakhtinian Critique of Gadamer's Dialectical Model of Conversation," delivered at the International Association of Philosophy and Literature in May 1989 at Emory University in Atlanta, Georgia.

14. I extend Rachel Blau DuPlessis's term designating white women as a group privileged by race and oppressed by gender to black men as a group privileged by gender and oppressed by race. In this instance, I use "ambiguously (non)hegemonic" to signify the discursive status of both these groups.

15. Black women enter into dialogue with other black women in a discourse that I would characterize as primarily testimonial, resulting from a similiar discursive and social positionality. It is this commonality of history, culture, and language which, finally, constitutes the basis of a tradition of black women's expressive culture. In terms of actual literary dialogue among black women, I would suggest a relatively modern provenance of such a tradition, but again, one based primarily on a dialogue of affirmation rather than contestation. As I see it, this dialogue begins with Alice Walker's response to Zora Neale Hurston. Although the present article is devoted primarily to contestorial function of black women's writing, my forthcoming work (of which the present essay constitutes only a part) deals extensively with the relationships among black women writers.

16. Zora Neale Hurston, *Their Eyes Were Watching God* (1937; rpt., Urbana: University of Illinois Press, 1978). All subsequent references in the text.

17. Geneva Smitherman, *Talkin and Testifyin: The Language of Black America* (Detroit: Wayne State University Press, 1986), 58.

18. Alice Walker, "In Search of Our Mothers' Gardens," in *In Search of Our Mothers' Gardens: Womanist Prose* (New York: Harcourt Brace Jovanovich, 1984), 232.

19. Not only does such an approach problematize conventional categories and boundaries of discourse, but, most importantly, it signals the collapse of the unifying consensus posited by the discourse of universalism and reconstructs the concept of unity in diversity implicit in the discourse of difference.

20. The arrogant and misogynistic Paul tells us, "I thank God that I speak in tongues more than all of you. But in church I would rather speak five intelligible words to instruct others [i.e., to prophesy] than ten thousand words in a tongue." Even though we are perhaps most familiar with Paul's injunction to women in the church to keep silent, the prophet Joel, in the Old Testament, speaks to a diversity of voices that includes women: "In the last days, God says, I will pour out my Spirit on all people. Your sons and *daughters* will prophesy. . . . Even on my servants, both men and *women,* I will pour out my Spirit in those days, and they will prophesy" (emphasis mine). I am grateful to the Rev. Joseph Stephens whose vast scriptural knowledge helped guide me through these and other revelations.

21. Sherley Anne Williams, *Dessa Rose* (New York; William Morrow, 1986), and Toni Morrison, *Sula* (New York: Alfred A. Knopf, 1973; rpt., Bantam, 1975). Page references for these two works are given in the text.

22. I draw on the distinction between the political connotation of *suppression* and the psychological connotation of *repression.* Suppression results from external pressures and censorship imposed by the dominant culture, while repression refers to the internal self-censorship and silencing emanating from the subdominative community.

23. Nehemiah, a minor prophet in the Old Testament, is best remembered for rebuilding the walls around Jerusalem in order to fortify the city against invasion by hostile neighbors of Israel. Under his governorship, Ezra and the Levites instructed the people in the law of Moses "which the Lord had commanded for Israel." He is represented as a reformer who restored the ancient ordinances regarding proper observance of the Sabbath and the collection of the tithes; he also enforced bans against intermarriage with the Gentiles. He is perhaps most noted for the reply he sent, while rebuilding the walls, to a request from his enemies, Sanballat and Gesham, to meet with him: "I am doing a great *work* and cannot go down" (emphasis mine). William's Nehemiah, like his prototype, is devoted to the completion of a project he calls *The Work*—in this instance a book entitled *The Roots of Rebellion in the Slave Population and Some Means of Eradicating Them.* Significantly, the

name of William's character, Adam Nehemiah, reverses the name of Nehemiah Adams, author of *A South-side View of Slavery* (1854), and a Boston minister who wrote an account of his experiences in the South from a point of view apostate to the northern antislavery cause.

24. The mark of the whip inscribes Dessa as a slave while she remains within the discursive domain of slavery—a domain architecturally figured by the prison from which she escapes, but also a domain legally and more discursively defined by the Fugitive Slave Act, the runaway ads, and the courts and depositions of the nation. Note, however, that within the northern lecture halls and the slave narratives—the spatial and discursive domains of abolitionism—the marks do not identify an individual, but signify upon the character and nature of the institution of slavery.

25. Monique Wittig, "The Straight Mind," *Feminist Issues* 1 (Summer 1980): 105–106.

26. Although the status of slave is not a "misreading" within the discursive domain of slavery, it is clearly a misreading according to Dessa's self-identification.

27. One might describe Sula's birthmark as an iconicized representation rather than, strictly speaking, an inscription. For our purposes, however, it has the force of a sign marking her birth or entry into black discourse.

28. Morrison's epigram to the novel highlights the cultural significance of the birthmark by quoting from Tennessee Williams's *The Rose Tattoo:* "Nobody knew my rose of the world but me. . . . I had too much glory. They don't want glory like that in nobody's heart." In "The Mission of the Flowers," Harper describes the rose as "a thing of joy and beauty" whose mission is to "lay her fairest buds and flowers upon the altars of love." Walker's protagonist Celie compares her own sex to the "inside of a wet rose." See Frances E. W. Harper, *Idylls of the Bible* (Philadelphia: George S. Ferguson, 1901), quoted in Erlene Stetson, ed., *Black Sister* (Bloomington: Indiana University Press, 1981), 34–6, and Alice Walker, *The Color Purple* (New York: Harcourt Brace Jovanovich, 1982), 69. In naming her own character Dessa *Rose,* Williams not only plays on the above connotations, but links them, at the same time, to the transcendence implicit in "arising" and the insurgence suggested in "uprising."

29. Signifying perhaps on Hawthorne's short story "The Birthmark," Sula's mark can be reread as a sign of human imperfection and mortality, a consequence of Eve's seduction by the serpent in the Garden.

30. The fire and water image, associated with the tadpole and ashes, respectively complement and contrast with that of the snake—a symbol of death and renewal—and that of the stemmed rose—an image suggesting not only love and sexuality, but the beauty and brevity of life as a temporal experience.

31. I do not develop here the interviewer's misreadings of Dessa in the early part of the novel, nor the specific insurgent strategies with which Dessa continually outwits him. These details are treated extensively, however, in my article on Williams's "Meditations on History," the short story on which the novel is based. It appears in Linda Kauffman, ed., *Feminism and Institutions: Dialogues on Feminist Theory* (London: Basil Blackwell, 1989).

32. Williams also uses onomastics to signify upon a less rebellious female heroine, somewhat more complicitous with female ascription by the Other. See Kaja Silverman's excellent discussion of Pauline Reage's *The Story of O,* in her article "Histoire d'O: The Construction of a Female Subject," in Carole S. Vance, ed., *Pleasure and Danger: Exploring Female Sexuality* (Boston: Routledge and Kegan Paul, 1984).

33. Williams, in her earlier version of this story, "Meditations on History," privileges orality (rather than writing)—as I attempt to demonstrate in my article "W(R)iting *The Work* and Working the Rites," in Kauffman, *Feminism and Institutions.*

34. Positing a kind of "mother tongue," Julia Kristeva argues that "language as symbolic function constitutes itself at the the the cost of repressing instinctual drive and continuous relation to the mother." This order of expression, she contends, is presymbolic and linked with the mother tongue. According to Nelly Furman's interpretation, the existence of this order "does not refute the symbolic but is anterior to it, and associated with the maternal aspects of language. This order, which [Kristeva] calls 'semiotic,' is not a separate entity from the symbolic, on the contrary, it is the system which supports symbolic coherence." Continuing, Furman quotes Josette Feral in establishing a dialogical relationship between the semiotic and symbolic orders "which places the semiotic *inside* the symbolic as a condition of the symbolic, while positing the symbolic as a condition of the semiotic and founded on its repression. Now it happens that the Name-of-the-Father, in order to establish itself, needs the repression of the mother. It needs this otherness in order to reassure itself about its unity and identity, but is unwittingly affected by this otherness that is working within it." Nelly Furman, "The Politics of Language: Beyond the Gender Principle?" in Gayle Greene and Coppelia Kahn, eds., *Making A Difference: Feminist Literary Criticism* (London and New York: Methuen, 1985), 72–73.

35. In contrast to Dessa, who disrupts the dominant discourse, Sula would seem to disrupt not only discourse but, indeed, language itself.

36. Adrienne Munich, "Feminist Criticism and Literary Tradition," in Greene and Kahn, *Making a Difference,* 245–254.

37. Rachel Blau DuPlessis uses these terms to describe the "tactics of revisionary mythopoesis" created by women poets whose purpose is to "attack cultural hegemony." "Narrative displacement is like breaking the sentence,"

writes DuPlessis, "because it offers the possibility of speech to the female in this case, giving voice to the muted. Narrative delegitimation 'breaks the sequence'; a realignment that puts the last first and the first last has always ruptured conventional morality, politics, and narrative." Rachel Blau Du-Plessis, *Writing beyond the Ending* (Bloomington: Indiana University Press, 1985), 108.

38. Bakhtin, "Discourse in the Novel," 271–272.

39. Gadamer, *Truth and Method*, 321.

40. Myra Jehlen, "Archimedes and the Paradox of Feminist Criticism," reprinted in Elizabeth Abel and Emily K. Abel, eds., *The Signs Reader: Women, Gender* and *Scholarship* (Chicago: University of Chicago Press, 1983).

41. See Harold Bloom, *The Anxiety of Influence: A Theory of Poetry* (New York: Oxford University Press, 1973); Sandra M. Gilbert and Susan Gubar, eds., *The Madwoman in the Attic: The Woman Writer and the Nineteenth-Century Literary Imagination* (New Haven: Yale University Press, 1979); and Joseph T. Skerrett, "The Wright Interpretation: Ralph Ellison and the Anxiety of Influence," *Massachusetts Review* 21 (Spring 1980): 196–212.

42. Andrea Stuart in an interview with Toni Morrison, "Telling Our Story," *Sparerib* (April 1988): 12–15.

Black Feminist Theory

1. Elaine Showalter, "Critical Cross-Dressing: Male Feminism and the Woman of the Year," in Alice Jardine and Paul Smith, eds., *Men in Feminism* (Methuen: New York, 1987), 127.

2. Hazel V. Carby, *Reconstructing Womanhood: The Emergence of the Afro-American Woman Novelist* (New York: Oxford University Press, 1987, 9.

3. Mary Helen Washington, "Introduction," in Mary Helen Washington, ed., *Black-Eyed Susans: Classic Stories by and about Black Women* (Garden City, N.Y.: Anchor Books, 1975), x–xxxii.

4. See Barbara Smith, "Toward a Black Feminist Criticism," *Conditions Two* 1 (October 1977), and Deborah E. McDowell, "New Directions for Black Feminist Criticism," *Black American Literature Forum* 14. Both were reprinted in Elaine Showalter, ed., *The New Feminist Criticism: Essays on Women, Literature and Theory* (New York: Pantheon, 1985), 168–185 and 186–199, respectively.

5. See, for instance, the reprint series that McDowell edits for Beacon Press and her Rutgers University Press reprint of Nella Larsen's *Quicksand* and *Passing;* Washington's three anthologies, *Black-Eyed Susans, Midnight Birds,* and *Invented Lives* and her Feminist Press edition of Paule Marshall's *Brown Girl, Brownstones;* Nellie McKay's edition of Louise Meriwether's

Daddy Was a Number Runner; and Gloria T. Hull's edition of Alice Dunbar-Nelson's diary, *Give Us Each Day,* to name but a few. Black women are not exclusively responsible for these kinds of editorial projects. See also William Andrews, *Sisters of the Spirit: Three Black Women's Autobiographies of the Nineteenth Century;* Henry Louis Gates's edition of Harriet E. Wilson's *Our Nig* and his Oxford University Press reprint series; and Jean Fagan Yellin's edition of Harriet Jacobs's *Incidents in the Life of a Slave Girl.*

6. Peggy Kamuf, "Replacing Feminist Criticism," *Diacritics* 12 (Summer 1982): 44.

7. Nancy K. Miller, "The Text's Heroine: A Feminist Critic and Her Fictions," *Diacritics* 12 (Summer 1982): 49–50.

8. Elizabeth A. Meese, *Crossing the Double-Cross: The Practice of Feminist Criticism* (Chapel Hill: University of North Carolina Press, 1986).

9. Teresa de Lauretis, "Feminist Studies/Critical Studies: Issues, Terms, and Contexts," in Teresa de Lauretis, ed., *Feminist Studies/Critical Studies* (Bloomington: Indiana University Press, 1986), 2.

10. Ibid., 9.

11. Ibid., 10.

12. Houston A. Baker, Jr., *Blues, Ideology, and Afro-American Literature* (Chicago: University of Chicago Press, 1984).

13. See Robert B. Stepto, "Teaching Afro-American Literature: Survey or Tradition: The Reconstruction of Instruction," and Henry Louis Gates, Jr., "Preface to Blackness: Text and Pretext," both in Dexter Fisher and Robert B. Stepto, eds., *Afro-American Literature: The Reconstruction of Instruction* (New York: Modern Language Association of America, 1979), 8–24 and 44–69, respectively.

14. Robert B, Stepto, *From Behind the Veil: A Study of Afro-American Narrative* (Urbana: University of Illinois Press, 1979).

15. Baker, *Blues,* 94.

16. Ibid., 101.

17. Elizabeth V. Spelman, "Theories of Race and Gender: The Erasure of Black Women," *Quest* 5 (1979): 42.

18. Deborah E. McDowell, " 'The Changing Same': Generational Connections and Black Women Novelists," *New Literary History* 18 (Winter 1987).

19. Mary Helen Washington, " 'Taming All That Anger Down': Rage and Silence in Gwendolyn Brooks's *Maud Martha,"* in Henry Louis Gates, Jr., ed., *Black Literature and Literary Theory* (New York: Methuen, 1984), 249–262.

20. Dianne F. Sadoff, "Black Matrilineage: The Case of Alice Walker and Zora Neale Hurston," *Signs* 11 (Autumn 1985): 4–26.

21. Washington, "Taming," 249.

22. Ibid., 260.
23. Sadoff, "Black Matrilineage," 5.
26. Mary Helen Washington, "Young, Gifted and Black," *Women's Review of Books* 2 (March 1985): 3.
25. Sherley Anne Williams, "Roots of Privilege: New Black Fiction," *Ms.* 13 (June 1985): 71.
26. See Susan Willis, "Eruptions of Funk: Historicizing Toni Morrison," in *Specifying: Black Women Writing the American Experience* (Madison: University of Wisconsin Press, 1987), 83–109.
27. Andrea Lee, *Sarah Phillips* (New York: Penguin Books, 1984), 3. Subsequent references to this edition are noted in the text by page number.

But What Do We Think We're Doing Anyway

The title of this chapter is a riff on Gloria T. Hull's title, "What It Is I Think She's Doing Anyhow," in Barbara Smith, ed., *Home Girls: A Black Feminist Anthology* (New York: Kitchen Table: Women of Color Press, 1983), 124–142.

1. *Black World* 23, 10 (August 1974).
2. Toni Cade, *The Black Woman* (New York: New American Library, 1970).
3. Alice Walker, "In Search of Our Mothers' Gardens," *Ms.* 2, 71 (May 1974).
4. Mary Helen Washington, "Black Women Image Makers," *Black World* 23, 10 (August 1974): 10–19; quote, 11.
5. Originally published as Barbara Smith, "Toward a Black Feminist Criticism," *Conditions II* 11 (October 1977): 25–44. Cited from Judith Newton and Deborah Rosenfelt, eds., *Feminist Criticism and Social Change* (New York: Methuen, 1985).
6. Ibid., 3–4.
7. Ibid., 5.
8. Ibid., 16.
9. Ibid., 8–9.
10. "The Black Sexism Debate," *Black Scholar* 10, 8–9 (May/June 1979): 14–67.
11. Audre Lorde, "The Great American Disease," *Black Scholar* 10, 8–9 (May/June 1979): 17.
12. Deborah E. McDowell, "New Directions for Black Feminist Criticism," *Black American Literature Forum,* no. 14, 1980.

13. Michele Wallace, "Who Dat Say Who Dat When I Say Who Dat?" *Village Voice Literary Supplement,* April 12, 1988, 18–21.

14. Barbara Christian, *Black Feminist Criticism: Perspectives on Black Women Writers* (New York: Pergamon Press, 1985).

15. Marjorie Pryse and Hortense Spillers, eds., *Conjuring: Black Women Fiction and Literary Tradition* (Bloomington: Indiana University Press, 1985).

16. Hortense Spillers, "Afterword: Crosscurrents, Discontinuities: Black Women's Fiction," in Pryse and Spillers, *Conjuring,* 249–261.

17. For a current overview of canonical issues in American literature see Frederick Crews, "Whose American Renaissance," *New York Review of Books,* October 27, 1988, 68–81. For an alternate view on the dangers of canonical formation in Afro-American literature, see Theodore D. Mason, Jr., "Between the Populist and the Scientist: Ideology and Power in Recent Afro-American Literary Criticism" or "The Dozens as Scholarship," *Callaloo* 11, 3 (Summer 1988): 606–615.

18. Spillers, "Afterword," 259.

19. Hazel Carby, "Woman's Era: Rethinking Black Feminist Theory," *Reconstructing Womanhood: The Emergence of the Afro-American Woman Novelist* (New York: Oxford University Press, 1987), 16.

20. Ibid., 17.

21. Valerie Smith, "A Self-critical Tradition," *Women's Review of Books* 5, 5 (February 1988): 15.

Reading Family Matters

I thank Susan Fraiman, Janice Knight, Cheryl Wall, and Richard Yarborough for their very helpful comments on an earlier draft of this essay.

1. See Wolfgang Iser, *The Act of Reading: A Theory of Aesthetic Response* (Baltimore: Johns Hopkins University Press, 1978); Susan Suleiman and Inge Crosman, eds., *The Reader in the Text: Essays on Audience and Interpretation* (Princeton: Princeton University Press, 1980); and Jane Tompkins, ed., *Reader-Response Criticism: From Formalism to Post-Structuralism* (Baltimore: Johns Hopkins University Press, 1980).

2. Mary Louise Pratt, "Interpretive Strategies/Strategic Interpretations," in Jonathan Arac, ed., *Postmodernism and Politics* (Minneapolis: University of Minnesota Press, 1986).

3. Mel Watkins, "Sexism, Racism, and Black Women Writers," *New York Times Book Review,* June 15, 1986, pp. 1, 35.

4. A significant and controversial exception from a woman is Trudier Harris, "On the Color Purple, Stereotypes, and Silence," *Black American Literature Forum* 18 (Winter 1984: 155–161. Though Harris focuses on *The Color Purple,* her assertions are echoed more broadly in readings of other novels by black women. She argues that *The Color Purple* satisfies white "spectator readers" by presenting stereotypical "black fathers and father-figures" who are "immoral [and] sexually unrestrained." See also Sondra O'Neale, "Inhibiting Midwives, Usurping Creators: The Struggling Emergence of Black Women in Fiction," in Teresa de Lauretis, ed., *Feminist Studies/Critical Studies* (Bloomington: Indiana University Press, 1986), 139–156. Male exceptions include Calvin Hernton's *The Sexual Mountain and Black Women Writers* (New York: Anchor/Doubleday, 1987), 37–58, and Richard Wesley " 'The Color Purple' Debate: Reading between the Lines," *Ms.,* September 1986, pp. 62, 90–92.

5. Jack White, chief of the Chicago bureau of *Time* magazine, compresses this oppositional tendency in his question: "Why were so many black women moved by *The Color Purple* and so many black activists/artists/militants [presumed to be male?] revulsed by the film—and the novel?" And not surprisingly, in his second question, White links these polar responses regressively to Shange's controversial choreopoem. He asks, "Why did so many black women walk out of *for colored girls . . .* shouting 'Amen,' while so many black men denounced the 'bitch' who wrote it?" "The Black Person in Art: How Should S/he Be Portrayed?" *Black American Literature Forum* 21 (Spring/Summer 1987): 22. Theologian Delores Williams's reading can be regarded as a response to Smith's question. She sees *The Color Purple* as "feminist theology" affirming the belief that "women's liberation is the key to the redemption of our society. This social redemption depends upon . . . changing our consciousness about the maleness of God, about divine validation of heterosexuality and about authority as it relates to the masculine and feminine dimensions of culture." For these reasons, she adds, "we black feminists leave the cinema knowing we have seen something painfully significant about ourselves, men, God and redemption." See "Examining Two Shades of 'Purple,' " *Los Angeles Times,* March 15, 1986. See also Williams's essay, "What Was Missed: 'The Color Purple,' " *Christianity and Crisis,* July 14, 1986.

6. Richard Ohmann, "The Shaping of a Canon: U.S. Fiction, 1060–1975," in *Politics of Letters* (Middletown, Conn.: Wesleyan University Press, 1987): 71, 75.

7. Cathy Davidson, *Revolution and the Word* (New York: Oxford, 1986), 111.

8. In Paul Smith, *Discerning the Subject* (Minneapolis: University of Minnesota Press, 1988), 34.

9. For discussions of gender and reading, see Elizabeth A. Flynn and Patrocinio P. Schweickert, eds., *Gender and Reading: Essays on Readers, Texts, and Contexts* (Baltimore: Johns Hopkins University Press, 1986).

10. Maureen Quilligan, *Milton's Spenser: The Politics of Reading* (Ithaca, N.Y.: Cornell University Press, 1983), 178.

11. Excerpts of Wallace's book were published in *Ms.* magazine in December 1979.

12. Quoted in Hernton, *The Sexual Mountain*, 44.

13. Among the most useful recent critiques of this tendency are Henry Louis Gates, Jr., "Preface to Blackness: Text and Pretext," in Dexter Fisher and Robert Stepto, eds., *Afro-American Literature: The Reconstruction of Instruction* (New York: Modern Language Association of American, 1979), 44–69, and idem, "Criticism in the Jungle," in Henry Louis Gates, Jr., ed., *Black Literature and Literary Theory* (New York: Methuen, 1984), 1–24.

14. Robert Staples, "The Myth of Black Macho: A Response to Angry Black Feminists," *Black Scholar*, March/April 1979, 26–27.

15. Janet Beizer, *Family Plots* (New Haven: Yale University Press, 1986), 7. I confine my comments to the few essays, the rhetoric of which is most insistently "pro-family." To these could be added the following essays and newspaper and magazine features that protest the treatment of black men in the literature of black women. Some of them object specifically to the film version of *The Color Purple*, but make no distinctions between film and novel: Gerald Early, "The Color Purple as Everybody's Protest Art," *Antioch Review* 44 (Summer 1986): 261–275; Richard Barksdale, "Castration Symbolism in Recent Black American Fiction," *College Language Association Journal* 29 (June 1986): 400–413; E. R. Shipp, "Blacks in Heated Debate over 'The Color Purple,'" *New York Times*, January 27, 1986; "Seeing Red over Purple," *People Magazine*, March 10, 1986; Abdul Wali Muhammad, "Purple Poison Pulses," *Final Call*, January 27 1986; Lynn Norment, "The Color Purple," *Ebony*, February 1986.

16. Christine Froula, "The Daughter's Seduction: Sexual Violence and Literary History," *Signs* 11 (Summer 1986): 621–644.

17. Despite abundant evidence that black women's "feminist" consciousness generally emerged organically from the material circumstances of their lives and can be documented well in advance of the second wave of the women's movement of the 1960s, this analysis continues to be perpetuated by black men. See bell hooks, *Feminist Theory: From Margin to Center* (Boston: South End Press, 1984), and Beverly Guy-Sheftall, "Remembering Sojourner Truth: On Black Feminism," in Pearl Cleage, ed., *Catalyst* (Atlanta, n.d.), 54–57.

18. David Bradley, "Telling the Black Woman's Story," *New York Times Magazine,* January 1984, p. 34.

19. Philip M. Royster, "In Search of Our Fathers' Arms: Alice Walker's Persona of the Alienated Darling," *Black American Literature Forum* 20 (Winter 1986): 357, 361. Royster keeps Walker's roles as daughter, wife, and mother clearly before the reader's eye, noting that she is a failed wife and an inadequate mother. See p. 353, especially.

20. Susan Willis, *Specifying: Black Women Writing the American Experience* (Madison: University of Wisconsin Press, 1987), 106.

21. Bradley, "Black Woman's Story," 30.

22. Royster, "Our Father's Arms," 363.

23. Watkins, "Sexism, Racism, and Black Women Writers," 36.

24. Ibid., 37, 36.

25. Richard Wright, *Native Son* (New York: Harper and Row, 1940), 140, 224.

26. Marilyn Butler, "Against Tradition: The Case for a Particularized Historical Method," in Jerome J. McGann, ed., *Historical Studies and Literary Criticism* (Madison: University of Wisconsin Press, 1985), 37. See also J. P. Stern, "From Family Album to Literary History," *Critical Inquiry* 7 (Autumn 1975): 113–131. After Wittgenstein, Stern describes writing literary history as analogous to "pictures from a family album, not as scenes from a single story or drama" with sufficient continuity.

27. The novel was reviewed by Robert Towers in the August 12, 1982, issue under the heading "Good Men Are Hard to Find," though Towers admitted then that "the two books have about as much in common . . . as one of Roy Lichtenstein's comic-strip blowups and a WPA painting of cotton pickers in the field." Reed's public conflicts with black women writers are well known, which piques my curiosity about this pattern of "pairing" his work with Alice Walker's in literary reviews. See also Darwin Turner, "A Spectrum of Blackness," *Parnassus* 4(1976): 202–218. For Reed's comments on this practice of pairing him with Walker see Mel Watkins, "An Interview with Ishmael Reed," *Southern Review* 21 (July 1985): 603–614. There Reed talks about his belief, captured in the title of a symposium which he sponsored, that "Third World Men [are] the Scapegoats of Feminist Writers."

28. Ishmael Reed, *Reckless Eyeballing* (New York: St. Martin's Press, 1986), 4.

29. See, as just one example, the courtroom scene near the end of Hurston's *Their Eyes Were Watching God* in which Janie is acquitted of murdering Tea Cake. One of the group of black men outraged at the verdict says, "Well, you know whut dey say 'uh white man and uh nigger woman is de freest

thing on earth.' Dey do as dey please" (1937; rpt. Urbana: University of Illinois Press, 1978), 280.

30. Haki Madhubuti, "Lucille Clifton: Warm Water, Greased Legs, and Dangerous Poetry," in Mari Evans, ed., *Black Women Writers: A Critical Evaluation* (New York: Anchor/Doubleday, 1983), 159.

31. Haki Madhubuti, "Sonia Sanchez: The Bringer of Memories," in Evans, *Black Women Writers*, 419–420.

32. Ibid., 159, 432.

33. Madhubuti, "Lucille Clifton," 150–151, 159, 156. With this gesture Madhubuti reveals unwittingly a central tendency and irony in this debate. In the name of the black family and the survival of the larger black community, there is a thinly disguised desire for personal, individual gratification and reflection.

34. Judith Fetterley, "Reading about Reading: 'A Jury of Her Peers,' 'The Murders in the Rue Morgue,' and 'The Yellow Wallpaper,'" in Flynn and Schweickart, *Gender and Reading*, 150, 147.

35. Hernton, *Sexual Mountain and Black Women Writers*, 38.

36. Peter Gay, *Education of the Senses* (New York: Oxford University Press, 1984), 436.

37. Houston Baker, *Modernism and the Harlem Renaissance* (Chicago: University of Chicago Press, 1987), 106.

38. Adolph Reed, "The Liberal Technocrat," *The Nation*, February 6, 1988, p. 168.

39. William Julius Wilson, *The Truly Disadvantaged: The Inner City, the Underclass, and Public Policy* (Chicago: University of Chicago Press, 1987), 7.

40. Reed, "Liberal Technocrat," 168.

41. Alice Walker, *The Third Life of Grange Copeland* (New York: Harcourt Brace Jovanovich, 1970), 9, 18.

42. All too little has been written about what black women experience within the family, a void partly created by the ideological discussions of the black family since the contoversial Moynihan report *The Black Family: The Case for National Action*. Moynihan's "black matriarchy" thesis is well known and need not be rehearsed here. It is enough to say that the flood of liberal repudiations it elicited, however well intentioned and sharply articulated, have done little to illuminate black women's subordination within the family. So strong has been the design and desire to refute with a mountain of "normalizing" data Moynihan's description of black families as "tangles of pathology" that black women's experiences, thought, and feelings have been buried. In his monumental *The Black Family in Slavery and Freedom* (New York: Random House, 1981), Herbert Gutman acknowledged that his study was "stimulated by the bitter public and academic controversy surrounding" the

Moynihan report. He traces the development of the slave family and enlarged kin networks from 1750 to 1925, describing long-lasting slave marriages. But, as Angela Davis notes in *Women, Race, and Class* (New York: Random House, 1981), Gutman's "observations about slave women are generally confined to their wifely propensities." Similarly, in *Labor of Love, Labor of Sorrow: Black Women, Work, and the Family from Slavery to the Present* (New York: Basic Books, 1985), Jacquelyn Jones is at pains to prove that the "two-parent, nuclear family was the typical cohabitation" in slavery and freedom that protected the community at large from racial oppression. Only briefly does Jones, in an otherwise commendable study, indicate that, while racial oppression "could bind a family tightly together," "it could also heighten tensions among people who had few outlets for their rage and frustration" (32, 34, 103).

43. Walker, *Grange Copeland*, 18.

44. Reed, *Reckless Eyeballing*, 77.

45. Darryl Pinckney, "Black Victims, Black Villains," *New York Review of Books*, January 29, 1987, p. 81.

46. Judith Fetterley, "Reading about Reading," and Annette Kolodny, "A Map for Misreading: Gender and the Interpretation of Literary Texts," in Elaine Showalter, ed., *The New Feminist Criticism* (New York: Pantheon, 1985), 46–62.

47. Kolodny, "Map for Misreading," 57.

48. Fredric Jameson, *The Political Unconscious* (Ithaca, N.Y.: Cornell University Press, 1981), 9. For a discussion of the extent to which what happens during reading has been "already limited by decisions made before the book is ever begun," see Peter Rabinowitz, *Before Reading: Narrative Conventions and the Politics of Interpretation* (Ithaca, N.Y.: Cornell University Press, 1987), 2 and following.

49. Alice Walker, "Source," in *You Can't Keep a Good Woman Down* (New York: Harcourt Brace Jovanovich, 1981). Subsequent page references are given in the text.

50. Shari Benstock, "At the Margin of Discourse: Footnotes in the Fictional Text," *PMLA* 98 (March 1983): 205.

51. Ibid., 221.

52. Margaret Homans, *Bearing the Word* (Chicago: University of Chicago Press, 1986), 160.

53. Ibid., 31.

54. Alice Walker, "In the Closet of the Soul," in *Living by the Word* (New York: Harcourt Brace Jovanovich, 1988), 82.

55. Shoshana Felman, *Writing and Madness* (Ithaca, N.Y.: Cornell University Press, 1985), 161.

56. Gloria Naylor and Toni Morrison, "A Conversation," *Southern Review* 21 (July 1985): 579.

57. *Massachuetts Review* 28 (Winter 1987): 688.

58. Reed, *Reckless Eyeballing*, 130.

59. There are striking parallels between the reception of contemporary black women novelists and that of their counterparts, black feminist critics in the academy. In a very insightful and refreshing article, Theodore Mason discusses the controversial issue of *New Literary History* featuring essays by Joyce Joyce, Houston Baker, and Henry Louis Gates. Mason invokes Ralph Ellison's *Invisible Man* to explain this controversy between two black men and a black woman, arranged by the white male editor of the journal who watches his orchestrated combat with amusement. See "Between the Populist and the Scientist: Ideology and Power in Recent Afro-American Literary Criticism or, 'The Dozens' as Scholarship," *Callaloo* 36 (Summer 1988): 606–615.

60. Anthony Barthelemy, "Mother, Sister, Wife: A Dramatic Perspective," *Southern Review* 21 (July 1985): 787.

61. I borrow this phrasing from Alice Jardine, *Gynesis: Configurations of Woman and Modernity* (Ithaca, N.Y.: Cornell University Press, 1985), 37.

Allegories of Black Female Desire

This chapter was made possible by support from the Faculty Research Program in the Social Sciences, Humanities, and Education of the Office of the Vice President for Academic Affairs at Howard University. This project was also supported, in part, by the Ford Foundation and the D. C. Commission on the Arts, the Honorable Marion Barry, Jr., Mayor. In addition, I thank my sister-critics: Vicki Arana, Carolyn Brown, Eve Hawthorne, and Alinda Sumers for criticizing my evolving manuscripts with compassionate candor. Also, Russell Adams and Arnold Rampersad read early versions of this essay and generously shared their comments. I also thank my research assistants: Michael Wahholtz, Hazel Ervin, and Klaus Braun. Lastly, I express my sincere appreciation to the staffs of the Moorland-Spingarn Research Center at Howard University and the Library of Congress for their dedication to the preservation of documents of Afro-American cultural production and for their patient assistance in making these documents available to scholars like myself.

1. Fredric Jameson, *The Political Unconscious* (Ithaca, N.Y.: Cornell University Press, 1981), 34.

2. Richard Wright, *Black Boy* (New York: Harpers, 1945), 186. All subsequent references are in the text.

3. The urgency of Richard's desire to escape becomes more emphatic when we recall that female entrapment and Jim Crow racism converge repeatedly in Wright's fiction, with *Native Son* (1940) serving as a notable example because of the marked similarity between the names of two black female characters in these novels. In *Native Son* Bigger Thomas ultimately kills Bessie Mears not because she threatens him specifically with domestic entrapment but because she undermines his dreams for autonomy by keeping his fear of white people foremost in his consciousness.

4. Zora Neale Hurston, *Their Eyes Were Watching God* (1937; rpt., Urbana: University of Illinois Press, 1978), 43. All subsequent references are in the text.

5. Robert B. Stepto, *From Behind the Veil: A Study of Afro-American Narrative* (Urbana: University of Illinois Press, 1978), 5, 178–191; idem, 'Introduction," in Dexter Fisher and Robert B. Stepto, eds., *Afro-American Literature: The Reconstruction of Instruction* (New York: MLA, 1979), 3–31.

6. I am defining traditional black literary scholarship as that of male authority, written during the middle decades of the twentieth century, that has regarded literature as purely a representational art form, thus that scholarship's preoccupation with explicating texts as works of social realism and didactic strategies for mitigating racism.

7. John Bouvier, *A Law Dictionary Adapted to the Constitution and Laws of the U.S.A.,* 3rd ed. (Philadelphia: T. and J. W. Jophnson, 1848), 116; 15th ed. (Philadelphia: J. B. Lippincott, 1883), 156; new ed., rev. Francis Rawle (Boston: Boston Book Co., 1897). *Judicial and Statutory Definitions of Words and Phrases,* collected, edited, and compiled by members of the editorial staff of the National Reporter System (St. Paul, Minn.: West Publishing Co., 1904–1905), 4390–93. All subsequent references are in the text.

8. Herbert Gutman, *The Black Family in Slavery and Freedom* (New York: Random House, 1977), 275.

9. Ibid., 411–431.

10. Ibid., 429.

11. These fictional texts include Frances Harper's "The Two Offers" (1859) and *Iola Leroy* (1892); Pauline Hopkins's *Contending Forces* (1900), *Hagar's Daughter* (1901), *Winoma* (1902), and *Of One Blood* (1902–1903); Victoria Earle's "Zalinka—A Story" (1892) and "Eugenie's Mistake (1892); Emma Dunham Kelley's *Megda* (1891) and *Four Girls at Cottage City* (1898); Amelia Johnson's *Clarence and Corinne* (1890) and *The Hazeley Family* (1894); and Katherine Tillman's "Beryl Weston's Ambition" (1893) and "Clancy Street" (1898).

12. See note 22. The following texts also discuss the ways in which women writers appropriated sentimental conventions to create a rational and pragmatic heroine: Janet Todd, *Sensibility: An Introduction* (London: Methuen, 1986); Jane P. Tompkins, "Sentimental Power: *Uncle Tom's Cabin* and the Politics of Literary History," in Elaine Showalter, ed., *Feminist Criticism* (New York: Pantheon, 1985), 81–104; and Ann D. Wood, "The 'Scribbling Women' and Fanny Fern: Why Women Wrote," *American Quarterly* 23, 1 (Spring 1971):3–24.

13. Late nineteenth- and early twentieth-century black women's writing is routinely marginalized in such texts as Benjamin Brawley, *Early Negro American Writers* (Chapel Hill: University of North Carolina Press, 1935), 290–292; Vernon Loggins, *The Negro Author: His Development in America to 1900* (New York: Columbia University, 1931), 211, 245–247, and 342–344; Hugh M. Gloster, *Negro Voices in American Fiction* (Chapel Hill: University of North Carolina Press, 1948), 30–31, 33–34, 131–139, and 141–146; and Robert A. Bone, *The Negro Novel in America* (New Haven: Yale University Press, 1965), 31–32, and 101–106.

14. Frederick Douglass's *Narrative of the Life of Frederick Douglass* (1845), Henry Bibb's *Narrative of the Life and Adventure of Henry Bibb, an American Slave* (1849), Solomon Northrup's *Twelve Years a Slave* (1854), Harriet [Linda Brent] Jacob's *Incidents in the Life of a Slave Girl* (1861), and Nancy Prince's *Life and Travels* (1850).

15. Jameson, *Political Unconscious*, 34.

16. Stepto, *From Behind the Veil*, 5.

17. Jameson, *Political Unconscious*, 34.

18. See note 12. Also see Deborah E. McDowell, "Introduction," in Jessie Fauset, *Plum Bun* (London: Pandora Press, 1985).

19. This is a revision of Lucius T. Outlaw's statement that "in general, hermeneutical understanding is an *experiental encounter* with a *heritage,* a tradition, which *speaks* through the work (say a text) or life-praxis/form of expression." See Lucius T. Outlaw, "Philosophy, Hermeneutics, Social-Political Theory: Critical Thought in the Interests of African-Americans," in Leonard Harris, ed., *Philosophy Born of Struggle: Anthology of Afro-American Philosophy from 1917.* (Dubuque: K. A. Kendall/Hunt, 1983), 60–87.

20. Jean Fagan Yellin, "Written by Herself: Harriet Jacobs's Slave Narrative," *American Literature* 53 (November 1981):479–486.

21. Harriet Jacobs, *Incidents in the Life of a Slave Girl,* with an introduction by Jean Fagan Yellin (Cambridge: Harvard University Press, 1987), 55. All subsequent references are in the text.

22. See Nina Baym, *Woman's Fiction* (Ithaca, N.Y.: Cornell University Press, 1978), 11–21; and Henry Louis Gates, Jr., "Introduction," in Harriet E. Wilson, *Our Nig* (1859, rpt., New York: Vintage Books, 1983), xi–lix;

and idem, "Parallel Discursive Universes: Fictions of the Self in Harriet E. Wilson's *Our Nig*," in *Figures in Black: Words, Signs, and the "Racial" Self* (New York: Oxford University Press, 1987), 125–166. All subsequent references to *Our Nig* are in the text.

23. Stepto, *From Behind the Veil*, 5.

24. See Joanne Dobson, "The Hidden Hand: Subversion of Cultural Ideology in Three Mid-Nineteenth-Century American Women's Novels," *American Quarterly* 38, 2 (Summer 1986):223–243; Judith Fetterley, "Introduction," in *Provisions: A Reader from Nineteenth-Century American Women* (Bloomington: University of Indiana Press, 1985), 1–40; and Wood, "'Scribbing Women' and Fanny Fern," 3–24.

25. See Sandra M. Gilbert and Susan Gubar, *The Madwoman in the Attic: The Woman Writer and the Nineteenth-Century Literary Imagination* (New Haven: Yale University Press, 1979), 3–93; and Margaret Homans, *Bearing the Word: Language and Female Experience in Nineteenth-Century Woman's Writing* (Chicago: University of Chicago Press, 1986), 1–40.

26. See Houston A. Baker, Jr., *Modernism and the Harlem Renaissance* (Chicago: University of Chicago Press, 1987), 1–47, for a discussion on the subtle ways black writers masked their authorial authority in blackface minstrelsey.

27. Gates, "Introduction," xl.

28. Frances W. Harper, *Iola Leroy; or, The Shadows Uplifted* (Boston: Beacon Press, 1987), 266. All subsequent references are in the text.

29. Mrs. N[athan] F. Mossell [Gertrude Bustill Mossell], *The Work of the Afro-American Woman* (Philadelphia: George S. Ferguson Co., 1894), 115; Anna Julia Cooper, *A Voice from the South* (1892; rpt., New York: Negro Universities Press, 1969), 29.

30. Sappho was an early classic author and the most famous colonist of the isle of Lesbos during the sixth century B.C. She was reputed by her contemporaries to have been greater than Homer and was called the Tenth Muse. However, her work was scorned because of her homosexuality, and by the eighth century only fragments of her large corpus of poetry survived early Christian book-burning. See Barbara G. Walker, ed., *The Woman's Encyclopedia of Myths and Secrets* (New York: Harper and Row, 1983), 535–536, 890.

31. Pauline E. Hopkins, *Contending Forces: A Romance Illustrative of Negro Life North and South* (Carbondale: Southern Illinois University Press, 1978), 260. All subsequent references are in the text.

32. Loggins, *Negro Author*, 247; Gloster, *Negro Voices*, 30–31; Bone, *Negro Novel*, 32.

33. Baym, *Woman's Fiction*, 11–21.

34. Amelia E. Johnson, *Clarence and Corinne* (Philadelphia: American Baptist Publication Society, 1890), 186. All subsequent references are in the text.

35. Emma Dunham Kelley, *Medga* (Boston: James H. Earle, 1891), 60. All subsequent references are in the text.

'The Permanent Obliquity of an In(pha)llibly Straight'

1. E. Franklin Frazier, *The Negro Family in the United States,* with a foreword by Nathan Glazer (Chicago: University of Chicago Press, 1966); Lee Rainwater and William L. Yancey, eds., *The Moynihan Report and the Politics of Controversy: A Transaction Social Science and Public Policy Report* (Cambridge: MIT Press, 1967), 47–94.

2. Maya Angelou, *I Know Why the Caged Bird Sings* (New York: Bantam Books, 1970); James Baldwin, *Just above My Head* (New York: Dell Books, 1979); Gayle Jones, *Corregidora* (New York: Random House, 1975); Ralph Ellison, *Invisible Man* (New York: Random House, 1952); Alice Walker, "The Child Who Favored Daughter," in *In Love and Trouble* (New York: Harcourt Brace Jovanovich, 1973); idem, *The Color Purple* (New York: Harcourt Brace Jovanovich, 1982). Hereafter, all citations to these works appear in the text.

3. François Roustang, "Uncertainty," *October* 28 (Spring 1984): 91–105.

4. Angela Y. Davis, *Women, Race, and Class* (New York: Random House, 1981); William Goodell, *The American Slave Code in Theory and Practice, etc.* (New York: American and Foreign Anti-Slavery Society, 1853; rpt., New York: Arno Press, 1969).

5. Robert Manson Myers, ed., *The Children of Pride: A True Story of Georgia and the Civil War* (New Haven: Yale University Press, 1972). This rich collection of letters, written between friends and family of the Rev. Dr. Charles Colcock Jones, from 1854 to 1860, provides a source of sporadic information on African-American women in slavery in the United States.

6. W. E. B. DuBois, *The Souls of Black Folk: Essays and Sketches* (rpt., New York: Fawcett Books, 1961; originally published in 1903).

7. Claude Lévi-Strauss, *The Elementary Structures of Kinship,* ed. Rodney Needham, rev. ed. and trans. James Harle Bell and John Richard von Sturmer (Boston: Beacon Press, 1969). W. Arens, *The Original Sin: Incest and Its Meaning* (New York: Oxford University Press, 1986). Though coming to my attention too late to inform this writing, Arens's text promises to correct our notions concerning the historic origins of incest.

8. Jacques Lacan, *Écrits: A Selection,* trans. Alan Sheridan (New York: W. W. Norton, 1977); Juliet Mitchell and Jacqueline Rose, eds., *Feminine Sexuality: Jacques Lacan and the école freudienne,* trans. Jacqueline Rose (New York: W. W. Norton, 1982). Terry Eagleton, *Literary Theory: An Introduction* (Min-

neapolis: University of Minnesota Press, 1983). Sigmund Freud, *Totem and Taboo*, vol. 11 of the Standard Edition of the Complete Psychological Works (London: Hogarth Press, 1981).

9. Houston Baker, *Blues, Ideology, and Afro-American Literature: A Vernacular Theory* (Chicago: University of Chicago Press, 1984).

10. Mary Douglas, *Purity and Danger: An Analysis of the Concepts of Pollution and Taboo* (London: ARK Paperbacks, 1984).

11. Frantz Fanon, *The Wretched of the Earth*, preface by Jean-Paul Sarte, trans. Constance Farrington (New York: Grove Press, 1968).

12. I borrow freely from the title of Annette Kolodny's brilliant study, *The Lay of the Land: Metaphor as Experience and History in American Life and Letters* (Chapel Hill: University of North Carolina Press, 1975).

13. Susan Suleiman, ed., *The Female Body in Western Culture: Contemporary Perspectives* (Cambridge: Harvard University Press, 1986).

14. Anthony Wilden, *The Language of the Self: The Function of Language in Psychoanalysis* (New York: Dell Publishing), 1975).

15. Harryette Mullen, "Daughters in Search of Mothers," *Cataylst* (from the Women's Research Center at Spelman College, Atlanta, Georgia) (Fall 1986):45.

16. Luce Irigaray, *This Sex Which Is Not One*, trans. Catherine Porter with Carolyn Burke (Ithaca, N.Y.: Cornell University Press, 1985.

17. Roustang, "Uncertainty," 99.

18. Ibid., 101–102.

19. Frances E. W. Harper, *Iola Leroy, or Shadows Uplifted* (rpt., New York: AMS Press, 1971). Pauline Hopkins, *Contending Forces*, afterword by Gwendolyn Brooks (Carbondale: Southern Illinois University Press, 1978); Charles W. Chesnutt, *The Short Fiction of Charles W. Chesnutt*, ed. with intro. by Sylvia Lyons Render (Washington, D.C.: Howard University Press, 1974); idem, *The Marrow of Tradition*, intro. by Robert M. Farnsworth (Ann Arbor: University of Michigan Press, 1969); Claudia Tate, "Pauline Hopkins: Our Literary Foremother," in Marjorie Pryse and Hortense J. Spillers, eds., *Conjuring: Black Women, Fiction, and Literary Tradition* (Bloomington: Indiana University Press, 1985), 53–67. A general perspective on late nineteenth-century fiction by African-American women writers is provided by Barbara Christian, *Black Women Novelists: The Development of a Tradition, 1892–1976* (Westport, Conn.: Greenwood Press, 1980), 35–62. See also Hazel V. Carby, ' "On the Treshold of Woman's Era': Lynching, Empire, and Sexuality in Black Feminist Theory," *Critical Inquiry* (Autumn 1985): 262–278.

20. Elaine Scarry, *The Body in Pain: The Making and Unmaking of the World* (New York: Oxford University Press, 1985).

Living on the Line

The research and writing of this chapter was made possible by a postdoctoral fellowship from the Ford Foundation.
1. Unless otherwise noted, all poetry quotations are taken from *Our Dead Behind Us* (New York: W. W. Norton, 1986), with page numbers given in parentheses in the text.

2. "There Are No Honest Poems about Dead Women," 61.

3. *The First Cities* (New York: Poets Press, 1968); *Cables to Rage* (London: Paul Breman, 1970); *From a Land Where Other People Live* (Detroit: Broadside Press, 1973); *New York Head Shop and Museum* (Detroit: Broadside Press, 1974); *Coal* (New York: W. W. Norton, 1976); *Between Our Selves* (Point Reyes: Eidolon Editions, 1976); *The Black Unicorn* (New York: W. W. Norton, 1978). The eight-year span between *The Black Unicorn* and *Our Dead Behind Us* was filled by *Chosen Poems—Old and New* (New York: W. W. Norton, 1982), three major prose works—*The Cancer Journals* (San Francisco: Spinsters Ink, 1980), *Zami: A New Spelling of My Name* (Watertown, Mass.: Persephone Press, 1982), and *Sister Outsider* (Trumansburg, N.Y.: Crossing Press, 1984), and two pamphlets for Kitchen Table: Women of Color Press.

4. *Choice* 16, 1 (March 1979):80.

5. *Black Unicorn*, 31.

6. "Outlines," 10; "Soho Cinema," 19; "The Horse Casts a Shoe," 33.

7. Mary J. Carruthers, "The Re-Vision of the Muse: Adrienne Rich, Audre Lorde, Judy Grahn, Olga Broumas," *Hudson Review* 36, 2 (Summer 1983):322.

8. Matthew Arnold's famous poem "Dover Beach" can be found in many sources.

9 "School Note," in *Black Unicorn*, 55.

10. Amitai F. Avi-ram, "*Apo Koinou* in Audre Lorde and the Moderns: Defining the Differences," *Callaloo* 9, 1 (Winter 1986): 206–207.

11. "From the House of Yemanjá," in *Black Unicorn*, 7.

12. "And What About the Children," in *Coal*, 46.

13. "Between Ourselves," in *Black Unicorn*, 112.

14. "Who Said It Was Simple," in *Chosen Poems*, 50.

15. "Scar," in *Black Unicorn*, 49.

16. "Vigil," 21; "Naming the Stories," 31; "For Judith," 42, and "Out of the Wind," 58; "Florida," 48.

17. "Dahomey," in *Black Unicorn*, 10.

18. "125th Street and Abomey," in *Black Unicorn*, 12.

19. "Mawu," 26.

20. "Memorial II" and "Suffer the Children," in *First Cities*, n.p.

21. "Burning the Water Hyacinth," 50. Lorde discusses "The Uses of the Erotic: The Erotic as Power," in *Sister Outsider*, 53–59.

22. R. B. Stepto, "The Phenomenal Woman and the Severed Daughter" (a review of Maya Angelou's *And Still I Rise* and Lorde's *The Black Unicorn*), *Parnassus* 8, 1 (1979):316.

23. Ted C. Simmons, *The Book Review/Los Angeles Times*, December 7, 1986, 4.

24. Kate Walker, "Outside In," *Village Voice*, September 14, 1984, 52.

25. *Publisher's Weekly* 221, 20 (May 14, 1982):214; JP, *Booklist* 83, 3 (October 1, 1986):184.

26. Michael T. Siconolfi, *Best Sellers*, January 1987, 327.

27. Hayden Carruth, "A Year's Poetry," *The Nation*, December 23, 1978.

28. Joan Larkin, "Frontiers of Language: Three Poets" (which included *From A Land Where Other People Live*), *Ms.* 3 (September 1974): 40; Andrea Benton Rushing, *Ms.* 7 (January 1979):43.

29. Rochelle Ratner, *Library Journal* 1976:354 and 1978:323; Stepto, "Phenomenal Woman," 320; Paula Giddings, "Books," *Essence* 17 (September 1986):31.

30. Andrea Benton Rushing, "A Creative Use of African Sources," *Obsidian* 5, 3 (Winter 1979):114–16.

31. I borrow this phrase from my colleague at Stanford University, Linda Garber, who (with a start by Martha Zingo) did the careful research for this essay.

32. Sandra Squire Fluck, *New Directions for Women* 16, 1 (January/February 1987):14.

33. Gloria Hull, "Poem for Audre," reprinted from *Conditions: Five* (1979) in Barbara Smith, ed., *Home Girls: A Black Feminist Anthology* (New York: Kitchen Table: Women of Color Press, 1983).

34. Fahamisha Shariat [Brown], "Review of *The Black Unicorn*," *Conditions: Five* 1979:176.

35. Novelist and folklorist Zora Neale Hurston, blues singer Bessie Smith, contemporary poets Sonia Sanchez, Nikki Giovanni, Pat Parker, and June Jordan.

36. I am constructing this "narrative" from three Audre Lorde interviews: Nina Winter, "On Audre Lorde," in *Interview with the Muse: Remarkable Women Speak on Creativity and Power* (Berkeley: Moon Books, 1978), 71–81; Karla M. Hammond, "Audre Lorde: Interview," *Denver Quarterly* 16, 1 (Spring 1981): 10–27; and "An Interview: Audre Lorde and Adrienne Rich," in *Sister Outsider*, 81–109. All of the quotes are Lorde's own words.

37. Initially published in *The First Cities*, "Coal" can be found in Lorde's volume of that name, p. 6.

38. "Outlines," 13.

39. These ideas are set forth in Julia Kristeva, "Revolution in Poetic Language," in Toril Moi, ed., *The Kristeva Reader* (New York: Columbia University Press, 1986), 90–136.

I Shop Therefore I Am

1. Toni Morrison, *The Bluest Eye* (New York: Washington Square Press, 1970), 19. All references are to this edition and are given in the text.

2. Barbara Kruger, "Untitled," 1987.

3. Toni Morrison, *Song of Solomon* (New York: New American Library, 1977), 312. All references are to this edition and are given in the text.

4. Kobena Mercer, "Black Hair/Style Politics," *New Formations* 3 (Winter 1987): 33–54.

5. Ibid., 46, 47–49.

6. bell hooks, "Overcoming White Supremacy," *Zeta,* January 1988, p. 24.

7. In embarking on this by no means complete interpretation of Michael Jackson, I draw on many conversations with Deborah Chay of the Graduate Program in Literature, Duke University.

8. Hazel Carby, *Radical America* 20, 4 (June/July 1986): 9–22. Carby specifically defines the blues singers as "part of a larger history of the production of Afro-American culture within the North American culture industry." In conceptualizing Afro-American culture as somehow autonomous with respect to dominant mass culture, Carby takes a very different position from my own. Her claim for the vitality of Afro-American cultural production has validity given the boldly radical nature of the blues singers and their music and given that the mass media culture in the 1920s was less developed than it had become by the late 1930s, the period Morrison documented in *The Bluest Eye* and certainly less homogenized than it is today.

9. Fredric Jameson, "Reification and Utopia in Mass Culture," *Social Text* 1 (Winter 1979): 135–148; quotation on p. 138.

10. Ibid., 137.

11. Nathan Irvin Huggins, *Harlem Renaissance* (New York: Oxford University Press, 1971), 286.

12. For a summary of the critical debate surrounding minstrelsy, see Eric Lott, "Blackface and Blackness: Politics of Early Minstrelsy," Paper delivered to the American Studies Convention, Miami, October 1988.

13. James V. Hatch, ed., and Ted Shine, consultant, *Black Theater USA* (New York: Macmillan 1974), 618.

14. Lott, "Blackface and Blackness."

15. Sylvia Wynter, "Sambos and Minstrels," *Social Text* 1 (Winter 1979): 149–156; quotation on p. 155.

16. Susan Willis, "Gender as Commodity," *South Atlantic Quarterly* 86, 4 (Fall 1987): 403–421.

17. Cultural critics have traced the challenge, the calling out, the duel motif to African tribal tradition. It is seen in Caribbean stick fighting, later makes its way into the challenges hurled by sound system DJs during the early years of reggae, and now may be found in rap music and breakdance competition. See Dick Hebdige, *Cut 'n' Mix* (London: Methuen, 1987).

18. Stuart Hall, "On Postmodernism and Articulation," *Journal of Communication Inquiry* 10, 2 (Summer 1986): 45–60. In a theoretical climate dominated by the notion of a postmodern subject, interpolated from many fragmented social positions, Hall recommends that in the final instance, marginalized peoples must and will function as concrete historical subjects, whose political engagement binds together multiple subject positions.

19. Stuart Ewen and Elizabeth Ewen, *Channels of Desire* (New York: McGraw-Hill, 1982), 167.

What Is Your Nation?

1. Paule Marshall, *Praisesong for the Widow* (New York: E. P. Dutton), 1984. All citations to this volume are given in the text.

2. Edward Kamau Brathwaite, "The African Presence in Caribbean Literature," in Sidney Mintz, ed., *Slavery, Colonialism and Racism* (New York: W. W. Norton, 1974), 73–110.

3. I borrow "diaspora literacy" from Veve Clark's exploration of the same knowledge in her paper "Developing Diaspora Literacy: Allusion in Maryse Conde's *Heremakhonon*," delivered at the African Literature Association Conference, Baltimore, 1984.

4. Nina Simone, in "Four Women": "he forced my mother my mother/ late/One night/What do they call me?" Remembered by Avey when, packing to defect from the cruise, she is confronted by the near-white Thomasina Moore, who had danced in her youth in the chorus line at the Cotton Club (19).

5. In many respects, the reason I am so powerfully attached to this novel is because when reading it for the first time, I experienced many powerful moments of recognition and could therefore feel the lyrical joy Avatara feels when she recognizes again elements from out of her childhood, which come also out of mine. The moment I first read the account of the Ring Shout, for instance, I recognized the outlines of the dance: I, like Avey, had been a visitor to my home, watching on the sidelines while only the old people took part.

The descriptions of the durbar in Ghana were so familiar, as were Lebert Joseph's ceremonies for absent children. Those supplications to the ancestors, performed for wandering children such as myself who seem to take a long time finding their way home again, have been done to ensure my safe return or to celebrate my safe arrival. My personal reading of this work then was in the first instance an "autobiographical" reading, which reminded me that all exiles can be transformed into homecomings.

6. On the many names and attributes of this god see Robert Farris Thompson, *Flash of the Spirit* (New York: Vintage Books, 1984), 18–33.

ABENA P. A. BUSIA is associate professor of English at Rutgers University; she has published articles on colonial discourse and on black women's writing. Her book *Song in a Strange Land: Narrative and Rituals of Remembrance in the Novels of Black Women of Africa and the African Diaspora* is forthcoming in 1990. A volume of her poems, *Testimony of Exiles*, has just been published.

BARBARA CHRISTIAN is the author of *Black Women Novelists: The Development of a Tradition* (1980) and *Black Feminist Criticism: Perspectives on Black Women Writers* (1985). She has written many essays on African-American literature, most recently "The Race for Theory." She is professor of Afro-American Studies as well as chair of the Ethnic Studies Ph.D. program at University of California at Berkeley.

MAE GWENDOLYN HENDERSON is associate professor in the African-American World Studies Program and the Department of English at the University of Iowa. She is author of several articles on black women's literature and coeditor of the five-volume *Antislavery Newspapers and Periodicals: An Annotated Index of Letters, 1817–1871* (1980). Her monograph on black expatriate writers will be published by Oxford University Press. Currently she is developing a black feminist theory of reading.

GLORIA T. HULL is professor of women's studies and literature at the University of California, Santa Cruz. The author of *Color, Sex, and Poetry: Three Women Writers of the Harlem Renaissance* (1987), she was coeditor with Patricia B. Scott and Barbara Smith of the landmark anthology *All the Women Are White, All the Blacks Are Men, but Some of Us Are Brave: Black Women's Studies* (1982). She also edited *The Works of Alice Dunbar Nelson*, three volumes (1988), and *Give Us Each Day: The Diary of Alice Dunbar Nelson* (1984). Most recently, Kitchen Table Press has published Hull's first volume of poems, *Healing Heart: Poems 1973–86*.

DEBORAH E. McDOWELL is associate professor of English at the University of Virginia. In addition to being the author of numerous articles and reviews, McDowell is the general editor of the Beacon

Press Black Women Writers series; this series has returned to print works by authors ranging from Frances Watkins Harper to Gayl Jones. The coeditor with Arnold Rampersad of *Slavery and the Literary Imagination* (1988), a collection of essays, McDowell has edited reprints of Jessie Fauset's *Plum Bum* and Nella Larsen's novels *Quicksand* and *Passing*.

VALERIE SMITH is associate professor of English at the University of California, Los Angeles; she was previously associate professor of English and Afro-American studies at Princeton University. The author of *Self-Discovery and Authority in Afro-American Narrative* (1987) and the editor of *New Essays on Toni Morrison's Song of Solomon* (forthcoming), she has written essays on black feminist criticism, Afro-American narrative, and black independent film. She is currently writing two books, one on slavery and recent Afro-American writing and one on black feminist theory.

HORTENSE J. SPILLERS is professor of English at Cornell University. She coedited with Marjorie Pryse a collection of critical essays, *Conjuring: Black Women, Fiction, and Literary Tradition* (1985). Spillers has contributed essays to a wide array of journals and volumes of literary criticism and theory and has recently been concerned with theorizing black women as subjects in Western discourse. She is at work on a book entitled *In the Flesh: A Situation for Feminist Inquiry*.

CLAUDIA TATE is professor of English at George Washington University. She is editor of *Black Women Writers at Work* (1983) and *The Works of Katherine Tillman* (forthcoming) and author of numerous articles, book chapters, and reviews. Among the most recent are "Laying the Floor; or, the History of the Formation of the Afro-American Literary Canon," "Anger So Flat: Gwendolyn Brooks's *Annie Allen*," and "On Black Literary Women and the Evolution of Critical Discourse." She is currently working on a book on the post-Reconstruction domestic fictions of black women writers, entitled *Domestic Allegories of Political Desire*.

CONTRIBUTORS

CHERYL A. WALL is associate professor of English at Rutgers University where she teaches Afro-American and American literature. She has published articles and reviews in journals such as *Phylon, Black American Literature Forum,* and *American Literature.* Her book entitled *Women of Letters of the Harlem Renaissance* will be published in 1990.

SUSAN WILLIS teaches southern and Caribbean writing at Duke University. She is most concerned with developing an approach to literature that brings historical, social, and cultural issues into the analysis. This is the approach taken in Willis's widely noted book, *Specifying: Black Women Writing the American Experience.*

Index

INDEX